Aspen's Fund Raising Series for the 21st Century
Edited by James P. Gelatt, PhD, CFRE

Successful Special Events

Planning, Hosting, and Evaluating

Aspen's Fund Raising Series for the 21st Century
Edited by James P. Gelatt, PhD, CFRE

Fund Raising Basics: A Complete Guide
Barbara Kushner Ciconte, CFRE, and Jeanne G. Jacob, CFRE

Planned Giving Essentials: A Step by Step Guide to Success
Richard D. Barrett and Molly E. Ware

Strategic Fund Development: Building Profitable Relationships That Last
Simone P. Joyaux, ACFRE

Capital Campaigns: Strategies That Work
Andrea Kihlstedt and Catherine P. Schwartz

Successful Special Events: Planning, Hosting, and Evaluating
Barbara R. Levy, ACFRE, and Barbara H. Marion, CFRE

Corporate and Foundation Fund Raising: A Complete Guide from the Inside
Eugene A. Scanlan, PhD, CFRE

Donor Focused Strategies for Annual Giving
Karla A. Williams, ACFRE

Aspen's Fund Raising Series for the 21st Century
Edited by James P. Gelatt, PhD, CFRE

Successful Special Events

Planning, Hosting, and Evaluating

Barbara R. Levy, ACFRE
Executive Director
Arizona Children's Foundation
Tucson, Arizona

Barbara H. Marion, CFRE
Principal
Marion Fundraising Counsel
San Francisco, California

AN ASPEN PUBLICATION®
Aspen Publishers, Inc.
Gaithersburg, Maryland
1997

Library of Congress Cataloging-in-Publication Data

Levy, Barbara R.
Successful special events: planning, hosting, and evaluating /
Barbara R. Levy, Barbara H. Marion.
p.   cm.—(Aspen's fund raising series for the 21st century)
Includes bibliographical references and index.
ISBN 0-8342-0935-7 (pbk.)
1. Fund raising—United States. 2. Promotion of special events—United States.
I. Marion, Barbara H.   II. Title   III. Series.
HV41.9.U5L49   1997
658.15'224—dc21
97-11358
CIP

About Aspen Publishers • For more than 35 years, Aspen has been a leading professional publisher in a variety of disciplines. Aspen's vast information resources are available in both print and electronic formats. We are committed to providing the highest quality information available in the most appropriate format for our customers. Visit Aspen's Internet site for more information resources, directories, articles, and a searchable version of Aspen's full catalog, including the most recent publications:
http://www.aspenpub.com
Aspen Publishers, Inc. • The hallmark of quality in publishing
Member of the worldwide Wolters Kluwer group

Editorial Resources: Brian MacDonald
Library of Congress Catalog Card Number: 97-11358
ISBN: 0-8342-0935-7

Printed in the United States of America

1 2 3 4 5

Table of Contents

Preface

Having survived over twenty-five years of special events, I thought it worth the time to accept this assignment and put my experience on paper. Throughout my career, special events have often been the tests before the lessons; but, without question, with the experience of each event, countless new lessons have been learned. It is the sum of these lessons that is contained in this book. The intent is to make life just a little easier for those who choose to learn first and to enable others to join them in the challenging arena of special events.

For some, special events are a way of life. For others, they are the worst nightmare. This book proposes a systematic way of approaching special events so that they may take an appropriate, productive role in the development process. There are certainly times to be cautious when special events are proposed, because they are not the answer to all problems, nor are they as simple as they most often appear at first blush. When special events become the watchword of your organization, and when volunteers propose new events with frequency and gusto, you may wish to suggest revisiting the development plan and the role that special events have been assigned in that plan. Having provided that warning, there is no doubt that special events have significant value when they are approached correctly, and with insight, good planning, and a strong volunteer base.

Some consideration must be given to the number of events planned for one year. Are staff and volunteers capable of executing the events planned alongside the ongoing development process? Weigh the value of spending six months to raise a net of $5,000 or $10,000 against the value of spending time with your donors and prospects. It may take only six requests to raise this same amount. How does that measure up to the time spent planning, managing, and executing an event? Or, does the status, number, and type of people involved in the event outweigh the extended time commitment? These considerations should be made at the time the board approves the development plan for the year.

This book will offer suggestions about how to design, plan, manage, and evaluate special events. Whether you are planning a press conference or a black-tie ball, the common elements will become obvious as you begin your adventure. With a good, solid plan in place, you'll be able to enjoy your experience and attain the goals you established at the start.

If you are new to the realm of special events, this is your opportunity to get off to a great start! Approached with caution and thoughtful planning, events can add a touch of spice to your development program, offer some nice visibility to your organization, and involve a new cadre of volunteers who may continue their involvement with your cause.

As you venture forth, good luck and happy planning to you and your volunteers!

Acknowledgments

Don't walk in front of me; I may not follow.
Don't walk behind me; I may not lead.
Just walk beside me, and be my friend.

Albert Camus

Throughout this endeavor, I have been fortunate to enjoy and appreciate tremendous support and encouragement from many wonderful friends who have walked beside me.

To my husband, Martin, who read, re-read, critiqued, endured less than wonderful meals, and supported me throughout this endeavor, thank you for your honesty, and most importantly for being my best friend.

To my co-author, Barbara Marion, thank you for being willing to set forth on this adventure with me and to explore ideas and thoughts with as much caring as I have experienced throughout our friendship.

To my mother, Jane Rifkin, whose editing and teaching skills were shared through countless hours of review, thank you for the years of teaching (not always appreciated at the time), and for your gentle touch that ensured that we would come through this experience and still be friends!

To Maurice Sevigny, Dean of The University of Arizona College of Fine Arts, who was willing to take a chance on a wild idea, who inspired his department heads and faculty, and who will always remain a true friend.

Thank you to Jim Gellatt, who read and responded from beginning to end, and whose responses helped to shape this work.

My gratitude to my colleagues in the National Society of Fund Raising Executives who have served as mentors and teachers throughout my career.

My appreciation to those who have contributed to this book. Your examples are a wonderful illustration of my thoughts.

And finally, thank you to Fred Chaffee, CEO of the Arizona Children's Home Association, for his encouragement and interest in this lengthy project.

I have been fortunate to enjoy such extraordinary friendship and support.

Chapter 1

What Is a Special Event?

*It is difficult to say what is impossible, for the dreams of yesterday
are the hopes of today, and the realities of tomorrow.*

Robert H. Goddard

Chapter Outline

- *Fantasy Flight 1029*

- What Is a Special Event?

- Fund Raising or Development?

- Organizational Needs

- Is a Special Event the Answer?

- Your Mission

- Types of Events

- Events and Capital Campaigns

- Event Definition

- The Advantages of Special Events

- Are There Disadvantages? Yes!

- How Do You Decide?

- Points to Ponder

Your excursion into the whirlwind of special events may be prompted by any number of circumstances. Perhaps you are following in the steps of a predecessor, producing an event that has been a tradition for your organization. Perhaps your creative juices started flowing and you are developing your own concept. Maybe an event was suggested by a board member as a solution to a specific problem. However you arrive at the experience of producing your special event, you will discover a world of creative and interesting opportunities, all of which are designed to bring people into contact with your organization.

As you explore this book, you will find that although many events are discussed, one event, *Fantasy Flight 1029*, is used as a recurring illustration of the points being made. This event celebrated the opening of The University of Arizona College of Fine Arts. The event was held on October 29 (hence the number 1029) and was every bit the fantasy flight that its designers hoped it would be. The following "travelogue" follows a guest through the adventure of *Fantasy Flight 1029*. As you experience this event through the travelogue, you will gain a foundation for the examples that will be recurring throughout this book.

Following the travelogue, you will find a definition of a special event, a clarification of fund raising versus development, a review of organizational needs, the question of whether a special event is the answer, types of events, your mission, an event definition form, and the benefits and disadvantages of special events.

Your organization or experience most likely will not resemble those of *Fantasy Flight 1029*, but if you use your imagination, new ideas and exciting concepts will come to light. So sit back, relax, and enjoy.

Fantasy Flight 1029

As we prepared for the evening of October 29, we speculated about what this event called *Fantasy Flight 1029* would involve. We'd been hearing enticing tidbits from friends who encouraged us to join them for this gala opening of The University of Arizona Fine Arts Complex. Nothing we heard, however, could have prepared us for the adventure upon which we embarked. Friends had convinced us that we should purchase first class passenger tickets to this event. An illustration of the theme of the event was the invitation, in the form of an airline ticket. We had the choice of "traveling" coach, business, or first class, with price differentials offering different benefits. Our friends were excited about the Dean of Fine Arts at the University, and they assured us that the Dean's Fund for Excellence needed our help. It was a compelling case when they told us that our two $500 tickets could make a significant difference in the life of a talented student. We did have to admit that we were impressed with the gifts of a matching hand-painted silk tie, cummerbund, and evening bag. Signed by the dean, these artistic gifts were both elegant and personal. Furthermore, we could enjoy identifying the other first class passengers by the art they were wearing.

When we arrived at the parking garage, I remember thinking that it wasn't a very convenient or attractive beginning to a black-tie event. But I immediately forgot the surroundings when I saw the uniformed Pep Band from The University of Arizona Marching Band. The students provided an energetic and exciting beginning to our evening, bringing smiles to our faces. As we made our way through the tunnel underpass to the Fine Arts Campus, we were escorted through the glittering silver and gold decor of the tunnel by the marching band flag girls and baton twirlers. The experience was the closest we will ever come to being treated like royalty. The tips of the flags touched over our heads as they waved us through. We hadn't reached our destination, but already we were enjoying the tremendous energy of these young college students. We smiled, wondering what next?

We were then greeted by someone dressed as an 18th century courtier, complete with powdered wig and velvet tails. He escorted us to a charming scene of children, three to eight years old, dancing in costume on the terrace of the organ recital hall. The children were a delight to watch. We were amazed to learn that the dance faculty worked with children so young. After a few moments, our escort directed us to the ticket check-in counter. We gave our boarding passes, decorated with a travel stamp motif, along with our names, and we were assigned two dots, each of a different color and number. Our boarding passes were returned with the dot assignments attached.

We were told to watch for the costumed guide carrying a colored lantern matching the dots. The dots signaled our flight plan for the evening and we should expect to find wonderful food and entertainment at our two designated destinations. A beautifully costumed Marilyn Monroe impersonator escorted us down a lighted runway to an outdoor courtyard where we found our friends, wonderful music, hors d'oeuvres, and wine. The festivities were especially exciting as everyone speculated about what experiences this evening might hold in store. The costumed student guides continued to come and go, escorting more guests.

After the cocktail hour, we were alerted by the flashing of lights that something was about to happen. A spotlight focused on a character in coveralls, carrying a ladder and making his way through the crowd. He began to mime a scene, and we realized that he was a construction worker illustrating the tasks involved in the building process of the new facility. Suddenly, he disappeared under his ladder only to reappear seconds later in a tuxedo as the master of ceremonies. His performance ended with a sweep of his hand, gesturing toward the new theater wing. What had been a dark glass wall was suddenly alight as the entire University Chorus came down the staircase and out into the courtyard. When lights swept across the courtyard, two dancers made their entrance from the side of the theatre wing. The brief dance and choral performance were enchanting. It was over in just a few moments when our master of ceremonies, the mime who had then found his voice, welcomed us to *Fantasy Flight 1029*. He invited us to look for the guide bearing a decorative staff with streamers and a lantern in the color of our first dot. As we looked around the courtyard, we saw that the guides and their standards were each more engaging than the last. The staffs were designed to represent royalty and totems as well as historical and Aztec designs.

The lighted lanterns and flowing colors were easy to spot, and as the crowd began to sort itself, we were on our way to our next destination. After a short distance, our group gathered at the steps of the Center for Creative Photography. The fifteen-member Brass Ensemble was seated on the porch, ready to play. The director introduced us to the musicians and treated us to a short performance, which our program identified as an in-flight vignette. The whole experience was both interesting and informative, and lasted no more than five minutes. Our nimble guide then led us off through the halls of the School of Music.

Shortly, we entered a room filled with large plants, soft lighting, brightly painted tablecloths, and an inviting buffet of delicious food from several of Tucson's favorite restaurants. We filled our plates and seated ourselves at a table enhanced by brilliant bougainvillea and lighted candles floating in clear glass bowls. The tablecloths, I learned, had been painted by a member of the art faculty. Truly an impressive effort! No sooner had we sat down than a waitress came by to pour from a selection of wines. Looking around, we realized that this room was actually a stage. Further, the auditorium, where we had expected to find seats, was empty except for a large movie screen hanging from the catwalk. Actually, we were in the newly renovated recital hall, which we had entered from back stage.

When the buffet was over, music started and two tango dancers began wending their way among the tables. Surprise! They were two of the faculty members from the Dance Department. They wove a spell upon the crowd. No one wanted them to stop. But the end of their performance signaled the beginning of a ten-minute film created by the Department of Media Arts. The audience was totally engaged. Several members of the University administration were in the audience. We certainly had never experienced an event as creative and exciting as this one. Had they? Fortunately, we had been forewarned that we were going to be dining at two different sites; therefore, we had saved room for what we would find at our next adventure.

This time the audience was divided into three groups. The logistics of moving people was truly a mystery. As instructed, we followed the guide holding the standard with a purple crown, the color of our second dot, and off we went on another tour. This time we stopped in a corner of the courtyard to experience another in-flight vignette, a pianist whose playing turned the courtyard into an enchanted space. The notes floated out into the night, creating a magical experience. We were then led into the new theater building housing the Laboratory Theater, a black-box facility. This room was decorated with a Mexican flair. Large hand-painted canvases depicting colorful, exotic Mexican designs and scenes were hanging from the balcony around the entire room. We later learned that they had been painted by students who had been to Mexico with their professor. They had painted these canvases just for this event. Because these paintings were too intricate for the tables, brightly colored cloths were used instead. Now we were enticed by food from one of the city's favorite Mexican restaurants, as we enjoyed the spirited music of a fourteen-member mariachi band. The music actually inspired some of the guests to dance. As we finished our food, the dim lights were lowered further and we heard the music of eighteen bass violins stationed around the balcony. When the lights came up, they focused on the catwalks of the theater. Dancers began wending their way across the wire grid while performing a lovely interpretation of *Dawn's Attic*, a dance choreographed just for this space and this event. The performance was over all too soon. The audience responded with a wildly enthusiastic standing ovation. We could hardly believe there was more to come. But when the theater doors opened onto the courtyard, we could hear music. It seemed to be coming from the rooftops and in fact, it *was* coming from rooftops, two of them. The antiphonal brass choirs stationed above were answering each other. People began pouring into the courtyard from all directions. All were engaged, discussing with friends the performances they had seen. It soon became clear that many combinations of experiences had occurred that evening, producing great excitement. Moments later, the brass choirs on the rooftops played in unison and once again the spotlights focused on a wall of the theater. This time, however, three men in tuxedos were sitting on the rooftop. Seconds later, they began their descent by rope, rappelling into the courtyard. As they reached the ground, a large company of dancers entered, the music began, and *Fireworks for Fine Arts* was underway. The dance composition brought into play each of the five departments using the travel stamp motif from the boarding pass. Flashlights were used most effectively by the dancers in their choreography. They created their own fireworks by striking their specially treated toe shoes against a rough surface, producing a shower of sparks with each step.

The dance could well have been the wonderful climax to the evening, but there was more to come. Guests now had a choice. They could enjoy dessert and dancing in the courtyard, or visit the Museum of Art for a Renaissance experience and the delightful refreshing music of Harp Fusion, the University's world-renowned group of thirteen harpists playing everything from classics to jazz to Dixieland music. The setting of Renaissance art, gold-leafed chairs, a beautiful table of sweets, plus a truly contented audience created the perfect environment for these musicians to weave a spell of tranquillity.

The subtle finale of the evening featured a wall of television screens in the courtyard with each screen offering an instant replay of a specific part of the evening. During the evening, I had noticed some students wearing black shirts decorated with hot pink identification of "Flight Crew 1029." Now I understood . . . these were the media arts students who had taped the entire evening. During the second round of performances (there were two seatings at every site), they had been editing the tapes so that guests could see what happened in areas they had not visited. It was, indeed, the perfect end to an incredible evening. As guests were leaving, I overheard their conversations. Enthralled with their experiences, they were enthusiastically recommending various departments to each other. I learned more about the Faculty of Fine Arts that night than I ever could have expected. I was now eager to learn more.

Guests who attended this special evening were so taken with the experience, that two and a half years later, people still ask the Dean of Fine Arts when they will be producing their next gala.

Fantasy Flight 1029 has been presented from the perspective of a guest. In fact, I *was* that guest, thanks to the capable many who melded their talents to bring this complex event to life.

What Is a Special Event?

Special events are "special" because they target an external market; they bring people from outside the inner circle of your organization into contact with your cause. Special events are usually suggested because they provide the opportunity to raise funds. Board members are typically more comfortable selling a ticket than they are asking for a contribution. When an event ticket is sold, the buyer is going to receive a tangible benefit. The benefits received from giving a contribution are much more intangible. It takes less effort to sell a ticket than to sell a contribution. Special events, however, are the solution to raising significant dollars only 50 percent of the time.

Fund Raising or Development?

Typically, the process begins with fund raising. The idea of a special event is usually proposed when an organization is in need of funds. The idea may be initiated during a discussion similar to that of the following scenario:

> After a difficult dialogue about how to meet the organization's financial goals, an enthusiastic board member suggests, "Let's do a special event!" The statement is made with energy and conviction. The committee responds in kind. The enthusiasm is contagious. To show less than full support might constitute an embarrassment or insult. The staff finds it has been swept along by the energy of the volunteers and an event is born. It is created, however, with very little thought or planning.

Will it be a solution or a problem? It might constitute fund raising, but it is unlikely to be classified as development. Development requires planning and asking questions before making decisions about an event. You will find some of these questions in Chapter 3.

Fund raising is just what it implies, raising money. You can do that any number of ways, for example, by setting up a table and conducting a bake sale, by enlisting the help of teenage children for a car wash, or by placing a collection canister on a business counter. However you choose to do it, when you are just fund raising and are raising dollars on a one-time basis, you are missing the opportunity to do much more for your organization.

The bird's eye view of development provides a much broader concept involving the identification, cultivation, and solicitation of prospects. Development promises to establish a relationship with a market that is right for your organization; it offers the opportunity to begin to cultivate that market and to move those people along the continuum from "suspects" to prospects to donors. Suspects include those who might have the capability to make a contribution if they have the interest. Prospects are those people whose interest and ability to give already have been established.

Organizational Needs

Organizations have complex needs. The following are primary among them:

- visibility

  –within the right market

  –public education

- opportunities to cultivate donors and prospects

  – create understanding and awareness

  – develop a pool of volunteers

- funds to support their work

  – a base of annual and special gift donors

It is not unusual for the urgent need for financial stability to take precedence over long-term de-velopment. When it does, the blinders go on and the field of vision is narrowed to the quickest way to raise dollars. These are the times when the loudest voice, the most enthusiastic voice, and the energy of the crowd take over. Then you are off and running, sometimes uncertain exactly where the finish line might be.

To understand the best approach for your circumstances, you might begin by understanding the needs of your organization. Involve your board, identify those needs, review each need, and ask the board to prioritize them. If you identify a need for human resources, whether a larger staff or larger pool of volunteers, then you'll approach satisfying that need with a specific appeal to those who you think can best help you. You'll want to be equipped with job descriptions, written plans about what you are asking people to do, and the vision of what a difference they can make. If you identify a need for larger offices, then conduct a search armed with the specifications you are seeking in your new space. If you need significant amounts of money (significant being relevant to the size of your organization or project), you'll want to document that need, build the vision of what will be accomplished with those dollars, and plan for how the dollars can be raised. These must be stated in writing before you begin your event or campaign. Whether this financial need should be met by producing a special event requires further consideration.

If you contemplate a special event, you may want to remind yourself that the cost of most special events is 50 percent or more of the dollars raised. And that is only the financial part. The cost in time and labor is always much greater than anticipated. It's important to ask yourself (and your volunteers) if you can afford a special event. For example, if the idea proposed is to meet emergency needs, can you develop a special event in time to meet those needs? Do you have the necessary cash to front the expenses of the invitations or other materials needed to produce the event? Would a failure compound the emergency? It's possible that you might raise more dollars by mounting an emergency campaign to ask for several large gifts. Such a campaign usually can be done in much less time than it takes to organize a special event. The exception, and there always is one, is an event such as Live Aid that is organized, produced, and performed by stars. This event, and others like it (such as Farm Aid), have raised millions to aid victims of disasters. Unfortunately, these events are atypical and beyond the reach of most organizations.

Is a Special Event the Answer?

Consider the fact that the most successful special events are those having a history in the community. When new events come along, they are typically more expensive to produce while less likely to raise significant net dollars. Producing an event for the first time will take longer, cost more, and yield less. So why do volunteers propose special events? Why should *you* consider becoming involved in a project that may well consume your time and energy as well as other available resources? There are many reasons. Primary among them are the following: (1) visibility, (2) cultivation, and (3) income potential. Each of these elements will be discussed in Chapter 2.

Your Mission

Any special event must be in keeping with the mission of your organization. You'll want to ensure that your event will convey the spirit and the purpose of your organization. For example, suppose your organization is a child welfare/mental health agency. Key to every program in such an organization is the issue of self-image. A beauty pageant certainly would be an inappropriate event because it would not support the philosophy that every person is beautiful and has something worthwhile to offer. Selecting the most beautiful can convey only a message that others are less beautiful.

One agency was approached by an organization wishing to conduct a golf tournament, identifying the agency as the beneficiary. Plans were well underway when, one day, the development office received a call from a concerned member of the agency's constituency. The caller asked whether the agency was aware that the organization producing

Your decision about the type of event you choose to produce should be founded on the goals you hope to achieve.

the tournament was planning to station bare-breasted women at each green! It took very little time to inform the benefactors that the agency would have to decline their generous offer!

Types of Events

There are many examples of special events. Your decision about the type of event you choose to produce should be founded on the goals you hope to achieve. If you are tempted to reproduce an event you have attended or read about, first consider your specific mission and goals, *and then* consider your resources. If you are looking more for broad visibility rather than dollars, or more for cultivation opportunities than visibility, you'll want to evaluate the potential offered by each type of event. In Chapter 2, you'll find a table listing examples of different events and their impact in the areas of visibility, cultivation, and fund raising.

Events and Capital Campaigns

Special events play an important role in any capital campaign. Because they bring people from outside the inner circle into contact with the cause, events are an essential vehicle for getting a message to a sizable number of people. Events also mark the phases of a campaign—the launch of the quiet internal phase, the kickoff or the public phase, and, of course, the victory celebration after the goal is reached. Events bring together those who have an important role in the campaign as a volunteer, community or civic leader, prospect or donor, or media representative. Large gatherings such as the kickoff and the victory celebration inform the community and recognize the leadership.

In addition to the large, more public gatherings, campaigns use events to accomplish other goals. Focus groups are used during the feasibility study to seek reactions to the campaign plan or the campaign material. Volunteers are prepared when events feature training and role playing. Small, intimate gatherings are used to cultivate major donors. Report meetings are vehicles for bringing together and remotivating volunteers with prospect assignments.

Each of these events requires the same, if not more, attention to process and detail as a stand-alone event that seeks to raise operating income as part of the annual fund. More is at stake, and more is riding on the outcome when the event is part of a capital campaign.

Event Definition

Until you know exactly what you are going to do, it will be difficult to know where to start. You might begin by defining the proposed event and by filling out the Event Definition Form (Exhibit 1–1). If possible, involve a combination of staff and key volunteers to help, discussing each of the issues as you write. The same form appears in Exhibit 1–2 as it was completed for a special event planned for The University of Arizona Faculty of Fine Arts for the opening of its new complex. The comparison of these two will provide you with some insight about the differences in special event purposes and will illustrate how various special events can offer different benefits.

It's essential to recognize that not every special event can be expected to produce a net benefit in the four to six-figure range. Your net figure will depend on the type of event and the purpose it's intended to fulfill. It's essential that members of your board understand these variances and that they fully embrace the purpose an event is expected to address. This will happen if they are involved with the planning from the very beginning.

The Event Definition Form may be used to confirm whether a special event is worth pursuing. Once that determination has been made, it's time to review the organization's capacity for producing the event. How you approach an event will determine the potential for successfully meeting those goals, because it brings a targeted audience to a site selected by your organization. Whatever form it takes, it should be designed to meet specific goals.

The Advantages of Special Events

A special event usually targets an external market, so it provides an opportunity to be more visible to the organization's target market. Identifying these markets is a critical first step. Another advantage of a special event is the opportunity to change the public perception of an organization. Internal impact follows success, improving public perception, and employee morale often enjoys a vital boost. In other words, an event brings the organization into the public eye, gets people talking about the organization, and creates a strong public image.

You have been asked to think about visibility, cultivation, and fund raising; but what else can a special event do for your organization? There are countless benefits to be realized. For example, production of an event has the potential to draw an organization's staff and volunteers together in a unifying effort. When everyone works toward the same goal, synergy is created, binding participants together. Each person contributes in his or her own way, and each feels responsible for the success of the event. Furthermore, the accomplishment of producing an event results in the confidence to tackle other, more challenging activities. A successful event will yield benefits beyond its stated original goals; it will empower members of an organization and its volunteers by providing them with confidence in themselves and their organization.

Are There Disadvantages? Yes!

The disadvantages of a special event must be considered as well as its advantages. Special events are unquestionably labor intensive. They can involve more people than you anticipate needing. They will become all-consuming for those involved. However, the disadvantages and challenges can be turned into opportunities. As previously noted, special events generally cost 50 percent of what they raise. This is particularly true when it takes place in a small town with a limited market, limited dis-

Exhibit 1–1 Event Definition Form

THE ORGANIZATION: _____

THE PROBLEM:

Rank organization needs using:

5=highest need, 4=significant need, 3=strong need, 2=moderate need, 1=lowest need

_____ **Money**   How Much? $ _____

_____ **Visibility**   With which market(s)? _____

_____

_____

_____

_____ **Cultivation Opportunity**   With Whom?

_____

_____

_____

_____

_____ **Mark an Occasion**   What Occasion?

_____

_____ **Honor an Individual**   Who? _____

Why? _____

_____ **Introduce an Individual**   Who? _____

Why? _____

The following may be answered yes or no:

_____ Date Restriction?   If so, when? _____

_____ Space Restriction?   If so, where? _____

Exhibit 1–2 Event Definition Form

CASE STUDY EXAMPLE:

THE ORGANIZATION: The University of Arizona Faculty of Fine Arts

THE PROBLEM: A new, but incomplete Fine Arts Complex.

Rank your organization needs using 1 (low) to 5 (high):

5=highest need, 4=significant need, 3=strong need, 2=moderate need, 1=lowest need

   4   **Money**   **How Much?** $50,000

   5   **Visibility**   **With which market(s)?**

Prospective audiences

Prospective donors

People with connections

Media

   5   **Cultivation Opportunity**   **With Whom?**

Prospective audience members and the people they influence

Prospects for major gifts

University administration

   5   **Mark an Occasion**   **What Occasion?**

The opening of the new Fine Arts Complex (unfinished interior)

        Honor an Individual   **Who?**_____

Why?_____

   5   **Introduce an Individual**   **Who?** The Dean of Fine Arts

Why? To interest the community

The following may be answered yes or no:

   yes   Date Restriction?   If so, when? Fall 1993

   yes   Space Restriction?   If so, where? Fine Arts Complex cretionary dollars, and fewer prospects for significant underwriting. Events have a way of becoming more complex and more expensive than expected and, therefore, may cost more than anticipated. Plan the budget very carefully, allowing for everything you will need, even if you think you can get services and goods donated. Budget income very conservatively. Consider all possibilities. For example, what if you don't sell as many tickets as you had planned? What if another organization plans an event for the same night and your market is split between the two events? There are some budget guidelines in Chapter 7 to help you consider all the possible financial pitfalls.

An even more serious problem arises when your donors choose to support your special event *in lieu of* a gift to the annual fund or other fund-raising efforts. In planning, you'll want to be certain that your timing is such that you are not competing with *yourself*.

However, make note of the fact that disadvantages can indeed be turned into opportunities. As noted in the list of advantages, special events offer the opportunity to engage and involve more people on your behalf. Good planning will not only prevent being short-handed at the eleventh hour, but will also provide you with an additional cultivation opportunity.

How Do You Decide?

How do you decide whether to do a special event? First, review your Event Definition Form (Exhibit 1–1). Determine if it confirms that you have good reason to do the event. Second, evaluate your resources. Third, consider your ability to attract key volunteer leadership as well as working volunteers. By the way, if you can involve volunteers at the start of this process, they will be quick to recommend others whose interest they can easily engage. Finally, if you believe that an event really is the answer to your problems, read on for help in moving forward through the planning stages.

Points to Ponder

Before you have your first conversation about producing a special event, consider having plac-ards printed, and tack them to your office walls (and the walls of the administration as well). These placards might read as the following:

Events raise significant dollars only 50 percent of the time!
Events normally cost at least 50 percent of the income generated!

A third placard might be useful and reads as the following:

Do not confuse the mission of the organization with the mission of the event!

The third placard reminds us of the basic rule that most people do not come to an event because of the cause, they come because of the event.

Fantasy Flight 1029 was successful in combining the mission of the University's College of Fine Arts because the focus of the cause—art, dance, music, theatre, and media arts—matched the values of the target audience with entertainment, elegance, and creativity. But that was a university spotlighting its College of Fine Arts. If the *why* of your event is major gifts, and your mission is to feed the homeless in the Bowery, do not plan to bring the guests to your shelter to feed them there! If the *why* of your event is cultivation of new friends of the forest, produce an event that uses multimedia to show trees in resplendent glory. Do not take your unfamiliar guests on a long trek into the dark, dank heart of the forest. If the *why* is to cultivate corporate executives and your cause is after-school play activities for latch-key children, do not invite your guests to join you for milk and cookies at 3:30 on a Monday afternoon.

Summary

Be Clear Regarding the Reason for Considering a Special Event

The goal of a special event is to elicit support for the organization. It is not to fulfill the expectations or ambitions of individuals or groups aligned with the organization. Nor is the event a substitute for the good, solid development programs of annual giving, major gifts, and planned giving. Special events are intended to be part of a rounded development effort, not the sole effort. Expanded visibility, enhanced cultivation, or increased income are legitimate reasons to undertake an event. Tradition, sociability, personal interests, and avoidance of personal solicitation are not good reasons.

Be Clear Regarding the Primary Goal

Whenever you first hear the words, "Let's do a special event," the first question you should ask is the one whose answer defines the reason behind the event—the *why* question. *Why should we have an event?* Is the event responsible to raise **visibility,** produce **income,** or increase **cultivation**? If the event is to accomplish more than one goal, you need to establish the numeric priorities so that when the difficult decisions have to be made, there is a clear understanding of the top priority.

Be Certain That Your Organization Has the Will and the Resources

Special events can consume more than they produce—of time, energy, good will, and even money. Now is the time to assess the disadvantages of producing an event, and to ascertain that the organization has the resources to undertake the size and complexity of the event being discussed.

Chapter 2
Goals: What Should This Event Accomplish?

Before you can score, you must first have a goal.

Greek Proverb

Now that you've given some thought to the pros and cons of special events in general, it's time to examine just why anyone would want to meet the demands on energy, time, pocketbook, patience, and fortitude just to produce a special event. In this chapter, you will explore the primary needs of visibility, cultivation, and income, and the importance of market identification, special event opportunity ratings, setting goals, the plan, and solicitation of prospects.

Visibility

Visibility is of paramount importance to any organization. For most not-for-profit organizations there is no such thing as too much visibility. An event must bring your organization into the public eye. You have the opportunity to provide the public with information about your organization as well as promote the event. Tell the public about your mission, what you do, whom you serve. They become informed whether or not they ultimately attend the event. Such visibility provides an opportunity to tell your story one more time and to one more audience, and this time you can include a call to action. This time, those hearing the story are invited to become involved as guests, volunteers, or contributors. When someone accepts your call to action, at a minimum, you have gained a more informed member of the community.

Evaluating the visibility potential of an event requires an assessment of the possible public and media interest in the proposed occasion. It also requires an assessment of the potential for pre-event media coverage. The visibility factor is affected by the type, or types, of media you choose to promote your event (for example, radio, newspaper, or television). The print media, for example, prefers to report in the society column after the event. Live media reporters will be interested when you have something unique to film or photograph, or someone special to interview. The length of the lead time provided, the number of invitations mailed, and the market to which invitations have been directed will all affect the visibility potential for your organization. You will find more about using the media in Chapter 14.

Public interest has the potential of building a public awareness and excitement about your event that will have many people talking about your organization and the activity surrounding your event. People don't have to attend to have an interest or know about what you are doing. This kind of visibility offers name recognition for your organization, and the next time you do an event or have an announcement to make, the public will be that much more aware of who you are.

Cultivation

Cultivation is the process of bringing people closer to your organization by raising their level of interest, information, and involvement. Just the act of sending an invitation brings your organization into the consciousness of the recipient. Cultivation opportunities abound for some organizations; but for others, opportunities are more limited. Successful organizations are those that develop as many strategies as there are individuals to cultivate. Cultivation reflects the individual's highly personal preference. Some people love the "rubbing of elbows" with society or fame; others prefer being part of a large gala; still, others would prefer a quiet evening with a key member of your organization. Knowing the preferences of each constituency will help you plan your event.

Special events offer the opportunity for others to learn more about your organization and possibly become more involved. It's not unusual to establish long-term relationships based on volunteer involvement. Many board members were first introduced to an organization at an event. The level of later involvement of guests will depend upon whom they meet and the kinds of information shared. Engaging a prospective volunteer or donor can also depend on who is doing the cultivating. For example, when a board member invites a guest to attend an event, the invitation might be delivered in a number of ways. The most effective invitation will be "person to person." It will include detailed information and will call for a response from the individual being invited. Another technique involves having a board member write a personal note on the invitation to an event and then follow up with a personal phone call. Further discussion of invitation techniques can be found in Chapter 11.

In planning your event, identify special opportunities to meet those whom you wish to cultivate. This could mean having a special reception before an event or having pre-event meetings or receptions at which a key figure is present. It could also mean assigning a special seat next to an important person, or providing a tour of "behind the scenes" happenings for a select few. Sometimes a tour of the event space before its public opening is meaningful. Providing the opportunity for the leadership of an organization to meet and acknowledge special guests is a form of cultivation. The key to all of these activities is that someone thinks to do them. You may think of some ideas for cultivation when you think about how *you* like to be treated. Remember when you went to a party and the host or hostess gave you special attention, introducing you and giving others just enough information so that they could begin a conversation by asking questions about you? As you recall, this attention helped you to feel welcome and comfortable. That is cultivation; that is an important part of the development process.

Income

And then there is the fund-raising element of special events. If you are more concerned about fund raising than development, you'll emphasize income opportunities rather than cultivation. Selling raffle tickets, for example, is a fund-raising event. You want to sell the greatest possible number of tickets to yield the greatest profit. But because people will not be gathering for the event, there is no cultivation taking place. A board is often lured by the potential to raise significant dollars by producing an event. What must be made very clear is that, like business enterprises, where there is income, there must always be expense. Just how much will it cost to raise those dollars? What size labor force is required to produce the event? How many of the expenses might realistically be underwritten or contributed? When all of these elements fall into place, special events can offer extremely effective fund-raising opportunities. In most cases, an event can provide visibility and cultivation *and* be a successful fund-raising event as well. This book will detail the process that can help you make it all happen.

Solicitation of Event Prospects

You are wondering just how solicitation plays a role in an event. Aside from the fact that you must invite people to purchase a ticket to attend (and that *is* a solicitation), you certainly are not going to ask your guests for contributions at your event. Or are you? How about a ticket price that *includes* a contribution, such as selling places at tables for more than the price of the tickets? What about the event raffle, an auction? These are solicitations. Furthermore, one of the concepts you'll want to understand is how to think about your event patrons as prospects for your other campaigns. One truism is that your best prospects are your donors. The people who have already invested in your organization are the people who are most likely to make another investment. So perhaps you need to consider which of your event guests are prospects for your next solicitation.

These are some of the differences between income generation and development. They are what separates the successful from the average. They are what brings a person closer to your organization. They are the differences that will provide you with the sign posts on the road, giving you direction and keeping you on target.

The Important Element of First-Hand Experience

Think for a moment about the cultivation of those closest to your organization. In the university setting in Chapter 1, it was mentioned that one of the goals was to generate a greater awareness within the administration of the talents of the Faculty of Fine Arts. You may think that to be somewhat redundant. "Because," you may be thinking to yourself, "they already know what is happening in Fine Arts. After all, the Dean reports to the Provost and, therefore, the Provost must certainly know what is going on." Such logic makes sense up to a point, and that point is the contagious experience of being a part of an enthusiastic audience.

Think about the last time someone told you about a movie. Remember how you related to it? Perhaps you thought "Oh, that sounds interesting. I'd like to see it." Now, think about how you felt when you went to that movie. Were you riveted to the screen? Did you experience sweaty palms during the tense moments? Did you experience these feelings when your friend told you about the movie? Most likely not. Well, you can be certain that neither the Provost nor the President of the University could possibly experience the fine arts without actually being personally involved. To hear, see, and feel are primary experiences that are simply not possible to duplicate. Without question, the experience of being at the event will carry over into those offices the next time a decision has to be made about the Faculty of Fine Arts! Furthermore, becoming personally involved in the audience response was to experience that all important sense of community interest and support.

Next time you're contemplating which constituents of your organization need cultivating, think twice! Maybe even three times! Your staff? Your board? Your clients? All can benefit from direct, in-person, experiential cultivation.

Board members have the ability to cultivate several people at once when they elect to invite people to an event as their guests. These guests are being cultivated even as they are introduced to others in attendance. Influential guests, board members, and the CEO of an organization all embody an opportunity for cultivation. Assessing the cultivation value of an event anticipates that you will have a plan for each prospect. Know what you want to accomplish. Whom do you want the prospect to meet? What is your purpose in cultivating this prospect? What do you ultimately want this prospect to do? Make a gift? Join the board? Open doors for you? Cultivation does not automatically happen just because a prospect attends an event. It requires a plan and people to implement the plan.

Market Identification

The identification of prospects, potential ticket buyers, or anyone else uses the same concepts as those used by people in the business world as they seek to identify their markets. For example, the following questions may be considered:

- Who is most apt to care about and support the mission of your organization?

- Who will want to attend your event?

- Who might want to be in the company of your board members, your CEO, or other staff?

- Who might want to be in the company of your hosts and hostesses?

- Who might want to be seen and be present because the cause is the "right" cause?

- Who might come just for the experience that you are offering (an entertainer, a tour, a food festival, or other experience)?

By identifying your market, you may help to define your event. For your event, it's important to build relationships with people who have reason to be interested in your mission. For example, someone having a history of cancer in the family is much more likely to be interested in supporting an event that funds cancer research, rather than one that supports heart research, the football team, or the history department. And constituents are not always the best market for your event. The homeless, for example, are not going to buy a ticket. But those who care about the homeless will be ready and willing to support your event.

It is helpful to be aware that not all of the patrons of your event are going to become your constituency. There are times when people will choose to attend simply because it is the "right" thing to do, or the "right" people will be present. There is nothing wrong with attracting these types of patrons—there is always the possibility that you might win some of these people over to your cause. But it is important to be aware of which of your patrons you should spend your time cultivating.

One of the advantages of producing a special event is the market awareness that it creates among the staff and board. This awareness can be further developed for the benefit of your organization in its daily operation.

Many events succeed simply because those producing it choose to honor an individual with a significant following in the community. This can be a good idea when done for the right reasons. However, some organizations have taken this idea to the extreme. One group chose to produce a luncheon at which they honored a volunteer from every organization in town. Other organizations suddenly found themselves supporting another cause because they wanted their honorees to enjoy the public recognition offered at the luncheon. Consequently, they felt compelled to attend. But an important element was missing—that of feeling good about the charity they support. Few of those attending this luncheon came away with good feelings about the sponsoring organization. After a few years, the event disappeared from the social schedule. There is reason to suspect that those who were selected as honorees began to refuse the honor. True, this organization had produced a fundraising event, but it certainly had not won any friends or cultivated any prospects. This event could *not* be considered a development effort.

Identification is a key element of the development process. Identifying the market for your event may actually help you open up new markets for your annual fund, capital campaign, or other related activity.

By their very nature, events offer the following three important opportunities for your organization: visibility, cultivation, and income.

Opportunity Ratings

Exhibit 2–1 is a list of events plus an evaluation of the benefit in each of the three areas discussed. A rating scale of 0 to 5 is used, with 5 being the highest. Naturally, many variables enter into the evaluation; therefore, the ratings are somewhat subjective. For example, a car wash is rated 1–1–1. Depending upon the size of the community and the cause for which funds are being raised, a car wash might offer much more visibility and culti-

Exhibit 2–1 Special Event Opportunity Ratings

Rating Scale
5=excellent, 4=very good, 3=good, 2=fair, 1=poor, 0=none

Event Type	Visibility	Cultivation	Income
Auction using Auctioneer who is a:			
Celebrity Figure	5	5	5
Local Figure	4	3	4
Committee Member	3	3	3
Presumption: High-quality, expensive items			
Bake Sale	1	1	1
Bowlathon	3	2	3
Car Wash (kids/local)	1	1	1
Church Bazaar	2	2	2
Competition	4	3	3
Conference or Workshop	4	4	3
Cultural Exchange	3	3	2
Dedication	4	5	0
Dinner			
With Speaker (of national stature)	5	5	5
With Dance	4	4	4
Drawing (expensive tickets for quality prizes)	3	2	4
Exhibition	4	3	2
Fashion Show	4	2	5
Food Fair (and/or competition)	5	2	5
Golf Tournament			
With Celebrity	5	4	5
Without	3	2	3
Groundbreaking	5	5	0
Kickoff	5	5	4

continues

Exhibit 2–1 continued

Event Type	Visibility	Cultivation	Income
Non-event Event	3	0	3
Performance	5	4	5
Press Conference	5	3	0
Rally	4	3	0
Reception	4	3	1
Rummage Sale	5	1	5
Run	5	1	5
Tea	2	5	2
Telethon	5	2	5
Tour/Site Visit	3	5	1
Victory Celebration	5	5	3
Walkathon	5	1	5

vation opportunities than is suggested by the rating of 1–1–1. If, for example, the town council members are washing the cars, there will be a much greater potential for visibility than is estimated on the rating scale. As you read through this list, determine if you can think of some examples from your own experience or conceptualize your proposed event and predict the benefits it might provide your organization.

Examining your organization's need and the basic purpose for producing your event will help you define the type of event, its market, and your approach. Defining what you want to accomplish will help you establish attainable goals. This is an excellent exercise in which to involve your volunteers. After your event is defined, you'll be able to explore your organization's ability to produce it. By all means, engage your volunteers in the spirit of planning and you'll avoid the pitfalls of

> **Engage your volunteers in the spirit of planning and you'll avoid the pitfalls of establishing unattainable goals.**

establishing unattainable goals that will only harm your organization. A failure can be costly in terms of volunteer relationships, dollar loss, and poor public relations. Strategic planning, however, can result in the many exciting benefits events have to offer.

Setting Goals

The Event Definition Form (Exhibit 1–1) helped to reveal some of your goals, but now that you've decided to go forward, those goals must be further developed. Following the case of the Faculty of Fine Arts (Exhibit 1–2), the following goals were identified:

1. To draw people interested in the arts to the new campus.
2. To raise $50,000 to endow the Dean's Fund for Excellence.
3. To demonstrate the exceptional talents of the five departments to audiences.
4. To interest the audience in the campaign to complete the interior of the facility.

5. To interest audiences enough to entice their return during the performance year.
6. To demonstrate to the administration the extent and caliber of talent within the faculty of fine arts.

These were six obvious goals, but to be certain that all of the objectives had been realized, a conversation was held among department heads who helped to confirm these goals. Also, two additional goals were identified. The conversation went something like the following:

Q. *Why do we want to bring people to this campus?*

A. Because we want them to see where we are so they'll know how to come back again.

Q. *Are there any other reasons?*

A. Yes, we want them to see and realize that the interior of this brand new campus is unfinished. And we want to excite them about the potential so that they'll want to help in the campaign to complete the facility.

Q. *Might there be even more reasons?*

A. Yes, it's important for them to meet the new Dean of Fine Arts because he has a great deal of charisma and is an articulate visionary.

Q. *So, people will get excited about Fine Arts just by talking with the Dean?*

A. Yes, and they'll also be excited by the caliber of work being produced here.

Q. *What markets are you targeting to attend this event?*

A. Several—certainly the current audiences of Fine Arts events, as well as people who are well educated and have discretionary income.

Q. *Do you mean that you'll have a plan for these people after you get them to the event?*

A. Of course. This is only the beginning. But, there's another market we need to attract as well, and that is the administration.

Q. *Why would an internal market be important to you? Don't they already know what you are doing?*

A. They know in theory, but the fine arts are experiential and until you have experienced a performance or an exhibition, you'll never really "know" what is being done.

Q. *So you think if you can get them here, they will have a better understanding of what we are doing?*

A. Yes, and not only that, they'll realize how important it is to complete these facilities to serve the present students, as well as to attract future students to these programs.

Q. *Now that you've established several strong reasons for producing this special event, can you think of anything you might have overlooked? Will there be any other impact of producing a successful event?*

A. With the kind of coordination and cooperation demanded by this event, there definitely will be some positive impact on the faculty and staff. The Faculty of Fine Arts has always been composed of five independent and, consequently, competitive departments. This event will demand the kind of cooperation and melding that have the potential to override any previous relationship. It is possible that this might ultimately unite the faculty as nothing else ever has.

At the close of this conversation, goals seven and eight emerged:

7. To bring cohesion to the five departments that have had a history of independent activity.
8. To demonstrate to the administration the significant community interest in the Faculty of Fine Arts.

The Faculty of Fine Arts was striving to regain their status as a college. The change had come about many years before when a previous administration had created the Super College of Arts and Sciences.

Now, both fine arts and science faculties were finding that when they operated with more autonomy, they achieved more of their goals. In addition to the arts and science faculties seeking separation, the departments were well entrenched in habits born of independence. The current dean had been planting the seeds, encouraging them to "act like a college." The proposed event would provide the perfect opportunity for furthering that concept.

With significant needs still not met in the new facility, it was critical that the university administration be aware of the importance of funding that completion to meet the needs of current students, as well as to attract new students to the college. Further, it was equally important for the administration to witness the community involvement and interest in this part of the University.

Your Goals and Your Plan

The plan for your event will emerge from its goals. Each goal will serve as a stimulus ensuring that the design of the event will achieve that goal. For example, to achieve the goal of attracting the administration to the fine arts event, it was necessary to put forth more effort than just sending an invitation. From the time the date was established, it was important to ensure that the key administrators had this date written on their calendars. In addition, if they had responded to this invitation, the committee had to be certain that these administrators were strategically seated with the "right" people. One technique used to involve people is to ask their help in involving someone else. In the letter in Exhibit 2–2, the President and the Dean are cultivating a fellow University President in the state. Whether or not she attends the event, she certainly will be flattered by the advance notice.

The goal addressing the unification of the five departments would be achieved only if all five departments were equally involved in this event. This goal had an impact on the structure of the planning committee. Each goal thereafter would serve as a guidepost in the constant evolution of the planning effort.

> **Goal setting can be energizing, enabling, and fun.**

Goal setting can be energizing, enabling, and fun. As volunteers and staff participate in the development of the goals for an event, they begin to see its possibilities. They are guided by the framework established, and they are inspired by the potential. An event without well-defined goals will remain a difficult challenge, almost impossible to achieve. It will leave too many exciting advantages unrealized.

There are always more questions to ask yourself during the goal-development phase. The following additional questions might be helpful to review:

1. Do we want to develop a relationship with the people who buy tickets to our event?
2. If so, what more do we want them to do?
3. Will we continue pursuing the people who do not come?
4. Is this the first of what might become an annual event?
5. How will our volunteers be impacted by the production of this event? Our staff?
6. Should we consider other markets in addition to our subscribers? For example: vendors, media people, facilities, people?

These questions open new areas for discussion and will probably encourage additional ideas. The importance of these questions is to stimulate dialogue and start the creative juices flowing. The next step is to realistically determine the potential barriers to a successful event (covered in Chapter 3).

Another Option

Bob Hopkins, president of *Philanthropy in Texas*, a fund-raising publication focused on Texas, suggests a simplified way to organize the development of an event. He suggests the "Five Ws and One How." If your committee can answer these questions about their special event, no questions will be unanswered. He does caution that you'll need to adjust the questions to your event. Questions about a golf tournament will vary from those of a fashion show or black-tie ball. Using this method

Exhibit 2–2 Sample Letter

DRAFT

June 24, 1993

Interim President Patsy Reed
Office of the President
Northern Arizona University
Flagstaff, AZ 86011

Dear President Reed:

We invite you to mark Friday, October 29, 1993, on your calendar for an opening that will be long remembered.

You will be invited to join The University of Arizona and the Faculty of Fine Arts for a unique celebration as we open our expanded fine arts facilities. An opening ceremony at noon will provide a dynamic start to festivities that will culminate in a creative black-tie opening gala at 6:45 p.m.

We promise you excitement, new performances, and installation experiences that will leave you wanting to know more about this exciting area of the University.

This is a most important event for the faculty, students, staff, and patrons of the fine arts. They have long anticipated this day as they have endured the inconvenience of construction in recent years.

The evening gala is to be a fund raiser to establish an endowment for the Dean's Fund for Excellence. Tickets will be $125, $250, or $500 per person.

Your formal invitation to this very special celebration of the arts will arrive in September. We hope that you will book promptly at that time since first class seating will be limited. If you have any questions, we invite you to call 555-8824 for information.

Yours Sincerely,

Maurice Sevigny   Manuel Pacheco
Dean of Fine Arts   President

also suggests that you will have already made some decisions about your event.

Many of the questions in Exhibit 2–3 will be addressed in the coming chapters. Once you have reviewed them, you may choose to return to this form and review its relevance to your event.

Points to Ponder

Decision Time

Now that the primary purpose (visibility, cultivation, or income) has been established, two essential questions must be addressed before moving forward. Those questions are the following:

Will the organization's needs be met by producing a special event?

Are there faster, less complicated, and less costly ways of fulfilling these needs?

Honest and realistic answers to these two questions should determine this, the first go/no-go decision point that the organization will encounter.

The Lodestar

Establishing the primary goal becomes not only the driving force behind the plan, but the lodestar, or magnetic north, by which all decisions can be tested. If the suggestion moves the event toward its goal, it deserves top consideration. If it does not, the suggestion merits no expenditure of significant time or money.

Summary

Having established your primary goal—visibility, cultivation, or income—you can now refine the goal for the proposed event by adding hard numbers and anticipated outcomes. You can also move into establishing the secondary goals, those objectives that will, of consequence, flow from your efforts to meet the primary goal. Once the primary and the secondary goals are articulated and accepted, a whole series of questions arise, questions that will help you get the desired results. These are who, what, when, and how questions.

Who do we want to reach? goes right to the target market issue. Once the market is defined, you can ask the next question about how to attract them. *What will get them in the door?* goes to the program or main attraction issue. *When is the right time for this event?* leads to the timing and competition issues. Then the essential, *How do we gain access to them?* question goes directly to the subject of volunteer leadership and the profile of the event committee.

The answers to these and other questions will encourage additional ideas, generate creativity, and inform the planning process.

Exhibit 2–3 Five Ws and One How

WHO	Is the chairperson?	**WHERE**	Will we have it?
	Is the honorary chairperson?		Will the head table be?
	Are the honorees?		Will the entertainment play?
	Will be benefited?		Will the raffle be held?
	Will be invited?		
	Will attend?	**WHEN**	Is the event?
	Will sell tickets?		Is the reception?
	Are the sponsors?		Are the pre-parties, post-parties?
	Will sell sponsor tables?		
	Will be the entertainment?	**WHY**	Is the event?
	Will pay for the pre-event expenses?		
	Will collect the money?	**HOW**	Details, details, details.
	Will order and plan the decorations?		Committees, committees, committees.
	Will coordinate the facility?		
	Will place people at tables?		
WHAT	Will be the event?		
	Is the reason you are having the event?		
	Will you serve?		
	Will be the entertainment?		
	Will be the program?		

Courtesy of Philanthropy in Texas, Dallas, Texas.

Chapter 3
Where to Begin?

I never lose an opportunity of urging a practical beginning, however small, for it is wonderful how often in such matters the mustard seed germinates and roots well.

Florence Nightingale

In this chapter, you will find information regarding institutional readiness to conduct a special event. The many questions that you will want to ask yourself and your volunteers include the following: Does the board of directors support this event? Do we have the human resources necessary to make this event a success? What is the target market that we are trying to reach? Are we looking at the best date? What are the financial considerations that we must explore? What kind of production time will this event require? What are the disadvantages of our plan? What are the potential barriers to this event? After the review of each of these issues in this chapter, there is a discussion about the special events planner. A joint proposal evaluation form is included.

Evaluating Event Readiness

You know what you want to achieve, but you're still wondering how to make it all happen. In fact, you are probably not convinced that your organization is ready to produce this event. The questionnaire in Exhibit 3–1 will help you identify areas to consider before you proceed further.

The readiness questionnaire includes the following issues.

Board Support

Board support is critical to the success of your event. If the board members have not been involved in discussing this event from the beginning, they will be much more cautious about getting involved. This suggests that having a few key board members involved from the beginning is going to make your work significantly easier.

Human Resources

In human resources, you are asked several key questions. What is the importance of board involvement? If you are expecting your board to support this event in any way (volunteer efforts, selling tickets, attendance) then you'll want to be certain that they are involved *from the start*. If you were to go to the board with the event on a silver platter, so to speak, there would be no opportunity for ownership. You may ask why board ownership is impor-

Exhibit 3–1 Event Readiness Questionnaire

AREA	YES	NO
Human Resources		
Has the board been involved in discussion and approval of this event?		
Do we have the number of people we need? # Staff?_____ #Volunteers?____		
Do we have the ability to recruit the "right" key leadership?		
Target Market		
What is the market for this event?		
Who is on the list?		
Can we find their addresses?		
Will they be motivated enough to come?		
Is the date relatively clear on the community calendar?		
If not, what is the competition?		
Will the competition draw from our market?		
Financial Consideration		
Do we know how much the event will cost? $_____		
Do we have enough financial resources to cover the up-front costs?		
Do we know the maximum potential net? $_____		
Do we know the minimum we must net to break even? $____		
Is the net gain worth the time and effort?		
Disadvantages		
Does this event have the potential to divert the attention of staff from ongoing responsibilities?		
Might this event conflict with our annual fund-raising efforts?		
What are the barriers to producing this event? _____ _____		

tant. It is critical because when there is no ownership, there is no involvement, and more importantly, no concern for success or failure. If the board can say to the staff at the end of an event, "Why didn't *your* event work?" you'll realize the difference ownership might have made. Board members have important contributions to make: fiscal responsibility, advocacy, and involvement. They know the community, they know the market, and they know the volunteers who will attract both workers and guests.

When you are asked to assess whether you have the ability to recruit the "right" key people, you are being asked to determine whether you or your board members have access to those people in the community who have a track record for making events work. These are people who know how to think about an event and how to attract and build the volunteer structure so that other people will want to work with them. The volunteers, in turn, will attract the guests who will pay to attend your event. Think for a moment about your own experiences. When you receive an invitation from an organization with which you have no ties, what is your reaction? If no one has written a note on the invitation, you'll probably look to see who the committee members are, and who the leadership is for this event.

Chapters 9 and 10 offer extensive detail on volunteer leadership. You'll learn how to identify, recruit, and involve your leadership from an honorary chair to the real workers for the event. However, you might want to make note at this point that it's your key volunteers who will draw the guests to your event. No matter how wonderful you and your committee believe this event might be, the primary force attracting the ticket buyers will be those people who are doing the asking and selling.

Target Market

Regarding target market, the questions will prompt you to think about how to sell this event and to whom it will be sold. Be aware of the target markets for your organization. Which group may or may not be the market for your event? If you are an organization serving the homeless, then your target market would be those identified as having a concern for human welfare or those living in a very comfortable home. If your organization is a hospital, which group of people is being served by your hospital? Who will be concerned about your success or failure? If you are an arts organization, who will be attracted by the nature of the event? More important, who is committed to your future success?

Many other questions were posed in Chapter 2, under "Market Identification." This is an area of tremendous importance to your success. It is well worth the time you invest in it now.

The Proposed Date

Before expending any more energy on this event, please look at the proposed date. You will want to check for events within a two-week period before and after the date you have identified. Check every community calendar you can possibly think of and call everyone you know to see if they are aware of any conflict on the proposed date. Think not only about your organization and its operating schedule, but also your target market. Are you certain that the date you have chosen doesn't conflict with a three-day weekend when people with children might be planning to leave town? Or, does someone on your list have a milestone birthday or wedding coming up to which many of your prospects will be invited? There will always be some event that suddenly pops up out of nowhere and conflicts with your efforts, but if you have put in your planning time and have already engaged the leadership you need, you will most likely survive the conflict.

Remember to seek broad reaction to the proposed date from your board, your friends, and your prospective leadership. Don't forget to check your community calendar and other organizations. *Use this opportunity to suggest that people save the date.*

When faced with a competing event on the date you have chosen, you'll want to assess whether that competition will draw from the same market you have identified for your event. If so, you may want to rethink your time frame. Obviously, the issue is not that simple. But further consideration would be prudent. How many people do you want to attract? How large is your market? How large is the market for the competing event? All are important questions, and it's *not* an understatement to state that they are important for you to consider *before,* rather than after the event.

Unfortunately, it's not a common practice to think about the impact of special events on the annual fund campaign.

Financial Considerations

The financial considerations are discussed in detail in Chapter 7. An important factor in your success will be the work you have put into budgeting. This means not only the expenses, but the evaluation of ticket prices. If you haven't given this aspect much thought, do not proceed until you first know all the answers on the questionnaire. This is not an idle exercise because your volunteer leadership, if they are savvy and experienced, will expect to know the answers *before* making a commitment to become involved.

Production Time

Now consider the production time you'll need for this event even though you're not entirely certain exactly what the event will be. Is there enough lead time to build a strong host committee? Do you have enough lead time to solicit significant underwriting? If you cannot answer yes to these two critically important questions, you should consider rescheduling your event.

Disadvantages

Finally, the disadvantages of any event are not as obvious as one might expect. If you plan to rely on a significant amount of staff time, have you (or they) given thought to how the event responsibilities will fit into their regular schedules? Should this event take more time than anticipated, what will suffer from lack of attention? How will the additional time required impact the operation of your organization? The Arizona Theatre Company staff engaged in lengthy discussions about the advisability of the Theatre Guilde producing an event called the *Taste of Tucson.* This three-day event required significant time from carpenters and scene painters, as well as electricians. Careful planning was required to fit this event into the production schedule to ensure that the required time and effort would not interfere with the main stage season.

Unfortunately, it's not a common practice to think about the impact of special events on the annual fund campaign. Development staff know that their organizations are depending on income from both efforts. Supposing a significant number of businesspersons in town support your golf tournament, how do you think they'll respond to the fund-raising appeal they receive three months later? If your donors at the $1,000 level decide that they will attend your black-tie dinner for $500, will they continue to give the $1,000 to the annual fund campaign? These are just a few examples of the thought process that must be used as you review all of the possible side effects of your event.

Your Event Program

When your event is not a sports event or other activity, you'll want to consider the kind of program you wish to offer. Some events define themselves; others leave room for variance. Whatever your decision, your event program should be smooth and fast paced. Entertainment can be performed during the reception and the meal. Speeches and presentations can begin while dessert is being served or eaten. Be aware that by the end of the evening (or the end of a meal) your guests will be less than enthusiastic about more speeches or awards.

Consider using a professional master of ceremonies. Television news personalities make excellent masters of ceremonies; they are accustomed to timelines, speak clearly, are relaxed, are viewed as objective, take instructions well, and can be a draw in themselves.

If the program includes an auction, consider hiring a professional auctioneer to motivate the participants and to keep the pace fast. Be certain to give the auctioneer, whether volunteer or paid, advance tidbits to put the members of the audience at ease and to entice them into the bidding. Point out the table of special guests and important staff. Keep the tone light and playful.

Progress on silent auctions should be reported with announcements of time remaining in which to enter a bid.

If the event is in honor of one or more individuals, position the presentations as the highlight of the evening, the crescendo to which other parts of the program build. Presentations should be at the end of the meal but not so long after that guests are preparing to leave.

Barriers to a Successful Event

Why think about the negatives? It seems that we are constantly advised to think positively, but such advice is not necessarily the best practice when planning. A good plan, like a good road map, will identify the hazards and the areas around which to detour. With goals established and *Fantasy Flight 1029* now in the future, it seemed prudent to consider the possible barriers. Knowing the detours is as important as knowing the shortcuts. Barriers are simply road signs inviting creative thinking and planning. Some of the barriers to the successful execution of this event included the following facts:

1. There was no budget for an event.

2. None of the performance facilities in the college were finished on the inside. Therefore, they were not suitable for performances.

3. The university football schedule eliminated many weekends, and those few available would have heavy competition from the community social schedule.

4. The members of the faculty were stressed enough without adding additional performances to their schedules.

5. Each of the five departments had its own fundraising plans and could barely find time for those. This event would require time from their schedules to raise money that ultimately might not even come to their departments.

6. There was no history or precedent for an event of this magnitude, hence there was no existing list of patrons.

But despite the barriers, this event would go forward because each one of the eight goals in Chapter 2 was determined to be critically important to both the present and the future of the Fine Arts Faculty.

Hiring a Special Events Planner

Another possible approach to producing your special event is using the special events planner. This is a person who contracts with organizations to direct their events. Typically, this person has a strong background in running events and can provide you with excellent references. When requesting proposals from event planners, you'll need to summarize a clear and concise description of your proposed event. Outline the detail of what, where, when, why, and who. Provide any information you may already have about potential expense and income. Let the prospective planner know more about your organization. Provide a list of your board, the number of your constituents, and some basic demographics about them. Is this an event that has some history, or that you have managed up to this point? Are you looking for a planner to propose event concepts or to produce a specific event? All of this information will need to be detailed for the prospective planners to better familiarize themselves with what they are being asked to do.

When sending out a request for proposal (RFP), send it to more than one events planner. Ask around the community to find out if other organizations have used people they find to be effective and trustworthy. Look up planners in organization directories or other books, or use word-of-mouth references. Be careful not to get into conversations with just one vendor who believes that he or she is the only one being asked to submit a bid. Until you have signed a contract, you may very well change your mind or receive a more impressive proposal.

And if you decide to use a planner, there's a whole new list of questions to ask. Assuming that this individual or firm offers a good proposal, you will realize that much more information is required, including answers to the following questions:

1. What other types of experience does this person have to offer?

2. Does this person provide the program or do you?

3. Who will promote this event?

4. What are the defined areas of responsibility?

5. What will the program cost? What additional costs will there be, such as advertising or printing?

6. Who will collect the money and pay the bills?

7. How will the money be reported?

8. If you are not selling the tickets, will you receive a list of ticket buyers?

9. How will these buyers be approached?

10. Who will do the design work for the printed materials?

11. Who will have final authority on all design and copy for printed materials? Remember the issue of fair market value (see Chapter 16).

12. How will volunteers follow-up the invitation? By calls? By personal approach?

13. When will you receive the money?

14. Who will acknowledge the ticket sales?

Also, it is imperative to check out the prospective planner with the Better Business Bureau. Remember that no matter how engaging the personality, no matter what promises are made, there is always the possibility that problems will arise. This person is not part of your organization and therefore cannot possibly have the same knowledge as you have about your constituents. Be alert for possible surprises. Before getting involved, it is worth putting research time into this proposed relationship. Once the contract is signed, it may be too late to correct any mistake.

When you have several proposals, it's helpful to have a board committee review them with you. Just as it's important to involve the board from the start when planning and producing your own event, it's just as important to involve them in making a decision about who to hire. Board involvement cannot be stressed too much. They will be the key to your successful event. Make no mistake, they must be part of such an important decision.

Collaborative Events

Aside from the event promoter, alliances may be proposed by other organizations or by businesses searching to affiliate with a qualified charity to promote their own business concerns. (Exhibit 3–2 depicts a collaborative proposal evaluation.) Some of these collaborations may provide the perfect vehicle for reaching a new market, a financial goal, or a cultivation agenda. Any of these reasons are valid and suggest that any proposal should be explored for its merits and opportunities.

Now that all of the issues have been reviewed, it is helpful to know about cooperative events that have worked out well for all concerned. Cooperative means just what it implies: the joining together of two organizations or groups to produce an event. Such events can be an exciting and positive experience and are usually events that have met the following key criteria:

1. A conceptual presentation is made to a committee of the board after initial screening by the staff.

2. The business, promoter, or organization presenting the concept has clearly defined responsibilities for each participant.

3. The business offers to cover all expenses by reimbursing the organization.

4. A financial goal is identified and a clear plan established for how to achieve that goal.

5. Each organization brings a proposed guest list to the table and is willing to check together for duplications.

Exhibit 3–2 Collaborative Proprosal Evaluation

EVENT CONCEPT

_____

_____

Proposed Date _____

Proposed Location _____

PROPOSED BENEFITS TO EACH ORGANIZATION

Financial_____

PROPOSED RESPONSIBILITIES FOR EACH ORGANIZATION

Invitations:

      Design _____

      Printing _____

      Addressing & Stuffing _____

      Mailing _____

Tickets:

      Design _____

      Printing _____

      Number to sell _____

Public Relations:

      Press Releases _____

      Talk Show Appearances _____

      Magazine Coverage _____

      Billboards _____

      Banners _____

continues

Exhibit 3–2 continued

Finance:

Bank Account_____

Budget Approval _____

Process for check requests—How does a vendor get a check?

_____

_____

_____

What is the process for advance underwriting of expenses? _____

_____

_____

_____

Process for budget adjustment_____

_____

_____

Periodic Reports _____

Final Report

Due by _____

To include _____

_____

TICKET PROCESSING

Processed by _____

Master List _____

Weekly Ticket Reports _____

LIST

Restrictions on use of list _____

_____

continues

Exhibit 3–2 continued

LICENSES AND INSURANCE

      Who files _____

      Who pays _____

BACK-UP PLAN _____

           _____

           _____

TROUBLESHOOTING

      Who do you call in case of problems? _____

           _____

           _____

6. Each organization agrees that those names new to each of them will not receive any other solicitation in that year.

7. Work is equally divided with approval for all copy and design cleared by a steering committee having representation from each group involved.

8. Checkpoints are established and progress reviewed at each checkpoint with a commitment on the part of all participants to uphold a fair share of the work.

Event Policies

Whether you produce an event on your own or cooperate with another organization, one of the most stabilizing factors will be your organization's event policies. If you don't have any, consider a few simple guidelines now that may enable you to avoid many future problems. The following policies, for example, might well prevent three different committee members signing contracts with three different vendors providing the same service!

Whether for your current event or every event, policies are the key to guidelines, just as they are for your agency's operation. When developing policies, consider the following questions:

1. Who is authorized to sign contracts?

2. Who is the official spokesperson for the event?

3. Are there any restrictions on the site where you might hold this event? Does it need to be accessible to the handicapped?

4. Are there any restrictions on the sponsorship of an event? Would you consider sponsorship from an entity that provides a service or product that is not supportive of your mission? For example, should a liquor distributor sponsor an event supporting a chemical dependency program?

5. What kinds of recognition might you provide sponsors? How many tickets should you set aside for them? What space can you allow in a program? Should they be mentioned during the event? If so, how often?

All of the previous questions pertain to issues that must be determined before, rather than after the fact.

When thinking of holding a collaborative event, there are many issues to consider. Following are some examples of collaborative events and the issues raised:

Scenario #1. A new business in town proposes holding a benefit at the opening of their new store. They offer to create a special event and all you have to do is sell the tickets. Ask all the questions listed for the events promoter because the circumstances are very similar. Proceed only if you and your board agree that this event will provide the opportunity for a positive experience for your organization. These opportunities are frequently brought to your attention with barely adequate lead time. Although you may feel some pressure to accept, you want to avoid any potential future problem. Do *not* be afraid to say no.

Scenario #2. Members from another organization (or business) approach one of your board members with a terrific idea for a fund-raising event. They suggest that the two organizations "partner" in producing this event because the partnership will offer the opportunity to share the work and the excess income. This idea is a potential nightmare in the making! If well thought out, it could work. However, there is a real potential for misunderstanding due to lack of clarity and a myriad of

> **Whether you produce an event on your own or cooperate with another organization, one of the most stabilizing factors will be your organization's event policies.**

other issues. The selling point for this type of proposal is most often related to providing visibility for your organization in a different market. Remember, if these people are not in your constituency now, *there is no fast way to build relationships* and make them instant supporters.

This warning is not intended to suggest that all such ideas are doomed to failure. There are times when a cooperative event delivers everything it promises, including dollars, visibility, and exposure with the right market. Be certain to define every detail in writing and develop signed agreements clarifying each issue.

Scenario #3. Members from still another organization approach you with an idea about how each of you can make a lot of money cosponsoring an event. The same rules apply. Check out every possibility. For example, is it possible that this organization has come to you because they would like access to your constituent list? Do they have an equally strong list to bring to the table? Caution must be your ally as you examine all the issues and review this proposal.

Scenario #4. A department store entered a new market in the late 1970s with an idea. They wanted to produce an opening gala for the benefit of the arts. Several leaders of the larger arts organizations were invited to a luncheon meeting hosted by the store, at which they presented their concept. They asked for feedback from the group. Not having had much experience with joint events, the group felt good about endorsing the idea. The concept was a preview night in the store with entertainment, wonderful food, and lots of prizes. Each of the five organizations was asked to guarantee 500 guests at a minimal ticket price of $5. The organizations were also asked to supply the volunteers who would make the event run smoothly. The store would guarantee $5,000 for each participating organization.

Clearly, this was an opportunity for the store to be sure that by offering a preview of their new property, they would be introduced to the "cream of society." They would enjoy media attention because, as the anchor tenant of the newest shopping mall in town and as a newcomer, they were making their entry with a philanthropic flair. No questions were asked, no agreements signed, no hard look at the mechanics of this philanthropic gesture. Fortunately, none were needed. Each organization was invited to set up a display with season ticket information, and each had an opportunity to promote itself in the store that evening. They set about finding their promised 500 people. What could have been an embarrassment was not, thanks to the competent involvement of the store representatives. The store continued to maintain its relationship with the organizations, keeping all apprised of its growth and maintaining relationships as well.

After that experience, the arts continued to enjoy several cooperative events sponsored by some of the larger department stores in town. Because each experience brought more organization and wisdom to the negotiations, every event has become a better designed cooperative event. These experiences have also led to a greater understanding of the nature of such cooperative events. It does stand to reason that some organizations began to decline participation in those events that did not measure up to the criteria that had become established.

Points to Ponder

First steps are often the most difficult. The beginning can be made more comfortable when the end is known, the target is in sight, the steps are illuminated. Although there is risk in suggesting a simplistic idea of a complex undertaking, the following analogy may be helpful.

The five rights of solicitation have been described as the following:

The right person asking the . . .
➡ right prospect for the
➡ right amount for the
➡ right purpose at the
➡ right time.

The four rights of special events might be described as the following:

The right audience invited by the . . .
➡ right volunteers to the
➡ right event at the
➡ right price.

Summary

As with all fund-raising efforts, institutional readiness determines the success or failure of special events. Because special events can be all consuming for those involved, it is essential to determine the organization's ability and readiness to undertake the event. Careful analysis now can forestall disaster evaluation later.

The organization must know the answers to the following questions:

Why is it undertaking the event?
What is the target market?
Can it reach and entice the market?
Can it produce the proposed event?

There are obstacles that make it difficult for an event to succeed. Lack of resources and lack of commitment top the list, with inadequate preparation time a close third. Obstacles need not cause the event to be abandoned but should cause closer scrutiny of alternatives such as collaborative efforts or the use of outside assistance in the form of an events planner.

Collaborative efforts are worth considering because they share the risk and the burden. Although the income would be shared with others, that can be more than offset by the additional ticket sales through a greater and broader number of people. Written advance agreements are key to a successful collaboration. Nothing should be left to chance or to interpretation. Each party must understand and accept their various roles and responsibilities.

Successful outside assistance, usually paid, also relies on clear, written understandings. Engaging the services of an event planner can give a greater certainty of success, can be a valuable educational experience for an organization with little background in events, and can be the factor that permits an organization to proceed. As with hiring any consultant, the organization should draft a plan, state its expectations, and then distribute an RFP. Ideally, the RFP should go to professionals who have been recommended because of the excellence of their work. Seek recommendations for other organizations and from local hotels and convention centers.

Whatever route you take, good solid planning is key. Depending on the complexity of the event, the number of partner organizations, and the use of outside assistance, the lapsed time—from concept to execution—can take up to twelve months.

Chapter 4

The Theme: What Will It Be?

If you will please people, you must please them in their own way.

Lord Chesterfield

In this chapter, you will find the building of an event revealed. You will learn about the "brainstorming soup party" and how to make it work for your event. You will find some discussion about the use of a star attraction, and then some information about a cultivation event.

You may have wondered whether you would ever get to this point. After all the conceptual work you have done and questions you have asked and answered, you still don't feel any closer to a decision about what your event will be! Enthusiasm is at an energized high, but you know that it won't last for long unless there's a realistic concept to support. You and several others have been talking about concepts for an event. But it still hasn't taken final shape. Following is the description of the technique used to develop the idea for *Fantasy Flight 1029*. Although the initial concept was in the germinating stage, it would never work unless those who could make it happen would contribute to it and make it their own. It was then that the "brainstorming soup party" was born. After the fact, this party proved to be well worth the time and effort.

The Building of an Event

Each of the fine arts department heads were asked to select three representatives from their departments. In some cases, a specific individual was requested. A volunteer who had been part of the initial discussion process agreed to host a soup party. Several people committed to making the soup, and committee representatives from each department were invited to the brainstorming soup party. The participants knew that the purpose of the evening was to talk about launching the new arts complex. The hostess had decorated several small tables throughout her house to seat the twenty guests. Although everyone was from one of the fine arts departments, they didn't all know each other. Name tags provided a level of comfort, and the social part of the evening was off to a good start. Guests were asked to sit with someone they didn't know. During dinner and after introductions, each person was asked to express his or her thoughts about what the gala might achieve. Because two of the departments were not located on the new campus, they were especially dubious about what this event might do for them.

Some of the initial gala concepts were explained. The Dean was asked to discuss the Dean's Fund for Excellence. He was very clear that the proposed endowment would provide financial support for each of the departments. He went on to illustrate the need for funds using examples such as the fact that Harp Fusion, the harp performance group, needed funds for their trip to perform in Japan. The dance department needed funds to help sponsor a workshop in jazz dance. Such a workshop would bring additional money to the department as well as provide national visibility. The Dean stated that he hoped to have monetary awards available to support excellence in teaching and to support strong research programs. Those present began to understand that the money being raised would benefit every department and that this event would provide an opportunity to establish credibility for all the participating departments.

After dinner, five discussion groups were formed. Each had a flip chart and had selected a recorder to take notes. The major goals for the event were written on the flip chart. They were reviewed for the group and posted for all to see as they worked. Although it was still open to change, the concept that this group discussed and ultimately embraced, was that which was first explained to them. This concept called for a significant number of mini performances. It required moving groups of guests from place to place. There was plenty of potential for disaster. Yet the proposed evening would be creative, exciting, and stimulating. Further, because of all the moving, it was participatory. Still, no one had never seen this concept implemented and many weren't certain that it would work.

In keeping with the goals for the event, the evening would include cameo performances by both students and faculty. When the guests had experienced several different performances, they would have an idea of the type of work produced by each of the five departments. They would be much more likely to return for more than they would if they had seen only one performance. This format would address the goal of creating enough interest to draw people back to the fine arts departments during the performance year (see the section on goals in Chapter 2).

They would also be led through the uncompleted portion of the complex where plans for completion will be displayed. In addition, it would be possible for guests to enjoy different eating venues as well as different performance sites. The evening could begin and end in the fine arts courtyard. During the evening, people would be led to several unfinished sites. This would address the goal of informing the guests about the uncompleted portion of the complex.

Up to that point, no theme had been developed for the evening. The only concept that had emerged from at least five previous meetings with the dean was an evening of unpredictable excitement. Finally, a theme emerged! "Expect the unexpected." From that beginning, the groups went to work developing ideas about what kinds of performances to have and at which locations they might be staged.

Each group was asked to brainstorm ideas and concepts for twenty minutes and to record all on the flip charts. At the end of that time, they were asked to review their ideas in the next fifteen minutes and prioritize them. Finally, the groups came back together to present their top five ideas. What was achieved that evening was a lengthy list of ideas and most important of all, group ownership of the gala. True, there were many doubts expressed about the feasibility, and there was significant concern whether the rest of the faculty would accept the proposal. People believed that the faculty would be resistant to the concept because of the work it would require. It would be critical to make a convincing case to the faculty; however, with the interesting and viable ideas put forth at the soup party, the case could easily be constructed.

It was important to give these ideas some time to percolate—but not much time, because this event was exactly one year away. At the end of the evening, there were scores of ideas, some terrific and some impossible. Everyone was thanked for their time. Then the work began of processing everything that had been suggested. Some of the idea highlights of that brainstorming session included the following:

- Start the entertainment in the parking garage.

- Do something interesting in the underpass from the parking garage to the campus.

- Seat guests on stage in the recital hall that had no seats and perform out in the house (where the seats should be).

- Feature dancers rappelling off the roof of the new theater (provided this would be accepted by risk management).

- Have antiphonal brass choirs performing on the rooftops.

- Have a commissioned dance taking place in the lighting grid of the ceiling in the new laboratory theater.

- Have vignette performances everywhere.

- Serve dinner backstage, in the scene shop of the theater.

At the next meeting of department heads, the results of the soup party were discussed. There was no immediate acceptance; but remember that these departments had not been accustomed to working together and this project was going to demand significant cooperation. Unlike most events, the committees for this event would have to be staffed by faculty. The community volunteers would be needed both to sell tickets and to solicit underwriting.

The next step was to shape the varying ideas into a workable format. It was critical to engender some excitement in the volunteer chairs of this event. A board member and his wife had been recruited to chair the event. Their exceptional sophistication about volunteer service prompted them to make it clear that because they were new in town, they would accept the task only if they had cochairs who had ties to different segments of the community. A second couple was enlisted to fill that void. This couple's long history in the community and their ties to various groups served as a nice complement to the talents of their cochairs.

The concepts were outlined to the two couples. They had some reservations because this type of event had never been done, but they were excited about the potential. The choice of five different eating and performance venues made it possible to handle the seating of as many as 400 guests. The idea of offering each guest two eating and several performance experiences meant that no one would be limited by a long evening at a table with the same people. With guests constantly on the move, the only concern was that they would not get to spend much time with their friends. On the other hand, the cocktail and dessert segments of the evening provided that opportunity. Despite the initial skepticism about this unusual concept, the volunteers demonstrated their faith in the faculty, their commitment to the quality of work being produced, and their willingness to explore something new.

The concept was now becoming more specific, but still there was no theme. It was another deadline that brought the committee to consult with the university graphic design class. The professor of the graphic design class had agreed to submit this event to his class for a competition to design the invitation. Although it was puzzling how to present this no-name concept to the class, the only option was to begin by describing the evening and suggesting that the design of the invitation might inspire a name as well as the elusive theme for the event.

What Was Learned?

- First and foremost, when people are invited to give their ideas, they become interested and take ownership. This means board members as well as outside volunteers.

- Second, the independent small group sessions probably produced many more creative ideas than one large group.

- Third, it is okay to invite participation in a project not "fleshed out" in advance because as you involve the people, you generate many more ideas from which to choose. Even those ideas that are not implemented contribute to the overall picture and broaden the perspective.

- Fourth, even the naysayers have a hard time dissuading a group that has developed forward momentum.

- Fifth, the initial brainstorming group does not have to be the final committee. Those who demonstrate the most active interest are those who will want to serve. Others will be just as glad to see someone else take a more active role.

- Sixth, don't be too concerned about the final shape early in the planning. In fact, this time it was the students working on the invitation concept who developed the final title and theme.

Three weeks after presenting the idea to the graphic arts class, the professor invited a small group, including the volunteer leadership, to class for the presentation. Seeing the initial concept now presented in visual form was fascinating. These senior-level students had developed extremely creative ideas. The most exciting was the one playing off the idea of an airline ticket. The invitation to the event was actually shaped like an airline ticket booklet with several pages. The students had designed a cover page with passport-type stamps depicting the five departments. The travel concept, an evening experience of different venues and fantasy performances in the arts culminated in the theme and title, *Fantasy Flight 1029* (the date for the event was October 29). This invitation promised passengers a journey to delight the senses. The initial idea of "expect the unexpected" was captured and, although no one was certain about how this was going to come together, anticipation was high.

Now that there was an agreed-upon theme, other pieces began falling into place. It was the volunteer chairs who recommended the next thematic concept. They thought that the travel theme should be reflected in the ticket pricing. It was suggested that "passengers" should be invited to select one of three ticket fares: coach class for $125,

business class for $250, or first class for $500. It was a wonderful suggestion, although some doubts existed about a market for the business and first class tickets. This suggestion would certainly help on the income side of the budget, increasing the potential ticket income from $50,000 to $60,000 (see the section on budgets in Chapter 7). There had to be a creative reason why someone would pay $500 to attend an event at which a pre-event party was not possible nor would there be access to star attractions, much less a special dinner. Finally, a solution was proposed. Business class passengers would be recognized in the event program and would receive a special fine arts ticket hot line number that would permit access to house seats or other special considerations. First class passengers would receive these benefits and, in addition, either a cummerbund and bow tie or an evening bag. These would be hand painted and signed by the Dean of Fine Arts. As a visual artist, the Dean rose to the challenge and was encouraged by the limited number of anticipated $500 first-class ticket holders. These benefits sparked some interest within the committee, especially after having had the opportunity to see the Dean's work.

Now you begin to see a picture of the unfolding of this event. It certainly didn't come together all at once, so be patient and give yourself and your volunteers the latitude and the time necessary to develop a truly wonderful event.

Remember, it was just about seven months before the actual event that the final theme and invitation were designed.

Making It Work for Your Event

If you are searching for a new event, the brainstorming soup party is a highly recommended process. If you are seeking to improve an existing event, you might want to first explore those areas in which you wish to make changes. The soup party process will work for you. The only time this process will not serve to improve your planning is when you are following a boilerplate event, which is an event that has been produced before, has a standard format in writing, and is not expected to vary from prior years. And there's nothing wrong with reproducing something that has proved itself in a past performance. However, even under those circumstances, it would be worthwhile finding some issue to present to your committee; it certainly will provide the opportunity to involve them, and *that* is the key to your success.

Now that you have some direction to your event, it is time to bring all of the ideas together and formulate the evening. The list of questions to be asked might include the following:

1. Are there other events similar to yours being produced in the community? If so, are they supported by the same market you are approaching? What ticket price has been established, and does it have a history of selling out? On what date is the event to be held?

2. Is the location you have selected the best one for your event? Is there adequate space for parking, eating, mixing, dancing, or whatever activities you have planned? Might you be planning the perfect event for the wrong site?

3. Have you considered the ticket price you will want to charge to meet your fund-raising goal? Will the market support that price? Are the same people being invited to too many other events in the same price range? Even if your committee will support the ticket price, how many of their friends will be willing to attend the event at the proposed ticket price?

4. Is this event politically correct or might you need to make some adjustments? This question should be asked even of events that have been produced for many years. The University of Vermont for many years conducted an annual winter event called "Cake Walk." It was an exciting weekend full of events that included the Cake Walk competition in which competitors dressed in silks, painted their faces black, and strutted their athletic steps to stardom. The walkers were revered; the event was a campus-wide phenomenon, and yet, in the late 1960s, the university realized that despite the respect given the competition and the walkers, this event did not reflect a spirit of diversity and respect for all cultures. The event was changed, a higher sense of purpose and philosophy prevailed, and today a new, and probably just as exciting, event involves students, faculty, and the community.

5. Does the proposed concept invite coordination of printed materials, decorations, food, and production ideas?

What About a Star Attraction?

Events that go down in history have typically engaged "star power." Most volunteers believe that tickets are more easily sold when guests will have the opportunity to see or be with a star. And many events lend themselves to including a star. It sounds appealing; it sounds like the solution to ensuring a sold-out event. But is it? Let's look at some of the issues.

The first issue will be how to engage a star. It certainly can't be done by writing a personal letter or even by picking up the phone. Stars have agents and for good reason! So where to begin? The library has books with lists of agents and those they represent. A few agencies are listed in Exhibit 4–1.

Once you have identified the agent, you'll want to know what fee the artist commands. You will also want to know the following:

1. What expenses does the agent expect to have covered? Certainly, travel and lodging expenses are to be expected. How many people travel with the artist, and will those expenses also be your responsibility? What class ticket are you expected to purchase?

2. When do they expect to arrive? Leave? What will the entourage do while the artist is performing?

3. Will the entourage expect complimentary tickets to your event?

4. How many cars will it take to meet the party at the airport? Or do they expect a limousine?

5. Will you need to hire security?

Exhibit 4–1 Finding Celebrities

The following are just a few resources through which you may either research or engage celebrities:

The Hollywood Reporter

5555 Wilshire Boulevard

Los Angeles, CA 90030

(213) 525-2000

This is a newspaper that publishes *The Blue Book* listing the names of actors and their agents, with addresses and phone numbers.

Celebrity Connection

Contact: Barry Greenberg

8306 Wilshire Boulevard, Suite 2859

Beverly Hills, CA 90211-2382

(213) 650-0001

International Talent & Touring Director
(800) 344-7119

Lists performing artists (music only), their booking agencies, management, and promoters.

6. What hotel accommodations and what accommodations at the event site are expected?

7. What unanticipated staging costs might you incur?

These are not exaggerated demands. These are the legitimate and sometimes not so legitimate expectations of some very well-known star entertainers. You and your committee will do well to consider all possibilities before you go too far down the road to stardom.

For example, a hospital had established a star-based event many years before. Its tradition was one of the first black-tie events in that city. Several years ago, when artists' fees became too high, the event became unreasonably expensive. In fact, there was no place in the city large enough to accommodate the number of people necessary to cover the cost of the star attraction. It no longer made sense to continue with the same event. The event committee finally recommended that local artists be featured.

Nonetheless, stars do draw people and if you have the capacity to accommodate a large audience, you may also have the potential to raise a great deal of money. The key factor is knowing your expenses before you get too far into the project. This entails asking lots of questions and having everything in writing from the outset. *You cannot be too cautious.* The gentleman's agreement is worth nothing if you do not have it in writing. A letter of confirmation that has been signed by both you and the agent is the only protection you have against some very unexpected expenses that could wipe out your profit.

Other Event Ideas

If you have exhausted all ideas and are still uncertain about the type of event to produce, explore the literature. In the bibliography, you'll find the names of a number of special event books that will describe different types of special events. The kinds of events that you will want to consider will vary depending upon the following:

- The dollars you want to raise

- The number of people you might want to attract

- The number of people available to you to help produce an event

- The physical resources available to you

- The lead time you have available to plan it

- The time you have available to produce it

- The mission of your organization

- Local considerations

Events can be as boilerplate or as creative as you want them to be. The bottom line is: how many paying guests can you attract, and what is your potential net? Does this event offer cultivation opportunities? Review the purpose of your special event in Chapter 1, and assess your plan to determine whether you can achieve your goal. Sometimes just letting go of the urgency to make a decision can result in the freedom to accept new ideas as they surface.

The Cultivation Event

It is productive to produce an event that is purely for cultivation and has no fund-raising intent. This type of event can build and cultivate your market for a future fund-raising event. Such events might be a press conference, a facilities tour, a work day (an opportunity to work with staff on a project), a performance, a discussion group, an opportunity to interview an expert, or a speaker who might validate your organization's work.

Whatever your decision, it's important that you know where you are going and how you want to get there. If you aren't following the road signs for your venture, you might think about creating some for others to follow after you. Translated, this is an effort to encourage you to write out the process of creating your event. Leave your thoughts and your experiences for those who will follow you. Build a record of everything you have done. This record will also be useful for an evaluation process to determine what succeeded and what didn't and why.

Further Development/Confirmation of the Selected Theme

Play with your event theme. Invite others who have not been involved up to this point to respond to your ideas. Let them make suggestions about what they believe your community will support. Try out your concepts, ticket prices, and other ideas to test the reaction. If there is any doubt, review your ideas. If there is interest, ask someone else to

review your concept and keep looking for improvements. Continue talking to lots of different people. Everyone brings something different to the picture, and you never know just how interested someone might become if they are involved in your event from the start.

Always remember that the image in your head is never the same as the image in the other person's head. And that's okay. In fact, that may well be to your advantage. If you doubt this statement, try it out on a few people. Pick a topic, idea, or scene that you have pictured in your own mind. Now try to describe this scene to a friend. Ask your friend to tell you what pictures come to mind. Now ask your friend to add something to the picture, perhaps a color or additional detail. I think that you will be surprised at what comes back to you; you may not even recognize it as the same idea. This is no new phenomenon. It's a reality that might be helpful to you if you can be open to the ideas that may arise. For whatever it's worth, try out this concept, just for the fun of it. You'll find yourself surprised and often delighted with the results.

Whatever you do, *don't assume anything*! It is tempting to think that if you don't fully describe something, no one will ask about it. Therefore, no one will disagree with you, and you will be able to make it happen just the way you have envisioned your event. That is a sure path to problems you really don't need. The best way to avoid these problems is to articulate all of your expectations, get them down on paper, and let your volunteers be a part of the process.

Points to Ponder

Target Market

Consider the words of wisdom David Nelson has shared with many of his clients, "Target the audience, then select the event." This approach allows the target market to become the driving force in every decision. Recruitment of volunteers is based on who has access to the market. The early involvement of the right volunteers brings forth ideas that will appeal to the market and helps ensure attendance. Selection of the theme is based on what will appeal. Selection of the location is driven by the event theme and program. Price is established by knowing what the market expects and tolerates. Acceptance by the market is virtually ensured because peers who know what will draw are creating the event.

Summary

The decision to proceed has been made. Now it is time to begin shaping the event itself, time to make those choices that will attract the target audience. This is the ideal phase for volunteer involvement. Using the volunteers in the process of determining and developing the all-important theme can have distinct advantages.

The board and volunteers who have access to the target market should be encouraged to get involved early in deciding the theme. These volunteers have essential knowledge about the perceptions and preferences held by the target audience. Their creative ideas and reactions to the ideas of others can illuminate that which will entice and that which will deter attendance. They are the early test market for ticket prices, location, program acceptance, and competition.

In addition to the practicalities, brainstorming with volunteers during this phase has two distinct positives. It brings forth a variety of ideas and solutions to problems and concerns, plus it presents opportunities to cultivate the volunteers, thereby reinforcing their commitment.

Chapter 5

The Site: Where Will It Be?

Location, location, location.

Unknown

This chapter presents the evaluation of the proposed site. In addition, you'll find a list of questions to ask about the site and an exploration of the equipment requirements of the site. There will be a brief discussion about tenting an event and another about diagrams.

Questions Regarding the Site

Now that you have an event to discuss, your next concern will be its location. You may have chosen an event that must take place at a defined site. Events such as a golf tournament or a performance of some kind will pretty much dictate where the event will be held. However, the location of most events is a matter of choice. Depending upon the size of your community, even the golf tournament might be booked at one of several golf courses. For the fine arts gala, there was no choice regarding where to hold the event because the purpose was to attract people to the site. True, there were many places within the facility that would be nontraditional, but they were deemed inappropriate for

various activities. For each proposed site, it was important to judge whether the number of people attending could be accommodated with a buffet service and tables at which to eat, while preserving enough performance space. Further, it was critical to have the service area close at hand, plus space to store food, dishes, and wine.

There are a number of factors that will influence your decision regarding the site for your event. As you examine the options, consider the following questions:

1. Will the space you have selected accommodate the number of people you intend to attract? The spacial relationships in facilities may be difficult to judge at first glance. Without actually placing tables and chairs on the floor space, you may not be able to judge the square footage needed. Help is available, however, because most hotels or rental companies can provide you with the number of feet required for a table seating eight or ten, including the space you'll need for wait staff to maneuver within the room. A rule of thumb is to figure the table size (such as a six-foot round table), add two feet to accommodate each seated person plus another three feet between the chair of one table and the chair at the neighboring table, to provide for service space. Hotel staff members usually know how many people they can squeeze in a room, or conversely, how many people would look lost in a room because of the empty space surrounding them. In the case of the fine arts event, the several proposed sites were nontraditional, so it was important to measure available spaces and create floor plans.

2. Is the site accessible to the people you hope to attract? If you are anticipating handicapped or elderly guests, will they be able to navigate the site? Knowing that there would be a number of elderly people who would have difficulty walking far, special accommodations were necessary for *Fantasy Flight 1029*. Because of the distance of the parking garage from the facilities where most of the festivities would take place, it was important to make alternate arrangements for the elderly and handicapped guests. Several handicapped parking places were secured next to the fine arts campus. Those requiring special parking were then notified of the location of the space saved for them. These guests also received a flight plan designed for their special needs. Another option might have been to arrange for transportation from the parking lot. Many attempts were made to engage the surrey carts used by the hotels for their big events, but none were available. Whatever the circumstances, you'll need to consider the logistics of movement during the event and the special requirements that will make a difference for those guests who need them.

3. Is there available parking? Just because you've seen the huge parking lot with your own eyes, don't assume that it will be available. You can relax only when you know that there will be no other events requiring parking at the time you need it. When you are given numbers, take time to assess the real parking potential. It's so easy to describe your parking needs when you are reserving the space, just remember to do it. Sometimes, available parking might be good enough reason to relocate your event. It can be a vital consideration.

4. Is the place you have selected for the event one people would like to see? Many special events are held in an especially elegant home for more than one reason. First, the home is likely to draw the attention of guests who would enjoy seeing it. Next, that particular home will provide a perfect background for the planned event. For example, when considering a golf tournament, have you selected a course where most people would prefer to play? Typically, the more exclusive the course, the more attractive it will be to those players who or-

dinarily might not have the opportunity to play there. Sometimes an event is held at an alternative type of site. A warehouse is a good example. In this instance, curiosity builds and people wonder how anyone can possibly create something attractive and interesting in such a large, empty space. This curiosity motivates them to attend.

5. What are the costs associated with the site you have selected? Will there be a room charge? What are the food costs? Are you required to use a certain caterer? Will there be a charge for parking? Is there an equipment charge? Will you be charged for setup, security, clean up, or any other costs? *Do not assume anything.* Ask every question you can possibly think of when you are negotiating for an event site.

6. What are the hidden costs for your event? Recently, a Phoenix fund raiser was planning an evening walk event. She was having a difficult time identifying the right site. The problems were the many hidden costs affiliated with various sites. One site had neither night lighting nor access to a power source for rented lights. The hidden cost for this site would be the rental of a power generator. When planning the fine arts gala, it became necessary to move some bike racks that were anchored in cement blocks. It was necessary to depend on maintenance, who charged by the hour, to use the special fork lift that could pick up and move the racks. If you are planning an off-site event, you will want to consider those hidden costs affiliated with the special event rider on your insurance policy. When you are planning your event, it's a good idea to do so with budget in hand. As you will discover in Chapter 8, the budget requires more planning than just the cost of food and beverage per person.

7. What about a cancellation policy? Although you are just engaged in the planning process for this event, consider the possibility that an unpredictable occurrence might cause you to cancel it. Where will such a calamity leave you financially? A freak circumstance in Arizona caused the cancellation of the Chicago Symphony Orchestra, scheduled to appear in Tucson after their Flagstaff engagement. The Tucson Symphony Orchestra (TSO) was sponsoring that performance in the Music Hall of the Tucson Community Convention Center. The event was anticipated to raise $10,000 for the TSO. There was a full house in the Music Hall the evening of the performance. The audience was stunned to learn that a snowstorm in Flagstaff had caused a significant delay for the performers. Some of the musicians had arrived, but their personal instruments and some of their colleagues were still on a bus that was stalled in the storm. Patrons were encouraged to return to the Music Hall in an hour and a half. At the appointed time, all returned only to learn that the delayed bus was not anticipated to arrive in time to permit a performance. Not only was the evening performance canceled but the orchestra was scheduled to leave Tucson the following day and would be unable to perform at all! The TSO was left with the expenses of engaging the hall for the evening, hiring personnel to usher and to run sound and light, and, of course, the cost of printing tickets and programs. Patrons were encouraged to exchange their tickets for one of the concerts remaining in the season, donate the cost of the tickets, or request a refund. In this particular example, the site would not have made a difference; however, it might be wise to discuss the possibility of a sudden cancellation with the director of the facility you are renting. Perhaps the cancellation policy discussed in Chapter 7 would have helped planners to absorb the financial impact of this unfortunate experience. Whatever the event, it's always helpful to consider seriously what the financial impact might be should the event not take place as planned.

8. About catering . . . will it be a problem? If your site is not in a hotel (where food can be arranged through the catering department, prepared, and served on site) then you will want to consider how to deal with the food necessary for your event. Does the site you have chosen have rules about who can cater? Will you be required to follow its suggestions? Can alcoholic beverages be served on this site or will you need to make other arrangements? Remember, there must be a food preparation area as well as space for cleaning up. What about keeping food hot? Or cold? Will water be available for cleaning up? Due to the alternative nature of the sites chosen for the fine arts gala, it was necessary to be creative with preparation spaces and wash tubs, garbage cans, etc. There were definite rules regarding food and beverage. Permission was re-

quested to bring in the donated food to be served by restaurant staff, as well as wine donated by local wine merchants. (Note: the Arizona laws regarding the donation of wine or liquor have changed since this event; it is no longer legal for a company to donate alcoholic beverages.) Once university permission was granted, the plans for food and beverage moved forward. In Chapter 7, you'll find a more complete explanation of how the donation of food and beverage was accomplished. When it became obvious that there was a need for a significant amount of ice to service six different sites, a volunteer secured the donation of a refrigerated truck. Otherwise, ice storage would have been an added budget item.

9. What are the equipment requirements for your chosen site? Following is a list of equipment that you might need for your event. Each of these items may be available from the facility you are renting or might need to be rented from an outside vendor. **(1) For your guests:** tables and chairs; dishes, silverware, and glassware; linens and napkins; and centerpiece components. **(2) For your program:** podium; display tables; programs; sound equipment; lighting equipment; and stage or platform. **(3) For your event:** registration tables; ticket stands; steps and ramps; curtains or booth dividers; garbage cans; dollies and/or hand trucks; and ropes and stanchions.

10. Is your chosen site accessible? This is not just an issue for the handicapped. Simply think about what you'll need to produce your event, and then consider the following questions: Is your site accessible by truck? Will you be able to get equipment and supplies on site without having to carry them for long distances? What about telephone accessibility? (Of course, with the cellular phones of today, this is not the issue it once was.) What about valet parking? Will patrons have far to walk? Are there safety hazards, dark stairways, or low railings?

11. Will weather be a consideration for your chosen site? If part of your event is out-of-doors, what will you do in the event of poor weather? Do you have a backup plan? Even if you have one, can the event actually be moved at the last minute? Will wind, sunrise, or sunset affect your event? If you are holding a marathon or bike race, it would be a good idea to research the almanac for every weather possibility.

Contracting

It's wise to accommodate as many needs as possible up front when contracting for a site. It's much more difficult to get concessions after contracts are signed. Another consideration will be other events happening at this facility before, during, and after your event. Nearly everyone can recall events where the music and/or applause from the next room made it impossible to hear, much less maintain the mood the event was trying to establish.

It's also helpful to inquire about the availability of the room before your event. You may find that your set-up time is limited by an event scheduled before yours in the same space. And if something is scheduled after your event, you may not have the time you need to tear down the event. Such an occurrence can impact the budget as you may have to hire more people to get the work done in time.

Tenting an Event

Another possibility for an out-of-doors event is tenting. A tent suggests something out of the ordinary. It may not be as expensive as you might think. When planning an outside event, it's time well spent to research both the cost and the availability, whether or not you use one. A tent also offers you the opportunity for creative and unusual decorations.

One drawback of tenting concerns the condition of the ground and the possibility of rain. Look carefully at the surface. Is it a grassy site that will turn to mud as the rain soaks in from the ground outside? Is it a hard-earth surface or a concrete surface that will serve as a conduit for the weather outside to get inside? Will your tent have flaps? Will it be stuffy or hot? Will there be time both to pitch the tent and to take it down? Will it require time that you have contracted for? Will the tent be equipped with electrical outlets, lights, more than one exit?

Diagrams

Can the facility provide you with diagrams? Although it sounds like a small detail, consider the intrinsic value of a diagram when you are meeting with a sound technician who has never been to the site or your florist who is trying to assess the impact of a table centerpiece on the total room. Whether or not you use one, a diagram is critical for any event that requires seating people. The importance of diagrams cannot be emphasized enough. No matter what your event or program, unless it is a bake sale or a car wash, a diagram is needed to help you recognize and determine other needs. Diagrams not only illustrate the placement of tables and chairs, but can provide helpful information regarding traffic flow. When reviewing the traffic patterns for *Fantasy Flight 1029,* the diagrams depicted in Figures 5–1 through 5–4 were used. They may not be meaningful to you, but they were indispensable when training the guides for the evening. The people-moving component was one of the most complex aspects of the event. It was essential that the groups of people being moved from place to place did not run into each other. There was considerable potential for confusion plus the possibility that people might decide to join a friend in another group, thus creating significant seating problems at the next venue.

In Figures 5–5 and 5–6, the seating plans for a local hotel illustrate how to make a room look different or accommodate different numbers of people. These illustrations are included to demonstrate that there is more than one way to set up a room, and that hotel banquet staff usually are able to provide many ideas for you if you just ask.

Points to Ponder

Expect the Unexpected

If you elect to go beyond the hotel and restaurant circuit for your site, anticipate the different worst-case scenarios that could happen, with a particular emphasis on comfort, health, and safety. For example, consider the following case scenarios:

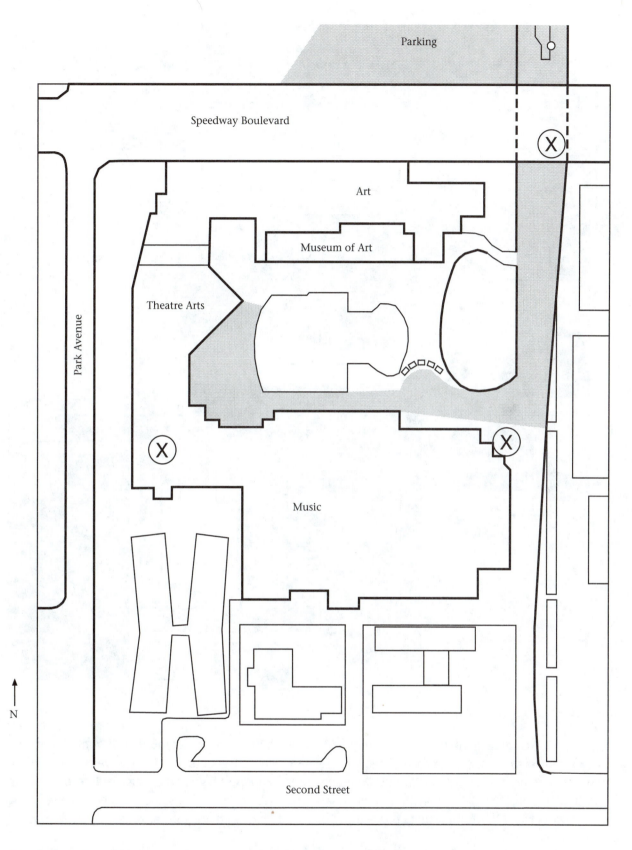

Parking

Speedway Boulevard

Art

Museum of Art

Theatre Arts

Park Avenue

Music

N

Second Street

Figure 5–1 This plan depicts the route guests of *Fantasy Flight 1029* would take from the parking garage to the Theatre Arts Courtyard. Courtesy of the University of Arizona College of Fine Arts, Tucson, Arizona.

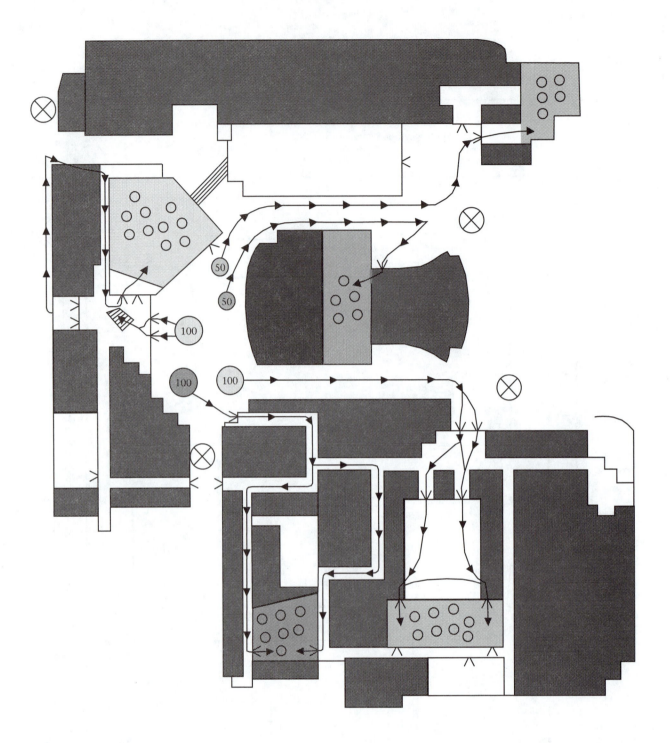

Figure 5–2 This diagram illustrates the routes to be taken by the various groups, differentiated by the color they were instructed to follow. There were four hundred guests in the courtyard. Each group (three groups of one hundred each and two groups of fifty) had to be guided through a different path to their first seating. The "Xs" indicate the location of the first performance vignette to be enjoyed along the way. Courtesy of the University of Arizona College of Fine Arts, Tucson, Arizona.

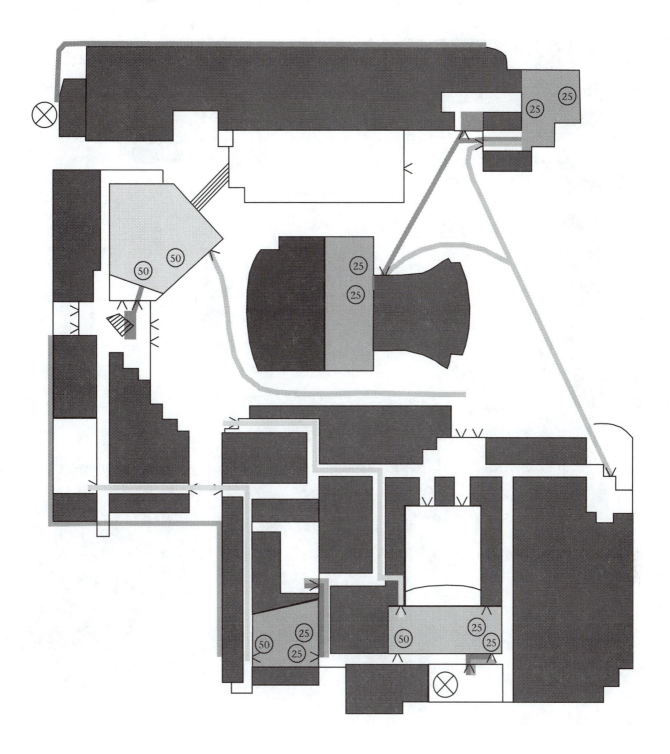

Figure 5–3 Now the guests required guidance from their first seating to their second vignette (on the way to their second seating). It was important to keep the numbers manageable for each performance site. Courtesy of the University of Arizona College of Fine Arts, Tucson, Arizona.

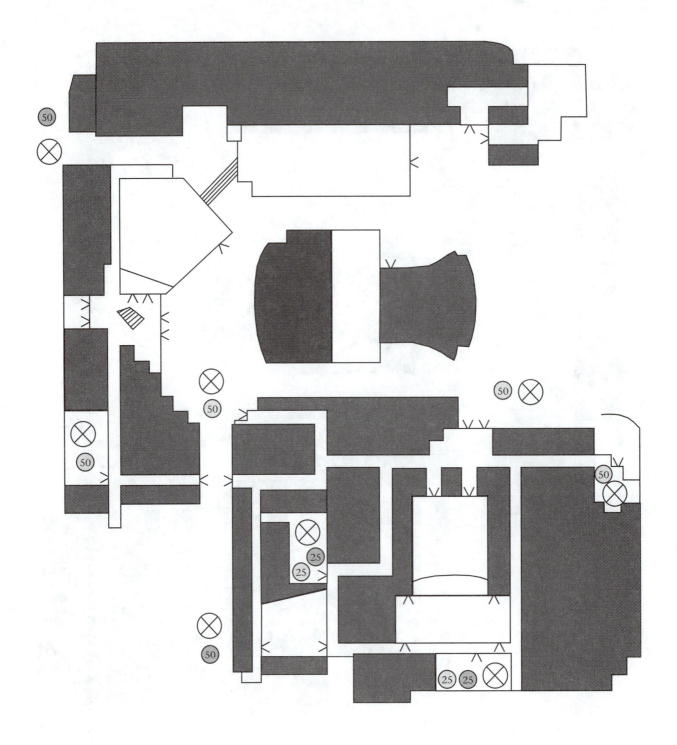

Figure 5–4 This diagram illustrates the number of people at each vignette site. Courtesy of the University of Arizona College of Fine Arts, Tucson, Arizona.

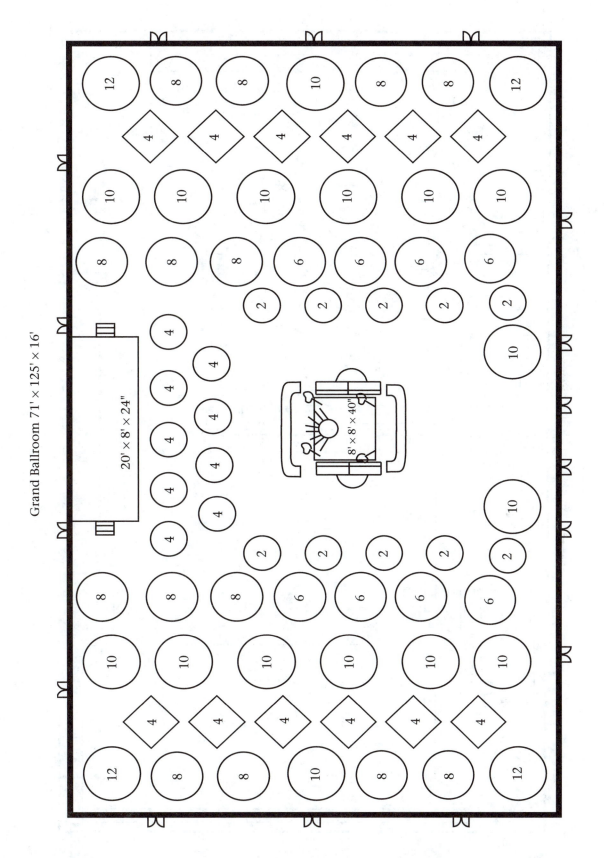

Figure 5–5 Diagram #1—The Grand Ballroom. This diagram demonstrates seating for 442 patrons. There is a platform for a production and a large decorative centerpiece in the center of the ballroom. This diagram demonstrates the use of tables of different sizes and how they can be complementary and decorative. Courtesy of Loews Ventana Canyon Resort, Tucson, Arizona.

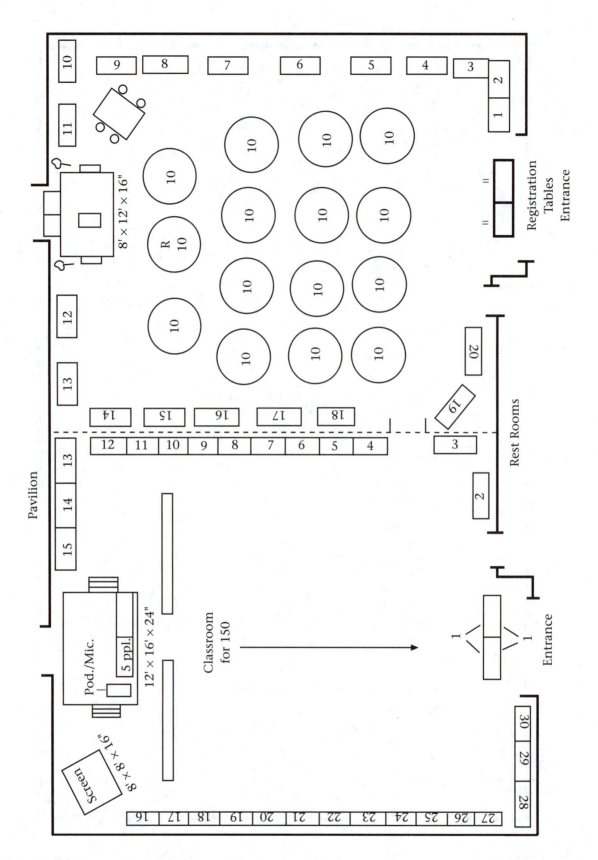

Figure 5–6 Diagram #2—The Pavilion. This diagram demonstrates a large room divided by a partition for a professional conference. It accommodates classroom seating on one side and table seating for meals on the other side. The numbered spaces around the edges are exhibits and vendor displays. Courtesy of Loews Ventana Canyon Resort, Tucson, Arizona.

Yachts are incomparable on a warm summer evening with a spectacular sunset. They are equally incomparable in a sudden squall with guests who left their sea legs on the shore.

The airplane hanger that housed the Spruce Goose, built by Howard Hughes, was perfect for an evening of buffet dining followed by dancing to music of the fifties under the broad wings of this relic of past dreams. Unfortunately, dancers who later drifted into the cavernous parts of the hanger failed to hear the final call for return transportation. Abandoned and alone in a strange industrial area at midnight, they quickly lost the glow and the warmth the organization had generated in their hearts.

The guest who decided to ignore the request to leave all champagne glasses outside when entering the newly restored mansion, tripped on a rug, sending herself and the glass flying. The glass landed first, just beneath her forehead, causing a minor but bloody cut. The mansion had no first-aid supplies and the staff was inexperienced in handling unsettled guests. The sounds of the ambulance brought the evening to a noisy end.

Expect the unexpected. Be certain to have contingency plans that make you appear the hero instead of the villain.

The site can be the appeal of the event, the program, and the decor, all in one. Consider the site that has intrinsic appeal in and of itself. A museum, closed to the general public for the evening, where the guests stroll from gallery to gallery, sipping wine and nibbling from food stations placed in each gallery, is program and decor all in one. A behind-the-scenes event at a winery, theater, firehouse, or zoo can entice individuals who enjoy the unusual. Consider a site not normally open to the public. The homes of the wealthy and powerful come to mind, perhaps as an add-on, extra-cost reception before the main event. A progressive dinner that moves from restaurant to restaurant appeals to those who like to sample the unusual and gives exposure to the restaurateur.

Summary

Unless the event has specific requirements such as a golf course or a performance, the site can be determined by a number of variables such as cost, suitability, convenience, availability, and ability to attract the target market. Considerations such as accessibility, catering, and optional services may play a role in site selection.

It may be that the site itself becomes part of the attraction. Unusual sites can create their own draw. Private homes of the wealthy, airplane hangers, yachts, warehouses, zoos, abandoned prisons, planetariums, museums, and parks all have been used to entice the market and serve as the backdrop for the program or even as the program itself.

The Black and White Ball in San Francisco, produced every second year for the benefit of the symphony, uses the very streets of San Francisco as its site. Revelers dine and dance in the cordoned-off streets surrounding the opera house and civic center. Tents are strategically placed for dining and for the variety of orchestras that offer music to please every ear. It is wonderful to see thousands of couples, each in formal wear of black and white, dancing in the streets until dawn.

Once the basic requirements are secured, you are limited only by your imagination when selecting a site.

Chapter 6

The Timeline: What Should Be Done by When?

You will never stub your toe standing still. The faster you go, the more chance there is of stubbing your toe, but the more chance you have of getting somewhere.

Charles Franklin Kettering

Chapter Outline

- Timelines

- Points to Ponder

In this chapter, you'll find an example of a planning calendar and you'll see that time is both the most controllable and the most uncontrollable aspect of special events. The challenge is to think ahead during the planning process. In fact, one of the most effective ways to develop a plan is to start from the event and work backwards. There will be times when you believe that it is much too early to order something or develop copy. But be advised that you can almost never be too early! Do your thinking well ahead, and build the calendar before you have too many distractions and deadlines begin to loom.

Timelines

This chapter contains several different types of timelines. All are included because each event is different and requires a different thought process.

The timeline form (Exhibit 6–1) is included for your information. The months are entered across the top and the activities or tasks are entered down the side. Exhibit 6–2 displays how the form was used for *Fantasy Flight 1029*.

There are some scheduling topics that are not covered in the foregoing timeline. Such topics as

when to reserve a facility were not relevant to *Fantasy Flight 1029*, but are critically important when you are using a facility that is not your own. Reserving space in major hotels generally takes place as much as a year or more in advance. If your event is small and does not require the grand ballroom, then you may find it possible to schedule something just a few months in advance. The larger the facility and your event, the further in advance you'll need to schedule the space. Other considerations must be taken into account. For example, think ahead to when you think you want to print your invitation. If it falls around election time, think again. That's when most printers are inundated with political work. If you think you might be printing around the holidays, check with your printer to see just how busy the schedule is. You'll need to plan for more time for printing during these periods of heavy use.

You'll notice that the planning takes place early on the calendar timeline. Board approval is necessary before making any arrangements. Planning is absolutely key to the success of an event. Other tasks that should happen early in the planning process include budgeting, list development, and volunteer recruitment. Accomplishment of these tasks will provide the solid groundwork necessary for a strong event. Arrangements with other departments or organizations must also take place early in the process. This includes any group or individual likely to have a full schedule and a tight calendar. Getting on that calendar early, with confirmation in writing, will add a dimension of security for which you'll be grateful. It's important to keep track of

Exhibit 6–1 Timeline Format

	Month from Which You Start			
Steering Committee				
Underwriting/Budget				
Program				
Invitation List/Printing/ Addressing				
Food & Beverage				
Host & Hostess				
Decorations				

continues

Exhibit 6–1 continued

	Month from Which You Start			
Arrangements/Setup				
Recognition/Thank You				
Checkpoints				

Exhibit 6–2 *Fantasy Flight 1029* Timeline

	November	December	January	February
Steering Committee	• Department selection of committee members	• First meeting of committee • Presentation of concept to volunteers • Discussion of committee chairs	• Introduction of volunteer chairs • Committee discussion of concepts	• Start regular meetings
Underwriting/Budget Equipment	• Presentation of preliminary budget to volunteer chairs • Discussion of ticket price	• Recruitment of F&B chairs to discuss concept of contributed food and beverage	• Finalize budget	• Budget distributed to steering committee
Performance Program	• Introduction of concept to department heads	• Discussion of concept to committee • Acceptance of assignments to enlist performers by department	• Written proposals from departments • Discussion of department representation by performances	• Review of proposals for performances and selection of balanced program
Invitations/Program List	• Staff review of database management for invitation list and reservations	• Staff preparation of existing lists from departments	• First volunteer review of list • Discuss new list sources • Class design project	• Gathering of additional names • Data entry by staff
Food & Beverage (F&B)	• Discussion of proposed concept of contributed F&B at selected venues • Develop job description for chairs	• Recruitment of F&B chairs and presentation of concept • Acceptance of concept • Request approvals needed	• Development of list of prospective restaurants, vendors, and suppliers • Assignments divided	• Development of letter of confirmation • Recruitment of participating restaurants

continues

Exhibit 6–1 continued

	November	December	January	February
Host & Hostess (H&H)	• Discussion of H&H concept with volunteer chairs • Initial list of people started	• Development of job description • Development of recruitment plan	• List development from invitation list • Additional sources identified	• Plan for H&H recruitment event • Discussion of program for event
Environment	• Development of job description • Recruitment of two chairs	• Discussion of feasible approach with limited budget (in and outside)	• Concepts for venues presented to steering committee	• Artists enlisted to paint tablecloths
Public Relations	• Information sheet developed • PR plan developed with PR staff	• Write letters to administration to get event on calendars • List dates for publications	• Discuss dedication ceremony for same date	• Discussion with campus press regarding special insert about fine arts
Arrangements/Setup		• Review of general event needs for evening • Security/equipment	• Disc with campus equipment and security • Permit for rappelling	• Reserve tables, chairs, linens, and dishes
Volunteer Support			• Begin list of human resources required for evening	• Discuss campus groups as resources for human resources required for event
Recognition	• Create donor recognition plan		• Develop recognition plan for F&B donors	

continues

Exhibit 6–2 continued

	July	August	September	October
Steering Committee	• Meeting of those still in town	• Spot meetings where needed	• Meeting—review status • Plan last six weeks	• Meeting as needed
Underwriting/Budget Equipment		• Review budget to date and adjust		
Performance		• Review logistics	• "Walk thru" with some performers	• Dress rehearsal
Invitations/Program List	• Address and mail "save the date" cards	• Address invitations • Stuff invitations	• Mail invitations • Fill in names in program	• RSVP due • Print programs
Food & Beverage	• Facilities and equipment plan	• Solicit food for volunteers	• Reminders mailed to participants	• Dress rehearsal and "walk thru" • Notify participants of delivery schedule
Host & Hostess	• Letter from Dean • Chair's letter and instructions for invitation notes	• Letter from chairs with reminder about tour	• Breakfast performance/tour	• Plan room assignments for VIPs
Environment			• Review equipment needs	• Move necessary fixtures • Install lights, etc.
Public Relations	• Stuff theatre program	• Press releases ready to mail	• Notice to departments regarding program page • Letter to upper level ticket buyers	• Release regarding impact of Faculty of Fine Arts on community

continues

Exhibit 6–2 continued

	July	August	September	October
Arrangements/Setup	• Notify grounds crew		• Recruit student helpers • Dress rehearsal	
Volunteer Support		• Enlist student help		• Dress rehearsal for all help • Distribution list for rental company
Recognition			• Plan thank-you notes	

where you are in the execution of your plan because it's much too easy for some small detail to slip by unnoticed, never to surface again. It could be an unpleasant surprise when you discover that the room you thought you had booked has not been reserved for you because you never confirmed the reservation.

Another illustration on the timeline is the number of tasks that must be completed at the same time. This is why the calendar format is so helpful. You'll notice that in November, eleven months before the event, there were tasks listed in nine of eleven areas constituting the plan. Whereas in July, there are tasks listed in only six of the areas. That is because 40 percent of the work is required early, 10 percent in the next phase, 40 percent around the time of the event, and just 10 percent in the "wrap up" and sending out thank yous. This balance is helpful to know as you look at the calendar to plan your event. Whether "early" is one year before or six months before your event, consider what else may be happening in your organization during that time and add it into the equation when you are considering the feasibility of your event.

Budgeting time does not have to be as graphic, but may be just as effective when composed as a list. The format might be to list items to be accomplished by month in a list like the one prepared for the No-Show Christmas Gala. This event is described in Exhibit 6–3, and its timeline is included.

Points to Ponder

Timelines are important management tools. It is essential that you have the discipline to create one with a relative deep degree of detail. Use the timeline to keep the project on track. Use it as a periodic reminder of where the project stands, what is coming ahead, and what is falling behind. There will always be deviations, but the probability of staying on schedule is greater with a timeline than without one.

Another value is that, should something unforeseen happen to the key staff person, someone else can pick up and carry forth more easily.

There are software products available for use with computers. For those who are particularly skilled with computers, there are project management products that may prove useful.

Exhibit 6–3 Special Event #1: No-Show Christmas Gala

Description: This is a non-event that involves a simple solicitation letter mailed by the organization. The mailing includes a large holiday greeting card, a donation/pledge card, and a return address envelope.

Special features/attractions: The solicitation letter is written like an actual invitation to a gala event, but the key is that no event is held. Instead, contributions are given in lieu of attending an event. The card is mailed to the organization's donor mailing list on the Monday following Thanksgiving. It is timed to be one of the first holiday cards that potential donors receive—and therefore grabs their immediate attention and interest.

Revenue raised: $12,000 to $14,000. (Expect less in the first few years until potential donors become familiar with the event.)

Estimated cost of hosting the event: $1,300 to $2,300, or 14% to 19% of the total revenues raised. This expense consists mainly of printing costs of the solicitation package and postage.

Net funds from event: $9,000 to $12,000.

Expenses covered or underwritten by sponsors/companies: $300. Currently, the printer donates production time to design the invitation package. A printer might also provide a special rate to print the package.

Time needed to coordinate the event: Two months.

Number of staff involved: Eight to 10 staff members hand-address the solicitation envelopes to give the mailing a personal touch.

Number of volunteers involved: 10 to 15. The organization serves people with disabilities. These individuals sort, fold, and stuff the envelopes. Other organizations could ask their volunteers to help with this project.

Size of constituency needed to make the event successful: Invitations are mailed to 4,500 potential donors.

Number of participants needed to make the event successful: 240.

Net: $9,000

Tips to maximize event effectiveness: The key to the No-Show Gala invitation letter is organization. Many staff and volunteers play a role in the mailing, so the coordinator must have a good plan of action and know what needs to be done, when, and by whom.

Pitfalls to avoid: Don't overdo it and make your potential donors feel like you spent too much money on the greeting card package. Carefully analyze the donor list. Don't send the letter to people who aren't capable of making a donation.

Additional information . . .

"Our year-end appeal letters weren't very successful," says the Flathead Industries development director. "When I first came here, I decided that we needed something besides a fund-raising letter.

"I did try to get an actual gala going. After some research, though, I found that the idea didn't fit with this low-key mountain community. So I combined the two ideas—a gala and an appeal—and the Holiday No-Show Gala was the result!"

This development director and her board designed an invitation that looks much like a holiday greeting card. The board chairperson's name appears at the top of the letter, and the names of other board members are printed down the left side. A red donation envelope—perfect for the season—with the chairperson's name and address on the front is also included.

continues

Exhibit 6–3 Special Event #1: No-Show Christmas Gala

"The first year of the no-show event, we printed 3,000 invitations," says the development director. "Board members and staff addressed them by hand, and I mailed them at bulk rates. Altogether, we spent $500 and raised $4,500. Now the No-Show Gala letter nets $9,000 to $12,000 each year!

"Timing is crucial to the success of this fund raiser," she adds. "We mail our invitation letter right after Thanksgiving, so it doesn't get lost in the thousands of holiday cards mailed in December." Since the invitation arrives at the end of November, prospects tend to put it with their gas and electric bills—and remember the organization when they pay their monthly bills!"

Planning List

Two months prior:
- ❏ Meet with board to plan and discuss the special "non-event"
- ❏ Write gala invitation and donation card
- ❏ Contact printer and discuss what is needed (may need to do earlier if you expect to find a printer to donate services in-kind)
- ❏ Meet with graphic artist to design holiday greeting card (in many cases, the printer will have a graphic artist on staff to help with design)
- ❏ Order paper
- ❏ Set print deadlines

One month prior:
- ❏ Proof all pieces of the mailing and ask a staff member not associated with the letter to review the package and provide feedback
- ❏ Send invitation package to printer
- ❏ Review printer's layout of invitation package
- ❏ Make necessary corrections and OK printing of package

Three weeks prior:
- ❏ Distribute envelopes to staff and board members to hand-address
- ❏ Contact volunteers to help with mailing process

Three days prior:
- ❏ Coordinate volunteer activities, assigning individuals to fold, stuff, seal, and stamp envelopes

Day of:
- ❏ Mail

Follow up:
- ❏ Analyze return rates and compare to average donation made; prepare cost analysis
- ❏ Report results of No-Show Gala to board
- ❏ Send "thank yous" to those who donated to the organization

Source: Reprinted from C. Elliot, *Aspen's Guide to 60 Successful Special Events: How to Plan, Organize & Conduct Outstanding Fund Raisers,* pp.1–3, © 1996, Aspen Publishers, Inc.

Chapter 7

How Much Will It Cost: How Much Can You Net?

There is no security on this Earth; there is only opportunity.

Douglas MacArthur

In this chapter, a budget-building process and a proposed format for that budget are presented. You will also find a worksheet on ticket income. From these tools, you'll be able to determine the potential net income to be realized from your proposed event.

Printing and Mailing

Thinking through the printing needs, you'll want to begin with ideas about the number of pieces to be printed. Will you want to send a save-the-date card or other event teaser? Will your invitation have a response card with an envelope included? Will you be mailing out tickets as they are ordered? What about posters? Will you want a program for your event?

Once these decisions have been made, you'll need to figure out how you want the printing done. Do you plan to solicit a contributed design as well as printing? If so, will this impact the kind of invitation you produce and the schedule of production? How many pieces will have to be mailed? Do you need two or three different envelopes? What size should your envelopes be? You'll find it helpful to write out in detail exactly what will be the demands of each job. If you intend to solicit the contribution of design and printing, you'll want to have this information at hand when you make the request. Because there are many variations of invitations, the prospective vendor will want to know exactly what you are asking. Writing it all out will be helpful to you as well. It is easy to go to a printer and request a contribution and then, upon returning to your office, remember that you did not ask for the save-the-date card or the program. Once you've made your request, it's difficult to go back and ask for more!

In your budgeting (as well as in your soliciting), don't forget the typesetting and paste-up. If the finished piece will require folding, be certain to ask if that is included in the price. If your contributed printing is in several colors, you may be asked to pay for the stripping. That is the process in which the colors are separated (by strips) so that they won't all run together. This is an exacting job and requires many hours of time, more than most printers can afford on a contributed job. If you have solicited an in-kind contribution of printing, don't be surprised if you are asked to pay for the stripping.

This is the time to consider signage. If you aren't producing the necessary signage on computer or by hand, you'll want to remember to include it in your budget.

The postage expense will depend on the number of pieces to be mailed and the projected number of responses requiring mailed tickets. Don't forget the postage necessary to communicate with your volunteers! If you do your job well, there will be many opportunities for communication.

Environment and Decorations

Will you need flowers? Plants? Aisle Stands? Swag ropes? Lighting or sound equipment? What about materials for special decorations? What about a stage? Platform? Signs? Will you need space heaters, fans? What about microphones and other audio visual equipment? Whatever your plan, *write everything down*, even those items that you expect to have donated. If you should have to pay for them, you want to know exactly what the cost will be.

Food and Beverage

In Exhibit 7–1, you'll find items from food to food service, tables, chairs, and linens listed. Plan for some breakage as well as theft. It's best to anticipate these unfortunate happenings rather than being unpleasantly surprised by them. They are almost inevitable.

One consideration that is not included in the budget is the guarantee that you will be asked to provide to most caterers and hotels. They will want you to guarantee a certain number of meals and you will be responsible for paying for those meals even if some of your guests do not show up. It is customary for the caterer or hotel to offer some allowance, perhaps three to five percent above the guarantee. Due to the inevitable last-minute cancellations, it is prudent to guarantee just a few meals less than you think you may need.

Another consideration is garbage! Be certain that you have the proper equipment on hand. If you have a caterer coming, discuss preferences with the person in charge. He or she may ask you to provide garbage cans or plastic bags. Whatever the caterer's requirements, you'll most likely be responsible for providing them.

Entertainment

If you are buying entertainment, be certain to ask what is included and what equipment, supplies, or other needs might be required. If you have secured the contribution of entertainment, the extras may be even more important. You can't always expect solo performers to bring their own sound equipment at their own expense. There is also the consideration of feeding the performers. If they are required to be on site during the time when your guests are eating, you'll want to attend to their needs. Sometimes performers prefer to eat after a performance and they may expect you to provide a meal. All of these details should be handled in *written* agreements between the performers and your organization.

Miscellaneous

Your event may require many special needs. Some events will require the use of walkie talkies to keep staff in touch with each other and so that they'll be able to be a step ahead of the guests. You may have a need to move large equipment or other supplies that require the use of a truck. Perhaps you'll be using a tent. No matter what you do, you'll definitely need janitorial help. And don't forget the staff necessary to help you the following day, or you'll find yourself and your volunteers doing a massive clean-up job.

If you decide to produce tee shirts to give or sell, or you wish to have this event recorded by a photographer, there will be added tasks to consider. There is also the possibility that you will require security or other such services.

Exhibit 7–1 is the budget used for *Fantasy Flight 1029*. The columns used were entitled Cash, In Kind, To Date (meaning budget spent to date), and Projected (meaning the total dollars projected to be spent for each category). The Projected column

Exhibit 7–1 Expense Budget, *Fantasy Flight 1029*

The X indicates that a budget item was contributed; the -0- means that there is no cash expense.

Expenses	Cash	In Kind	To Date	Projected
PRINT AND MAIL				
Save-the-Date Card (2,500)				
Design	-0-	X	X	-0-
Typeset and Paste-Up	50		22	22
Paper	-0-	X	X	-0-
Printing	-0-	X	X	-0-
Postage	725		725	725
Invitations (2,500)				
Design	-0-	X	200	200
Materials	50		51	51
Typeset and Paste-Up	-0-	X	X	-0-
Paper	-0-	X	X	-0-
Printing	250	X	X	-0-
Envelopes (# 9 and 10)	418		335	335
Postage	725		900	900
Reservation Cards (H&H)				
Design	-0-	X	X	-0-
Typeset and Paste-Up	-0-	X	X	-0-
Paper	-0-	X	X	-0-
Envelopes	62		X	-0-
Invitations				
Printing	-0-	X	X	-0-
Postage	116	X	86	86

continues

Exhibit 7–1 continued

Expenses	Cash	In Kind	To Date	Projected
Boarding Pass				
Printing	-0-	X	X	-0-
Postage	58		58	58
Stripping	1,400		1,284	1,284
Programs (500)				
Design	-0-	X	X	-0-
Materials	50	X	X	-0-
Typeset and Paste-Up	-0-	X	X	-0-
Paper	-0-	X	X	-0-
Printing	200	X	X	-0-
Stapling	-0-	X	X	-0-
Signage	350		350	350
Event Correspondence	200		225	225
TOTAL PRINT AND MAIL	**$4,655**		**$3,853**	**$4,236**
ENVIRONMENT				
Flowers	-0-	X	X	-0-
Plants	-0-	X	X	-0-
Aisle Stands (40)	207	X	X	-0-
Lights/Sound	-0-			1,000
Stage	-0-	X	X	-0-
Materials	2,500		1,968	2,500
Scotchgard				150

continues

Exhibit 7–1 continued

Expenses	Cash	In Kind	To Date	Projected
PERFORMANCES				
Scenery			374	374
Costumes	200	300	300	
FOOD AND BEVERAGE				
Entrees	500		54	150
Ice	100	X	X	-0-
Catering Managers	225	X	X	100
Service Rentals				
702 Dinner Plates	248			210
216 Black Plates				100
400 Dessert Plates	108			108
800 Knives	165			-0-
918 Dinner Forks	165			190
400 Dessert Forks	82			82
500 Spoons	125			41
1,316 Wine Glasses	269			356
Breakage	50			50
Salt and Pepper Shakers (5)	3			-0-
300 Cups and Saucers	162			162
Linens				
8 Extra Skirts				66
Underskirts (50)	414			414
Skirting, Banquet (24)	265			265
Banquet Whites (24)	127			171
Napkins (918)	400			400
Napkins (paper) 1,000	40			40

continues

Exhibit 7–1 continued

Expenses	Cash	In Kind	To Date	Projected
EQUIPMENT				
12 Card Tables	32			32
8 Round Tables (36")				39
54 Tables	247			267
700 Chairs	976			139
20 Serving Tables		X	X	
20 Prep Tables		X	X	
MISCELLANEOUS				
Walkie Talkies (8 × $10)	80			80
Truck Rental		X	X	
Tent				
Custodial	500		500	500
Security	2,180			2,180
Space Heaters	356			356
Photography	1,000			
Tee Shirts	-0-			850
TOTAL EXPENSES	**$15,449**		**$6,550**	**$16,723**

will help you keep track of where you are financially and can possibly forewarn you of the possibility of going over budget. You'll notice that some items were over budget and some were not even included in the original budget. But remember, a budget is a working document, a guide, and a tool—not an inhibitor. Exhibit 7–2 provides a blank budget.

Potential Income

When you estimate the expenses, you should also figure the potential income. This will give you an idea about how many tickets you'll need to sell to break even and then how many to make a profit. This requires that you multiply varying numbers of guests by each possible ticket price until you find just the right combination. When calculating the ticket income, remember that you will probably give away some complimentary tickets, so you must factor those into the possible number of seats available. Complimentary tickets might be considered an expense, and forgetting to note that could cause miscalculations.

If you are planning additional sources of income, those should be factored in as well. For example, you may choose to sell ads in your program to help cover the cost of the program and possibly make additional money. You may also elect to solicit underwriting to cover the event expenses, and if you put a line on your response card inviting contributions, you may realize some income from that source. This income, however, is more difficult to budget, and normally it's best not to try guessing what those contributions will be, unless your organization and the event have a track record for receiving them in the past.

Sponsorships

Sponsorship is about relationships that are mutually beneficial and profitable for both partners. Sponsorship constitutes a transaction between a business and an organization. The not-for-profit organization receives a fee or fees in return for supplying the for-profit organization with a ready-made audience that will be exposed to the sponsor's product. As with any commercial transaction, there should be a written agreement between the parties, one that explicitly covers the rights and obligations of each partner. The agreement should cover the expectations of the sponsor for access to the event and for ad visibility, as well as the expectations of the organization for fees payment.

One part of the agreement addresses the issue of access. Sponsors want access to key or exclusive markets that are of interest to the sponsor. The attraction for the sponsor is the audience, the guests, or the constituency—whoever is potentially interested in the sponsor's product. This access has value. The value is determined by the profile of the audience, the interest of the sponsor, the sales potential, and the degree of exclusivity. Because the profile of the audience determines the sponsor's interest, it is wise to fix the audience and then target the sponsors that have an interest in the market niche represented by the audience. There is little interest in wine at an event produced by a twelve-step program.

The organization must offer the targeted sponsor enticements to purchase access. Enticements could include recognition in the form of announcements from the stage, acknowledgment in the program, and acknowledgment on advance marketing material.

The second part of the agreement addresses the issue of visibility during the event. The sponsor may want to negotiate event visibility through the use of signs, distribution of samples, distribution of marketing material, demonstration of the product, or on-site sales opportunities.

A third part of the agreement addresses the issue of after-event benefits. For consideration, the sponsor may request ongoing visibility in the organization's year-round communications; the organization may offer preferred status for its next event; or the organization may offer to mail follow-up material to the attendees or to its entire database.

Sponsorship is not a philanthropic transaction. It is a business relationship and, therefore, subject to negotiation and profit. The not-for-profit organization must be true to its values and enter into only those sponsorship transactions that reflect honor on the organization's mission and do not compromise the organization's independence or programs.

Exhibit 7–2 Expense Budget

Expenses	Cash	In Kind	To Date	Projected
PRINT AND MAIL				
Save-the-Date Card				
Design				
Typeset and Mock-Up				
Paper				
Printing				
Postage				
Invitations				
Design				
Materials				
Typeset and Paste-Up				
Paper				
Printing				
Envelopes				
Postage				
Reservation Cards				
Design				
Typeset and Mock-Up				
Paper				
Envelopes				
Programs				
Design				
Materials				
Typeset and Mock-Up				
Paper				
Printing				
Stapling				

continues

Exhibit 7–2 continued

Expenses	Cash	In Kind	To Date	Projected
Signage				
Event Correspondence				
TOTAL PRINT AND MAIL				
ENVIRONMENT				
Flowers				
Plants				
Aisle Stands				
Lights/Sound				
Stage				
Materials				
Scotchgard				
PERFORMANCES				
Scenery				
Costumes				
FOOD AND BEVERAGE				
Hors D'oeuvres				
Entrees				
Beverage				
Ice				
Catering Managers				
Service Rentals				
Dinner Plates				
Dessert Plates				
Knives				
Dinner Forks				

continues

Exhibit 7–2 continued

Expenses	Cash	In Kind	To Date	Projected
Dessert Forks				
Spoons				
Wine Glasses				
Cups and Saucers				
Salt and Pepper Shakers				
Creamer and Sugar Bowl				
Breakage				
Linens				
Table Cloths				
Underskirts				
Skirting, Banquet				
Banquet Whites				
Napkins				
Napkins (paper)				
EQUIPMENT				
Card Tables				
Round Tables				
Tables				
Chairs				
Serving Tables				
Prep Tables				
MISCELLANEOUS				
Walkie Talkies				
Truck Rental				
Tent				

continues

Exhibit 7–2 continued

Expenses	Cash	In Kind	To Date	Projected
Space Heaters				
Photography				
Tee Shirts				
Custodial				
Security				
Cultivation Events				
TOTAL EXPENSES				

Return on Investment

In simplistic terms, a special event is an activity designed to produce income in excess over expenses, in other words, a profit. The amount of profit can be stated as a return on investment (ROI). Most professionals seek to have, as a minimum, a 50-percent net profit; therefore, for each dollar spent, one dollar and fifty cents must be raised. This net profit goal usually excludes indirect costs, specifically labor costs for staff and volunteers. If indirect costs were included, most events would show little, if any, net profit.

It's important to have the individuals responsible for budget, expenses, and contract agreements understand the implications of exceeding costs in any area. One successful event producer tells his volunteers that they can expense an item only if they have offsetting income in hand. The volunteer that wants to hire an orchestra must find an underwriter or angel. The individual that wants to have elaborate centerpieces with balloons must get them donated or sell advertising in support of the cost. Harsh, but his events result in a very favorable ROI.

How Many Guests Do You Need?

Table 7–1 helped to define how many host couples were needed for *Fantasy Flight 1029*. If the goal was to attract 400 people, then forty host couples would be the ideal. Because it was unlikely that all would be able to bring an additional five couples, there was no concern of going over goal.

Exhibit 7–3 demonstrates the potential ticket income from sales of the several different priced tickets.

The goal was to net $50,000 with probable expenses of roughly $20,000. That clearly defined the ticket goals.

> One successful event producer tells his volunteers that they can expense an item only if they have offsetting income in hand.

Given the goals of this event, the only acceptable scenario was number 3. This selection was a choice of the cochairs who knew the capacity of the host committee to attract people who would purchase the more expensive tickets. These then became the goals for the ticket sales. Had this scenario proved unrealistic or unachievable, the next step would have been to establish realistic goals and then to determine how to raise more money. This may be accomplished by underwriting, or selling program ads, adding a silent auction, raffle, or other creative solution. Another option would be to reduce the expense budget. In fact, many professionals develop the income potential first. However, the reality is that income and expenses must be developed together. If income and expenses aren't in proper balance, the financial goal for the event must be reduced.

A budget is meant to provide a guideline. It must be taken seriously; but in the event of realistic changes in circumstances, there must be flexibility to adjust accordingly. Use your budget as a tool; it will be helpful for your volunteers, but you must alert them to any necessary adjustments. Such an alert is best provided when you first realize the change will occur. Volunteers are supportive when they are not presented with surprises that require them to make significant adjustments. The following chapters will help you to select volunteers who have skills that will support your budgeting efforts. Exhibit 7–4 presents a sample budget for a special event.

Another type of budget format may be found in Chapter 17, Exhibit 17–1. This format is part of a check list and provides a good budget control tool. However, this format is not intended to replace the initial budgeting process.

When Budgets Indicate That an Event Should Be Canceled

Canceling an event is an unpleasant thought and one that is considered to be the last resort. However, canceling an event may be much more prudent that trying to produce an event that is not

Table 7–1 Host/Guest Chart

No. of Host Couples	No. of Invited Couples	No. of Invited People	No. of Host People	Total No. of People
40	× 5	= 400	+ 80	480
40	× 3.5	= 280	+ 80	360
30	× 3.5	= 210	+ 60	270
20	× 3.5	= 140	+ 40	180

Exhibit 7–3 Income Worksheet, *Fantasy Flight 1029*

Scenario 1

People		Price	= Total
200	×	$125	= $25,000
100	×	$250	= $25,000
Total 300			$50,000

Scenario 2

People		Price	= Total
250	×	$125	= $31,250
100	×	$250	= $25,000
Total 350			$56,250

Scenario 3

People		Price	= Total
40	×	$500	= $20,000
75	×	$250	= $18,750
295	×	$125	= $36,875
Total 410			$75,625

Exhibit 7–4 Sample Budget for a Special Event

INCOME	EXPENSES
Event	**Event**
Tickets	Cost of facility rental $_____
____Patron tickets @ $____ = $_____	Cost of entertainment $_____
____Sponsor tickets @ $____ = $_____	Cost of food $_____
____Regular tickets @ $____ = $_____	Cost of decorations $_____
____Donations	Cost of invitations $_____
(From individuals not coming)	Cost of mailing $_____
	Cost of patron's party $_____
	Cost of posters $_____
	Cost of photographer $_____
Total Income $_____	Total Expenses $_____

Income $_____ Less Expenses $_____ = Funds Raised $_____

Raffle	**Raffle**
____Chances @ $_____ = $_____	Cost of printing $_____
	Cost of prizes $_____
	Cost of license $_____
Total Income: $_____	Total Expenses: $_____

Income $_____ Less Expenses $_____ = Funds Raised $_____

continues

Exhibit 7–4 continued

INCOME	EXPENSES
Advertising Booklet	**Advertising Booklet**

INCOME

Advertising Booklet

_____1/4 pages @_____ = _____

_____1/2 pages @_____ = _____

_____Full pages @_____ = _____

Inside front cover @_____ = _____

Center spread @_____ = _____

Inside back cover @_____ = _____

Outside back cover@_____= _____

Total Income: $_____

EXPENSES

Advertising Booklet

Cost of ad forms $_____

Cost of typesetting $_____

Cost of printing $_____

Total Expenses: $_____

   Income $_____   Less Expenses $_____   =   Funds Raised $_____

TOTAL EXPECTED INCOME FROM ALL SOURCES: $_____

Courtesy of California Pacific Medical Center Foundation, San Francisco, California.

supported by the necessary attendance. It is a foregone conclusion that by the time you realize that people are not coming and that you have tried everything you know to improve the attendance figures, the money spent will be lost. However, if you were to proceed with an event that is not supported by enough of an audience, you stand to lose even more money. This is a difficult decision and one that must be made in consultation with the board. Not only is it embarrassing, but it's a costly decision as well. Be certain that you have explored every avenue to save the event before deciding to cancel.

Should you decide to cancel, there are several important steps. The first is to refund the ticket money that has been collected. This may be done in writing or by phone, offering each person the option of a refund, exchange, or donation. Next, it will be important to notify any sponsors of your event. If they have given money to underwrite the event, you'll need to explain your decision, make a suggestion about how you might still be able to offer them visibility, and ask if they would like their money refunded. There is a possibility that an underwriter might suggest that you should keep the money to help defray those expenses already incurred. But there is also the possibility that they might want their money refunded. This is one of the considerations that will influence your decision whether to cancel.

When a Special Event is Not a Fund-Raising Event

There are circumstances when you might want to offer something special for your patrons. Perhaps you chose to bring in a special speaker. However, the cost to provide that speaker should not be part of your organization's budget. A widely-acclaimed speaker will draw a crowd even if they have to pay. But all you want to do is break even. You'll still need a budget to help you price this event just to cover expenses.

Points to Ponder

The basic rule for answering the question, "How much will it cost?" is to avoid thinking about how much it *should* cost. Now is the time to be prudent

and careful, but it is not the time to scrimp and save to the detriment of the event and its goals. Spend whatever it takes to get the right people, the *who*, to attend your event. As David Nelson so bluntly puts it, "Spend whatever is necessary to get the right butts into the seats!"

At the same time, think creatively and take advantage of every opportunity to save without impairing the event. Acquiring "freebies" in services and supplies is one of the ways. Most events provide opportunities for service industries to expand their markets and gather new customers. Restaurants that want to entice new diners may, as a marketing strategy, donate or supply their services at cost. Vineyards may want exposure for a recent bottling. Florists may enter into competition to offer visibility for their decorating talents. Recognition in the event program may be cost-effective advertising for companies that want visibility within the same market that you have targeted for the event.

With events that are produced as "annuals," let the expense/income ratio be only one of many considerations when planning the second or third annual event. For each new event, there is a three-year learning curve in which mistakes are made, audiences refined, volunteers and staff trained, and efficiencies instituted. Wait until the third or fourth year before making decisions based on income and expense.

For events that are repeated, view the income as an expanding resource. Each year, add a new income-generating opportunity. For example, year one focuses on producing a successful but basic dinner dance that was well received by the target market. In year two, something new is added, perhaps a silent auction. In year three, entertainment is added to the silent auction. In year four, the silent auction plus entertainment is supplemented by sponsorships. Planned growth for income permits the basic dinner dance to remain fresh while staff and volunteers, relieved of the "let's do it all now syndrome," work at the added revenue streams over a period.

Summary

The budget is an essential tool for the event. It establishes expectations and guidelines for all involved. Deviations should be justified before the budget is modified. It may be that responsibility for budget control is assigned to a different individual than the person responsible for arrangements. Certainly, an increase in expenditures should entail a commensurate increase in income or some other compensating measure.

Except in rare cases, special events are not intended to lose money. They are not always income generators, but must at least break even financially. The budget should be viewed as the tool that determines decisions, including the decision to abort the event if the income-to-expense ratio becomes insupportable. Line item changes can be negotiated, but the income-to-expense ratio should remain constant unless it changes to a more favorable ROI. The budget becomes the reason to say "No, we cannot agree to that suggestion."

Chapter 8

Human Resources: How Many People Will You Need?

A division small in size but unified in commitment will win. Remember, weaponry and manpower are important, but it is the general's commitment that determines victory.

W. Chan Kim and Renee A. Mauborgne

Chapter Outline

- Tasks Requiring Volunteer Support

In this chapter, you'll find help in organizing your thoughts about the following:

- tasks for which you'll need volunteer help

- types and qualifications of volunteers you'll want to recruit

- organization of volunteers

Tasks Requiring Volunteer Support

Conceptual and Creative Work

From the beginning, volunteer support is critical to the success of your event. Why? Volunteers will be your idea bank. They will generate interest from others in working on and attending this event. The more volunteers you have involved, the larger your audience will be. One example is the fashion show. Using volunteer models who are known in the community will generate interest among the friends and family of each model. Each model can probably sell ten tickets, enough to fill one table. With twenty or more models, you can go into your event with approximately 200 tickets already sold.

Of course, you'll want to make ticket selling easy for them. Explain the process to your volunteers, providing printed material they can use when selling.

But before you even consider the models, you'll want some volunteer involvement in planning the event. If you already know what you want to do, you'll need to sell your ideas to the volunteers so that they have some ownership. This is step one on your way to success. If you aren't certain what you want to do, as in the case of *Fantasy Flight 1029*, the volunteer contribution will be both critical and challenging. This is the circumstance under which you have the risk of an idea appealing to the volunteers but sending red flags up for you and your staff. Your relationship with your volunteers might be tested at this point. Your experience could be terrific, but it never hurts to be prepared for possible pitfalls. This is the group that will recommend, endorse, and develop your concepts and set or confirm the ticket price for your event. The *conceptual and creative work* is the backbone of your event. Thinking through ideas will help you determine the best market for your event. When that important determination has been made, then you'll be able to move to the next step.

The Steering Committee

This group may be comprised of those individuals who helped conceptualize your event, or it may be an entirely different group of people. Whatever its makeup, the steering committee will be those people who will track the event and keep abreast of the timeline, ticket sales, etc. The group might be composed of all of the committee chairs or it may be an independent group. The steering committee will be concerned with the oversight of your event. Not every event requires a steering committee. If, however, you have a complex event that depends on attracting a large number of guests, the more people involved in planning, the more people are likely to support the event.

The Honorary Chair and The Working Chair

Your honorary chair, if you have one, should be so widely recognized in the community that some will attend your event just to be part of the same social scene as the chair. Your working chair is typically one who will roll up sleeves and tackle anything and, in general, will keep the rest of the volunteers motivated. Should you have both? When you have access to just the right people for each of these positions, then you would do well to consider having both. It isn't necessary, but it can extend your reach into the community and add some nice visibility for your organization.

The Host and Hostess Committee

This is the group that will make (or break) your event. How many will you need? That depends on how many you want to attract to your event. The host committee members are your front line salespeople, your public relations team, and your best customers. You'll find more about this important group in Chapter 10, but at this point, you'll want to determine how many people you'll need to achieve your attendance goals. The more you have out there talking about your event, the more potential you'll have for selling out. For example, if you have a host committee of forty couples and each couple is responsible for bringing five couples with them, then you'll have the potential to attract 400 people to your event! Of course, there are times when you will want all women or all men; this composition will influence the composition of the committee. Whatever your goal, let it help

you determine your requirements for this committee.

Invitation Design and Production

You may choose not to involve volunteers in this arena. However, if you have some individuals with artistic talents, you may enjoy having some help with the design elements. Once again, the same principles come to bear—the more volunteers involved, the more interest will be generated in others. There is definitely such a thing as too large a committee for this task. Design by committee can be challenging! So select the members judiciously, and be sure to let them contribute. It can be a real turn off when a committee member is expected to rubber stamp the staff's decisions. Volunteers don't appreciate putting their time and effort into a project and never being given the opportunity to participate in a meaningful way.

Underwriting

This is where volunteer help can bring new contacts into the picture. This committee is generally composed of a few people who are well connected and able to ask for contributions of dollars as well as goods and services. Remember that the more underwriting you secure, the more ticket dollars will be raised free and clear. A reminder: just because your event is completely underwritten, the fair market value of the event is still whatever a person would pay for the same service or product in the community and, hence, the amount that is not tax deductible.

Event Schedule and Program

Depending on the type of event you choose to produce, you may wish to have a committee that will review and facilitate the event schedule and program. In some organizations, this committee comprises staff members. For the fine arts gala, the program was produced by staff and the committee served not only to approve but to coordinate the department offerings, coordinate all of the performances, and keep a "reality check" on the complexity of the technical requirements of the multiple performance groups. For example, could lights be set for musicians and then reset to meet the needs of the theater department when both were using the same performance space? Were there enough microphones and, more importantly, was there enough power to drive the desired sound and light plans? If your program is being produced by volunteers rather than by your organization, the support of this committee is critical.

Food and Beverage

This may be a group who selects the food and beverages for your event or solicits the same. In the case of *Fantasy Flight 1029*, this committee was composed of two restaurateurs. They determined whom they would ask, and for what, and then proceeded to do it. Of course, it helped considerably to have them contribute from their own restaurants. Further, they solicited some of the more expensive food items from their purveyors to help out the restaurants that were volunteering to prepare the food.

Environment/Decorations

Wherever you have chosen as the site for your event, it is certain to require a boost in the area of decor. The larger the area, the greater the need and the greater potential expense. This is where you'll need some creative and resourceful people. Whether the need is limited to table centerpieces or you are trying to brighten up a warehouse, creative energy that has been tempered with a good understanding of budget limitations will be a must. If you don't have access to such talents within your organization, it may be necessary to contract for this expertise.

Public Relations

These are the people who will make recommendations regarding appearances on talk shows, society photos, and notes. This group may propose some gimmicks to generate interest in your event. These might include a teaser sent before the invitation or a sample performance created just to whet the appetite of volunteers. More ideas will be discussed in upcoming chapters.

Phone Follow-Up

No matter what type of event you produce, you can be certain that its success will be enhanced by phoning. Whether you are phoning the host committee, the board members, or other groups who may be selling tickets, phoning will play an important role. Each audience to be phoned will respond more positively when the right person calls. Therefore, it is important to assign only the most appropriate callers to this important committee. For example, board members will respond to other board members, but not to staff.

Signage

Signs are an important part of any event, and the creation of these should not be left until the last minute. On the other hand, there will be times when you will not know what you need until the last minute. This may be clearly a staff function or, if necessary, independently contracted. It is important to think through the event early enough to allow the time necessary to create professional looking signage. Will you need signs on the streets, in the parking area, on the path, or in the building? Will you need signage with directions to the rest rooms? Many signs may be computer-generated; however, there may be convincing reasons to purchase better quality signs. What about sponsorship signs? Will you need banners? What about table tents? All are too important to be left to last minute detail.

> No matter what type of event you produce, you can be certain that its success will be enhanced by phoning.

Arrangements and Setup

This area is often left to the imagination until the week or even the day of the event. Yet, this is the area in which you'll need significant support. Although the arrangements may be emblazoned on your own mind, you'll be in serious trouble if you haven't managed to get them on paper so that you are able to determine where you will need the most help. No assumptions about what you *think* other committee members understand will help. The necessary arrangements must be written down. Exhibit 8–1 presents a chart that will help you work through your event.

Recognition

This activity may or may not require a committee. It depends on the number of people you'll want to be recognized and the chosen method of recognition. It may be accomplished in a printed program or by acknowledgment from the podium; a gift may be presented, or some visible designation of status may be provided. For *Fantasy Flight 1029*, you may remember the tee shirts that identified the artists filming the event. Decisions must be made regarding how, what, where, and when recognition will occur.

Thank Yous

Last, but not least, are the thank yous. Creative thinking will help to produce a thank you process that will demonstrate sincere appreciation for the efforts expended by these many volunteers. This may not require a committee's work but will need some coordination. Plan this just as you would any other part of the event—in advance. These essential recognition pieces must be executed in a timely fashion so they do not appear to be an afterthought, weeks or months later.

The Human Resources Working Chart

Exhibit 8–1 is an example of a chart that will help you to organize your volunteer lists. Each volunteer task is briefly described. Each task has a designated staff person in charge. There is a date designation to indicate the time when this particular group of volunteers is needed. This is one of those lists that needs to be developed, reviewed, and then revised. For several days, you're likely to be thinking of additional needs. After you've given yourself plenty of time to review this list of tasks, you'll want to begin recruiting the people to fill the slots.

Summary

Volunteers are the essential component of all development programs, including special events. For events, volunteers are critical to success because they have access to the target market, they are the validating force, they are ticket sellers, they are advocates, they are a source of creativity, and they are the core attendees. They become your salespeople, your public relations team, and your first and best customers.

The depth of volunteer involvement varies from organization to organization and from event to event. For a high-level social event that is an annual occurrence with many attendees, volunteers can be involved from the earliest planning stages. They can perform the crucial role of being the "host" on behalf of the organization. An invitation, especially one with a handwritten note from a host is more compelling than an invitation from the organization.

The correct volunteers can be a resource about community perceptions and community preferences. Their advice on price, location, competition, and programs can be invaluable. As the planning evolves, the volunteers become weather vanes, alerting to changes in the environment. Their ability to access the right people is just the recruitment tool needed to approach any honorees or other notables whose presence will make the event a "must do."

There are many tasks in producing an event, tasks at which volunteers can excel. Tasks that may be undoable or unproductive for staff. Volunteers become the arms and legs of the event.

Reference

Kim, W. Chan and Renee A. Mauborgne. 1992. Parables of leadership. Harvard Business Review, July/August: 123–128

Exhibit 8–1 Human Resources Requirements for *FANTASY FLIGHT 1029*

Tasks	Staff Volunteers	Dates	
Moving Team	J. Bassnett	10/28–11/1	1. Bill L.
	1-1302		2. Louis S.
Pick up and deliver chairs and equipment			3. Brett
Load and unload			4. Ian
Deliver to sites			5. Jose
			6. John D.
Event Set-Up	B. Levy	10/28–29	1. Lisa
	1-8822		2. Darlene
Direct deliveries, loading and unloading miscellaneous items, see that they get to the right site, run errands, etc.			3. Diana
			4. Marjory
			5. Mary Ann
			6. Pat B.
			7. Rhea
			8. Ellen
			9. Cande
			10. Carrol
Ticket Booth Staff	L. Ferguson	10/29	1. Brett
	1-8824		2. Darlene
Greet guests and assign first and second seatings			3. Diana
			4. Ian
			5. Peter

continues

Exhibit 8–1 continued

Tasks	Staff Volunteers	Dates	
Event Guides	P. Bjorhovde	10/28–29	1. Susan W.
	1-9507		2. Andy P.
Appear in costume			3. Jerry D.
Guide guests through evening			4. Jane W.
Attend training			5. Mikelle O.
			6. Amy G.
			7. Dan U.
			8. Sahku M.
			9. Alexa S.
			10. Paddie E.
			11. Heather T.
			12. Renate D.
			13. Greg L.
			14. Eric J.
			15. Allison J.
			16. Andrew L.
			17. Ron V.
			18. Gloria R.
			19. Annie S.
			20. Rob J.
			21. Merrie G.
			22. Alan P.
			23. Ricardo E.
			24. Lori H.

continues

Exhibit 8–1 continued

Tasks	Staff	Volunteers	Dates	
Food Service Managers	B. Levy	11/28–29	1. Daniels
	1-8822		2. El S.
Set up each prep and eating area			3. Ovens
Train servers and bussers			4. Joy Hicks
Supervise shift to second seating			5. Boccata
Supervise breakdown at end of evening			
Servers and Bussers	B. Levy	11/28–29	1. Turner D.
	1-8822		2. Paul P.
Work with restaurants to set up buffet, set tables, bus tables	Food Service Managers		3. Barbara M.
			4. Philip S.
Clear first seating and reset for second			5. Sue S.
Clear and pack rentals			6. Larry L.
			7. Joanna M.
			8. Dolores S.
			9. Martha R.
			10. Katie A.
Cocktail and Dessert Servers	Food Service Managers	11/28–29	1. Joan N.
			2. Aggie A.
Pass trays of hors d'oeuvres			3. Paul I.
Set up and serve desserts			4. Randi K.
			5. Lev O.
			6. Donna A.

continues

Exhibit 8–1 continued

Tasks	Staff Volunteers	Dates	
			7. Lyneen E.
			8. Caroline M.
			9. Millie G.
			10. Kay C.G.
			11. Stacie W.
Costumes	Theater Dept.	11/28–29	1. Gwen W.
Supervise and help guides get into costumes—supervise return and hanging of costumes			
Hospitality Room	J. Reeves	10/29	
Pick up donated food			1. Jerry R.
Supervise delivery of donated food			2. Julia DeJ.
Keep food tables clean and replenish food			
Remind volunteers of time schedules			

Chapter 9

Who Should Be the Key Players?

There is something that is much more scarce, something rarer than ability. It is the ability to recognize ability.

Robert Half

In this chapter, you will find a discussion about the leadership you'll need for your event. You'll find a description of the "key" people, how to identify them, and how to recruit them.

Who Are the "Key" People and How Do You Reach Them?

The key people are those who will be able to draw the people you'd like to attend your event. Therefore, the right people are going to be those most likely to have contact with the markets you are trying to reach. If you are seeking sports fans for your event, then you'll want people whose friends and associates are sports fans. On the other hand, if you are seeking high society for your event, you'll need high society represented on your steering committee. You will always be safe striving for the top echelon for your special event leadership.

But how do I reach them?

Begin with a small group of volunteers who will help you strategize about the best possible chair for your event. This group may include people from the community, board members, and donors. These people will want to know what you hope to achieve and whom you are seeking to involve. They will be able to offer recommendations only when you are very specific about your needs. Are you interested in reaching several different markets or just one market? What kind of commitment will you be asking your volunteers to make? Do you have a case statement for your event and a job description for the chair or members of your steering committee? The case statement is your reason for producing the event, describing the need for the dollars to be raised, the markets to be cultivated, and the visibility to be sought.

Because of the information contained in most event programs, these programs provide an excellent research tool. When you are looking for a person's connections, an event program may provide that important information. For example, you might know that an individual is involved with the symphony. By looking through a symphony program, you could find out if this person is a member of the board or even an officer. If you are seeking a way to contact your prospect, perhaps you can find another board member, with whom you have a relationship, to help make the necessary introductions. You also may be able to find the donor category of your prospect.

Perhaps you know from the start just whom you would like as chair. The person you have in mind was probably selected because of prominence, affiliations, and interest in your organization. Or, you may have chosen this opportunity to acknowledge the work someone has done for your organization. Whatever the case, consider the best recruitment scenario. Perhaps it's a lunch meeting including someone considered influential by your prospect. When you are ready to ask, it is most effectively done if and when you have some of the following materials in writing:

1. a case statement including a description of your organization and the event concept

2. goals of the event

3. a job description for the event chair

4. a timeline of the commitment you are seeking from the prospect

5. financial expectations you are seeking from your prospect

Exhibit 9–1 presents a job description for an event chair. The job description should reflect exactly what you hope your event chair will be willing to do. When you first meet, it is important that your expectations be clearly stated. You gain nothing by holding back one of your expectations until the prospect has said yes. Remember, volunteers can abandon a project at any time! Each area of responsibility merits a job description. You'll find job descriptions for the committee chairs in Chap-

Exhibit 9–1 Event Chair Job Description

- Serve on steering committee, which will approve event concept and financial plan.

- Attend two meetings per month until concept and budget are approved.

- Attend bi-monthly meetings up to a pre-determined time before the event when meetings may be more often.

- Help to recruit committee chairs.

- Invite hosts and hostesses to participate.

- Sign pre-event correspondence.

- Help to develop event invitation list.

- Maintain contact with committee chairs through development staff.

- Purchase tickets to the event.

- Make some fund-raising calls with development staff.

- Attend the event.

The time commitment for this project is anticipated to be over nine months. The average meeting time per month will be three hours. Telephone time will add an additional three hours per month. Staff will support all activities of the chair of this event by drafting and producing correspondence as requested, producing mailings, and recording and distributing minutes of meetings.

ter 10. The planning and time that you put into these descriptions will amply reward your efforts.

Some of these tasks may not be set in stone, but they are probably ready enough to be labeled "draft." Plan this meeting with your recruitment partner. Who will open the conversation? Who will bring the conversation around to the event? Who will present the rationale for this event? Who will describe the event? Who will ask your prospect for a commitment?

Although it's true that you are asking this prospect for help in the form of time, talent, or contacts, remember that being affiliated with the event offers some benefits for your volunteer. Consider the exposure you are offering your prospective chair. The event may provide your prospect with some valuable visibility. The position of chair sends a message that this is someone who cares about the community and works on its behalf. The social or economic rewards can be significant.

If yours is an ongoing event, you may wish to consider the future when recruiting your event chair. At the same time, you may wish to ask your prospective chair to recommend a vice chair who will learn the ropes this year and move into the position of chair next year. When you can achieve this positioning, your search for the next vice chair is made much easier because you have someone in leadership recommending someone else with compatible capabilities.

How to Equip Your Volunteers

We have just covered the necessity of the job description and its value to your volunteers. There are other pieces of information that will ease the minds of your volunteers and make their jobs fairly simple. As much detail about the event and its logistics as you can provide them in advance will save both your volunteer and yourself time and effort.

A Case Statement

Those in the fund-raising profession know the importance of the case statement. The case statement states the reason why an organization should be supported. Each of your leadership volunteers should have a short but descriptive case statement for the event they are selling. These are the words they can use when convincing their friends that this event is worthy of support. Review your goals for the event, and out of those goals you will be able to develop the case statement. This is particularly important if you are working with an organization that is not well known to the public.

Exhibit 9–2 provides the case statement for *Fantasy Flight 1029.*

Exhibit 9–2 Event Case Statement for *Fantasy Flight 1029*

> The College of Fine Arts is nationally respected for the quality of its departments and their programs. Locally however, the College is not as well known. There are so many excellent arts organizations in the community that people have not taken the time to explore the wealth of excellence in this College.
>
> *Fantasy Flight 1029* is designed to offer the community a glimpse of each of the departments and the fine entertainment they offer. The entertainment produced for this event will spotlight the top faculty and student performers. The varied program will provide something for everyone and is designed to stimulate interest in coming back for more at a later date.
>
> The funds raised from this event will secure an endowment for the Dean's Fund for Excellence. That's the fund available to students and faculty to ensure that they might enjoy opportunities when they are presented. This fund has paid travel expenses for artists invited to national and international competitions. It has paid for supplies and materials that an artist is unable to afford. It has provided educational opportunities for faculty and students. But the fund today is limited to a very small budget and the needs are far greater than the total budget. An endowed fund will ensure the extra support required by the artists and will be available in perpetuity.
>
> This event will open the eyes of the community to a wonderful resource they may never have known before; further, it will open significant opportunities for students and faculty, thereby increasing the level of excellence within the College.

Timeline

The full timeline (like the example in Chapter 6, Figure 6–2) might be overwhelming to a newly recruited volunteer. But it would be extremely helpful for a volunteer to see how well you have planned your event. So, you might take the work of just one committee and discuss its timeline. If volunteers feel well supported, they are comfortable in accepting assignments they might otherwise pass up.

Other Printed Materials

Any mock-ups or drafts of designs are helpful. Even if it isn't the final version, people are engaged by a work in progress. Diagrams of facilities will help a volunteer visualize an event. Photographs will interest people and help them to sell tickets.

Providing your prospective leadership with information ahead of time is a form of cultivation. When you educate someone about your organization, whether you wind up with a chair or not, you will have another person educated about your organization. The material engages people, catches their interests, helps them visualize, and helps them to feel involved. You are not only cultivating people for the event, you are cultivating them for your organization. At various times during the committee meetings, remember to bring your senior staff members by, introduce them, and tell your volunteers a little something about each one. You could not find a more valuable cultivation opportunity if you tried. It also provides the opportunity for your staff to thank the volunteers and reinforce the message that they are making an important contribution of their time, effort, and connections.

Involvement of Key Volunteers from the Start

There is a slightly different approach to requesting board or volunteer involvement from the one just covered. It works best for those individuals who have had considerable experience in volunteering, and who have definite opinions about how their time and talents should be used. Those who like a hands-on experience will want information from the beginning. They will want to be consulted about everything. They will give opinions and advice that will require your careful attention and your action. Although this kind of volunteer may provide the

best possible support for you, it's also possible that the ideas proposed may be counter to your expectations. This can result in a challenging situation, so it's best to know your volunteer well *before* asking advice. Be prepared to make adjustments to your own plans to honor the volunteer's recommendations. If you know in advance that you work well together, the experience can be a positive and rewarding one.

Whatever you are asking, be certain that you are making the best use of the volunteer's time. You will gain considerable credibility by sticking to your plan. When you have asked for thirty minutes of someone's time, do not stretch that. If volunteers realize that you will honor their time and do what you have promised, they are much more enthusiastic and willing to commit their time.

Asking advice for the recruitment of additional volunteers is generally a good involvement technique. Is there anyone who doesn't like to be asked for advice? Advice-seeking is an excellent cultivation tool. The volunteer world is a small world of many connections. People who are generous with their time and their connections are certain to know others of the same philosophy. Flattered by your request for help, your volunteer is much more likely to play a key role in the recruitment of others. In addition, people who have been asked for advice generally choose to involve themselves further, offer other suggestions, and even recruit some of the individuals whom they have suggested. There is always the possibility that the person you ask will choose not to become more deeply involved. This individual may make many recommendations, but may not be willing to ask people to attend.

Revisiting the issue of exposure, the more you can offer up front, the more involved your volunteer will become. This isn't such a surprise, for when a person's name is publicly affiliated with an event,

> **People who have been asked for advice generally choose to involve themselves further, offer other suggestions, and even recruit some of the individuals whom they have suggested.**

the individual will have a greater investment in its success.

The *Fantasy Flight 1029* Volunteer Recruitment Experience

Initial discussions regarding the conceptual design of *Fantasy Flight 1029* involved one volunteer and three staff members. After lengthy discussions, the brainstorming soup party, plus one more follow-up meeting, the time had come to invite the participation of a couple who would be key to the event. A meeting was scheduled with the couple and the dean. There was enough of a draft concept presented to engage these volunteers. However, they were firm that they would consider the assignment only if we were willing to recruit another couple who would draw from a different market. This idea had merit, so, the recruitment of the second couple was successfully undertaken. At this juncture, ideas really began to flow.

With enthusiasm high and the volunteer chairs in place, the time was ideal to recruit two restaurateurs to take charge of the food and beverage component of the evening. It was the combination of the people involved, the uniqueness of the event, the fact that it was not going to be an annual function, and the nature of the audience being developed that won the interest of these two entrepreneurial individuals. They committed their own restaurants and succeeded in attracting thirty-four of their fellow restaurateurs and their suppliers to donate food and beverage for 400 people.

Recruitment of Hosts and Hostesses

Success in recruiting your front-line volunteers, the ones who will be selling your event, will depend on the manner in which they are recruited. You could have the volunteer chairs talk to people to get them enthusiastic about your event, but when this is done one on one, you lose the excitement and momentum of a group process. Consider the following scenario and think about what would cause *you* to want to become involved. One of the two couples chairing *Fantasy Flight 1029* offered to host a party at their home, a lovely place in a gated community. They sent invitations to all of those who had been identified as important hosts and hostesses to be recruited. The party was for cocktails on a weeknight. The entertainment was a performance by several students who provided some background music during the social period and was followed by a brief solo piece for the guests when they were seated and able to pay more attention. The dean talked about the faculty of fine arts and the importance of the upcoming opening. All guests were given packets of information. The hosts for the evening explained why this particular group of guests had been invited. A staff member described the process of using the forms in the packets to send in names and addresses for those who should receive invitations to the upcoming opening.

The evening was exceptional; the guests looked around the room at their friends and realized that they were all going to have a terrific time at this event because they would be going together. It was obvious that being identified as a host or hostess for this event would be prestigious. They were sold. Some guests began to make commitments by ordering their ten tickets. The benefits of the higher ticket price were explained and many signed up for them that evening. The group process was an important component to the success of this event. If the same people had been approached one by one, the momentum, excitement, and enthusiasm of the prospective hosts would have been much more difficult to achieve.

Exhibit 9–3 depicts a recruitment letter. This letter was composed entirely by volunteer Marjory Slavin. Note her use of some key phrases such as "in on the ground floor" "your personal responsibility will be minimal" and finally, "as decision makers and community leaders."

What Benefits Accrue to Your Volunteers?

For many people, the opportunity to work with friends is enough motivation. However, when you

> **When you can provide a benefit for your volunteers, you will endear your organization to them for a long time to come.**

Exhibit 9–3 Recruitment Letter

April 6, 1993

Dear Janet and Steve,

On April 28, 1930, The University of Arizona Drama Department dedicated its new home—under the football stadium seats. The production on that occasion was *He Who Gets Slapped.* The intervening 63 years have seen theatre and the other fine arts coming a long way and culminating this fall in *another landmark dedication.*

The new eighteen-million dollar Fine Arts Complex will be formally opened, allowing three of the five Fine Arts Departments to be under one roof. The entire community will participate in saluting Fine Arts' diversity and excellence by paying tribute to its exceptional programs and their contribution to our lives and to the lives of all Arizonans.

As part of the dedication weekend, a black-tie gala—a unique event, like none seen before—will take place on October 29. A true movable feast. . .for our bodies (with food coordinated by Ellen Burke Van Slyke of Boccata, and Cande Grogan of Ovens) and for our minds and spirits (with performances and installations by faculty and students). . .will showcase the complex.

Give us the opportunity to tell you more about the Gala and how you can become part of the Host & Hostess Committee for the dynamic, exciting, and creative scene. We think that you will be as excited as we are to be in on the ground floor. Your personal responsibility will be minimal—your own attendance, of course, and your effort in obtaining the attendance of five other couples.

Please come to hear about this celebration of the arts. Share in the fun by joining us for cocktails and a brief, informative program at the Slavin's home on Thursday, May 13 at 6:30 p.m. We hope that you will not make a decision concerning your participation until you hear all the details.

Thank you for taking the time to consider this invitation. As decision makers and community leaders, your support will underscore the significance of the complex and aid in demonstrating to all the vitality of the arts at The University and their importance in university education and in our lives. Please call the Slavins at 555-3507 to let us know whether you will be able to attend.

Warm regards,

Louis and Marjory Slavin   Darryl and Mary Ann Dobras
Cochairs, Host & Hostess   Cochairs, Host & Hostess
   Committee   Committee

Courtesy of Marjory and Louis Slavin

can provide a benefit for your volunteers, you will endear your organization to them for a long time to come. You have the opportunity to provide leadership benefits for your volunteers at the same time you develop a relationship with them. When you are able to gather your hosts and hostesses, you can engage them in discussion with some inside information about experiences to be offered at your event. The live performances at the *1029* recruitment party were a critical component. Most of the guests were unfamiliar with the Faculty of Fine Arts. It was essential that they understood the caliber of talent that would be presented at the event. When people hear "student," they typically think of someone who is a learner and not very proficient. When the guests listened to the artists who performed at their recruitment party, they felt confident of the exceptional artistic quality promised for the event.

The hosts and hostesses were then asked to complete a form with names and addresses of the friends whom they planned to invite to the event. Save-the-date cards were sent to all, and when the invitations were mailed in September, they contained notes from the hosts and hostesses encouraging their friends to join them for a spectacular evening.

At this point, it is important to confirm volunteer participation. The letter in Exhibit 9–4 was sent to a couple who had been unable to attend the host and hostess party, but who had made a commitment to participate. It was the first of many pieces of correspondence that were to flow from the dean, the cochairs, and the staff.

Honorary Chairs and Working Chairs

There will be times when it will be essential for you to have a high-profile personality as your honorary chair. This position carries prestige and power as well as a good deal of exposure. Sometimes, the honorary chair will be the only reason someone buys a ticket. That phenomenon can be attributed to a couple of reasons. Perhaps the ticket buyer simply wants to attend an event with your honorary chair. Or perhaps your ticket buyers want to be certain that the honorary chair knows they were present at this particular event.

Think through your options and select the honorary chair who will offer the greatest draw and widest visibility. Honoring deserving people is certainly one of the most effective reasons for a successful event. When your honorees are widely respected in the community, many from the community will attend to pay their respects and show their admiration for the honorees. Honorary chairs are typically chairs in name only. The name of your honorary chair will appear on everything printed. It's even possible that your honorary chair might be willing to make an appearance. But, if you have an honorary chair, it's advisable to also have a working chair. This is the person who will actually implement some of the plans, not just ap-

---

Exhibit 9–4 Sample memo to committee members

Dear Louis and Ruth Ann,

We are delighted that you have accepted our invitation to become a Host & Hostess for the Fine Arts Gala in October. We are sorry that you are unable to attend the informational gathering at our home on May 13. However, we will be meeting with you at your convenience to discuss the exciting details.

We'll be in touch soon!!

Louis and Marjory

prove them. It is a little more difficult to recruit this individual because there is limited visibility in the working chair's position. However, there are some volunteers for whom this arrangement works nicely. In fact, there are those people who would just as soon have no visibility at all!

Most likely, the circumstances surrounding your event will determine the need for an honorary chair. If you have chosen to honor someone, then a friend or peer in the field might be an appropriate choice. If you have chosen to honor a teacher or mentor, then a widely recognized student might be the best choice for the working chair.

Committee Chairs

Once you have recruited the event chair, you'll want to discuss filling the committee chair positions. It is possible that your event chair will have ideas about who might fill these roles. You'll want to agree on the best people to provide the leadership. Think through the tasks. What do you want the committee chairs to do? Who should they know? From whom can they call in favors, and whom can they reach that you can't reach? In the best of all possible worlds, your committee chairs will have influence over just the right people you need to make your event a success. In other words, your committee chairs can be your assurance of a successful event. In the following chapter, you'll find a discussion of the techniques you can use to attract these people and keep them involved.

Training Volunteers

Volunteers can be more effective and successful if they are adequately trained for their roles. It is the responsibility of staff to train volunteers. Event leadership should be trained in recruitment techniques with concentration on handling objections, acknowledging the objection, paraphrasing the objection, and answering with sentences beginning, "I am glad you asked that question because. . ." or "I can see where you might get that impression, but. . ." The strategies for recruitment of event volunteers are identical to those used in the recruitment of fund-raising volunteers: giving information, asking opinions, inviting questions

about the event, and seeking involvement. Assure prospective volunteers that they will receive support and training. Everything will be done to make them comfortable in their role and ensure their success, which, after all, is the organization's success. Training for selling tickets is similar to training for solicitation, which is why major gift volunteers are so successful at selling event tickets. In fact, selling tickets is easier for some because of their perception that a value, the ticket, is transferred. Volunteers should be trained through group participation, which builds comfort, and should receive the following:

- information about the cause and the programs that will benefit

- clarification about value that the event offers

- techniques for handling objections

- detailed facts about the event

- written statement of roles and responsibilities

- the organization's expectations

- communications and reporting information

- experience through role playing, if appropriate

Volunteers should leave the training with a sense of comfort in their ability, enthusiasm for the event, optimism about their success, and security in the support they will receive from staff and other volunteers.

Problems With Volunteers

As with any personnel issue, "problem" volunteers can be avoided by careful recruitment and attention to training, especially regarding roles and responsibilities. It is essential that volunteers be recruited with a clear understanding of the task they

> **Problems arise when decisions about the event are made in response to internal pressure or conditions.**

are undertaking, their role within the organization, and the limitations upon their responsibilities. Job descriptions, a definitive charge to the committee, and a clear chain of command will help avoid conflict or illuminate the path to resolution when conflict arises.

Events are special because they target an external market with the intention of bringing outsiders into the organization's sphere of influence. Problems arise when decisions about the event are made in response to internal pressure or conditions. Three decision areas particularly susceptible to internal pressures are ticket pricing, amenities, and the crucial go/no-go decisions.

The price of tickets should be determined by the value of the event, the prevailing practice, and the target market. Price should not be determined by internal pressures such as "My friends cannot afford that," or "Our clients will be excluded," or "We will never be able to ask that much." All such comments arise out of self-interest or lack of understanding. Events are intended to raise money, cultivate major donors, or gain visibility. Events are not intended to be low-cost or cost-comfortable social gatherings for clients and volunteers. Ticket pricing requires difficult decisions that are firmly grounded in economic reality of return on investment and analysis that determines what the market place will bear.

The second area for potential friction surrounds the amenities and their cost. One person finds a bargain for centerpieces that are different from what is planned, another believes that token gifts should be more than token, another wants to upgrade the entertainment. These are scenarios that invite conflict and budget-breaking. Commitment to adherence to the budget is essential to keep friction at bay. The individual responsible for decorations must remain in control and within budget as must the individual responsible for entertainment. Authority should be designated to one person, and there must be total acceptance of the rule that no one else is permitted to contract or purchase without the expressed permission of the individual in authority.

The third area for potential friction surrounds the go/no-go decision. Part of good planning includes points when progress is assessed and benchmarks reviewed. Occasionally, an event is at risk for failing in its objectives. Early warning signs include failure to recruit volunteers as ticket sellers, failure to engage the main attraction, failure to stay on target with the timeline, failure to sell sufficient tickets, or changes in the local environment such as competition, natural disaster, economic downturn, and community unrest. Whatever the cause, it may mean that the prudent action is cancellation. Volunteers may argue that too much has been invested, too much exposure has been created, or that the embarrassment would be too great. The decision to abort must be based on economics. Better to suffer embarrassment (cancel the event) than to suffer embarrassment and lose money (a poorly attended event).

Points to Ponder

When surveying the recruitment possibilities, consider two overlooked sources of volunteers. Previous attendees of the event have a built-in understanding of what the event should accomplish and how it unfolds. In addition, they are a good resource for suggestions for improvements and variety. Major gift donors are another resource; their commitment to the organization may be strong enough to induce them to serve, even in a modest way. They are most likely to bring friends who have the capacity to give a major gift.

Recruit volunteers who are compatible and who can work in concert with each other. Friction and dissension among the volunteers can ruin an event before the doors open.

For any event, the people who will be at the event are the strongest draw for prospective attendees. There is greater reason to buy a ticket and actually go if the other attendees include friends, socialites, celebrities, the rich and famous, or the powerful. The successful recruitment of volunteers from any of these groupings can ensure the attendance of others.

> **For any event, the people who will be at the event are the strongest draw for prospective attendees.**

The volunteers should be a resource for early sales of the most expensive reservations at tables or tickets. The volunteers should be asked to pledge that they will do certain tasks such as recruit two new people to the committee, sell reservations at one or two of the expensive tables, add their friends and associates to the invitation list, write personal notes on the invitations, make ten follow-up calls, and attend three meetings.

Summary

Having the right people connected with your event can ensure its success. The key to recruiting the right people is, as with all development, culti-vation, which is the process of taking the individual from awareness to understanding to acceptance to commitment.

The steps are all too familiar. Identify the prospective volunteer leadership. Present them with information, the case for both the organization and the event. Pique their interests in the possibilities and how they would benefit from this activity. Secure their involvement in tasks that are appropriate to them and at which they can succeed.

The role of staff includes efforts to support volunteers and to ensure that volunteers benefit from the experience. The benefit can be social, experiential, educational, or emotional (satisfaction in furthering the mission of the organization).

Chapter 10

Who Will Do the Work and How Do You Keep Them Involved?

Collectively we can do what no person can do singly.

Leland Kaiser

Event chairs, honorary chairs, and high visibility people are all part of an event; but the workers are the people who will ensure its success. Both are necessary; one without the other will not work. In this chapter, you'll find the substance of job and people descriptions. Who is the best person for a particular job? What does that volunteer want to know when being asked to serve on a committee? Realize how your planning will impact the work you expect of your volunteers.

Determining what role each volunteer will play is only the beginning. How will you keep volunteers enthusiastic over the long timeline required for special events?

Attracting Working Committee Chairs

There are a number of methods of attracting people to work on a committee. The most effective one is to find someone with whom your prospective committee member or chair would like to work. If your chair recommends some people, it's likely that he or she would be willing to work to help your volunteer be successful. Recruiting volunteers is much like attracting people to governing boards; you'll need to articulate the case. Perhaps one of your prospective members is deeply committed to your organization or cause. Such a commitment would certainly help when you make an appointment to recruit this individual. But when you go for that appointment, you'll be best served if you are prepared to answer all the questions certain to come up. It is vital to have the same tools available that you needed to recruit your key leadership.

When you ask a busy person to undertake another task, the person is customarily impressed when you've done your homework and done the thinking ahead of time. When you can intelligently answer questions and have demonstrated your personal commitment to this event, the volunteer will realize that a staff member is fully supportive and ready to help. A much greater chance exists now that the volunteer will readily agree to serve your cause.

Job Descriptions

This is your opportunity to make perfectly clear just what you expect from your working volunteers. They'll be pleased, because when you ask them to serve, they'll want to know their responsibilities. Your descriptions may be brief or complex, depending upon the task. Generally, the more succinct the description, the better understood the task.

When defining the role of a committee, it is advisable to define the role of staff as well. Only then will a committee member know whether staff will be there to provide back-up support. When developing job descriptions, be clear, be thorough, be careful! Be sure to think ahead and include the benefits for each committee member, whether perceived or real. Exhibits 10–1, 10–2, and 10–3 provide sample job descriptions.

These are but a few examples of committee job descriptions. Your event may not be a seated meal as implied by these descriptions, but the thought process for any event will be the same. From the beginning, as you think about the selection of your working committee chairs, keep in mind how important it is for the committee chairs to have the respect of their peers. Are they held in such high regard that when they make a request, the committee members will respond? Are these prospective working chairs people who will give credit to others?

Although these lists may appear daunting in number, it is well worth your time to go through this process. Remember, the committee chairs are the keys to the success of your event. They deserve special treatment and extra "TLC." Watch for opportunities to offer these volunteers a fun or interesting experience, or find a reason to express a public accolade. Do not hesitate to offer your recognition of a volunteer's contribution or achievement. The time you invest in cultivating them will prove to be rewarding. Not infrequently, the relationships developed during a special event become stronger, and you'll find that you may have just recruited a new board member—and not just any board member—you've recruited the best kind, an involved and tested board member.

Cultivation Opportunities or Maintaining the Enthusiasm of the Entire Volunteer Structure

Keeping people enthusiastic and energized requires special attention. Not long after the recruitment party for *Fantasy Flight 1029*, the hosts and hostesses received a news flash from the dean. This

Exhibit 10–1 Job Description, Invitation Committee

This committee will do the following:

- select and approve the invitation

- recommend the process for name gathering

- initiate the gathering of names and addresses of prospective guests to be invited to this event

- conduct follow-up phone calls to those who have not submitted names

- recommend and oversee the note writing and addressing process

The staff will support this committee by doing the following:

- sending memos to committee and board members

- compiling the address list

- eliminating duplicate entries

- providing requested materials with which to work

- providing the space needed to accomplish that work

one-page communication offered information about the Tucson restaurants that would be participating and some of the artists who'd be entertaining, plus the suggestion that readers save the September date scheduled for a breakfast tour of the complex. There, they would enjoy some performances and have the first chance to select and purchase hand-painted tablecloths to be available after the event. Furthermore, all first-class

> **When developing job descriptions, be clear, be thorough, be careful!**

Exhibit 10–2 Job Description, Decorations Committee

The committee members will do the following:

- draft a plan for the decor

- work with staff to ensure that the plan fits within the budget

- review the plan with event chair and staff

- enlist the aid of other volunteers to implement the plan

- work with staff to recommend the most cost-effective way to obtain materials

- solicit vendors for contributed or borrowed materials

- plan the installation of decorations

The staff will do the following:

- apply the proposed plan to budget and report back to volunteers

- review plan on event site to ensure that implementation is feasible

- draft letters of solicitation for volunteers to use with vendor prospects

- document items that must be returned when event is over

- ensure return of all borrowed items within a reasonable time

- draft and produce thank you letters for donated and borrowed items

Exhibit 10–3 Job Description, Event Arrangements Committee

The members of this committee will do the following:

- review event timeline with staff and chair before development of arrangement plan

- develop the floor plan with staff and site-coordinating staff

- arrange seating plan with event cochairs

- review schedule for the decorating and program committees

- oversee and/or implement placement of table signs or place cards

- meet facility staff and become familiar with the site

- Ensure that all contracts are signed by staff

The staff will do the following:

- make arrangements with facility staff

- introduce volunteers to facility staff

- ensure that the plan is documented on paper

- assist committee with seating assignments

- document both table arrangements and seating assignments on paper

- Seek committee approval for any requested or necessary changes

- provide staff for welcoming guests

- handle last-minute requests and changes

- accommodate unexpected guests

passengers would have the opportunity to choose their personal colors for the hand-painted cummerbunds, ties, and purses they'd be wearing.

Sharing the many successes and notes of progress was a terrific key to involvement. A fun bit of news was shared when the University approved having the dancers rappel from the roof of the new theater building! Other stories began to filter back to the planning committee. They were all encouraged as they realized how much excitement was beginning to build in the community.

As reservations began to drift in (before the mailing of the invitations), the event chairs started to feel like they were part of a truly successful event, an event that would keep the community involved for many years to come!

The memorandums in Exhibits 10–4, 10–5, and 10–6 were used to maintain and increase the involvement of volunteer hosts and hostesses. Since a long, hot summer lay ahead, it was of considerable importance that these influential people keep talking about the coming fall event.

Each time a memo went out, the resulting calls with questions and new people to invite reflected the mounting enthusiasm for the coming event. When September arrived, a cultivation party was held at the site. Hosts and hostesses were invited to a breakfast at which they saw a sampling of the hand-painted tablecloths, heard some harpists, and enjoyed a dance performance. They were able to preview the tie and cummerbund sets and evening bags that were hand-painted by the dean. Those who had already purchased their first class tickets were invited to select the colors of their event gift. The selected product was to be hand delivered two weeks before the event.

The hosts and hostesses for *Fantasy Flight 1029* enjoyed some special opportunities from the time of their recruitment to the events that they were invited to attend as the event took shape over the next several months. These opportunities were not the only method of involving the people who will sell your event.

There are other ways to recruit and involve table hosts; one of the most popular is the corporate breakfast. For this event, a highly visible corporate leader is recruited to chair the event. This person then hosts a breakfast to which all peers and prospective table hosts are invited. At the breakfast, recruits learn about the organization involved, hear a first-person testimony about the value of the services delivered by this organization, and are then asked either to sell a table to their friends or to call on a handful of people, all of whose names and phone numbers are on cards.

This method is most successful when the chair of the event is calling in chits. In other words, when the people being asked to attend the breakfast are those who have benefitted from the work of the chair in another venue, they feel an obligation to repay the chair and support this new event. It also works well when the honoree at an event is someone to whom many people feel indebted. Typically, they want to recognize the honoree with their own attendance as well as demonstrate their support by inviting additional guests to join them for the event.

Remembering the principal of obligation, you may be able to consider other ideas to create a sense of obligation so that people want to return the favor you have provided. When people have enjoyed a breakfast, lunch or other form of entertainment, they feel somewhat obligated to return the favor by selling the requested number of tickets to fill a table. Awareness of this principal also suggests that if you know why you're being invited to such a breakfast, it's probably a good idea to attend only if you intend to help sell the event being promoted.

Other cultivation opportunities may be employed if you have the opportunity to introducce your table hosts to a noted personality, or give them a preview of an activity that their guests will enjoy at the event. In the case of a performance, attendance at a rehearsal is considered a privilege. Any opportunity that you employ will motivate your hosts to become enthusiastically involved and will make it easy for them to help sell your event.

Training Volunteers

As stated in Chapter 9, training volunteers can only help them become more effective. With some volunteers, there is little training to do. But when you have steps in the process with which they are not familiar, it's critical that they feel equipped to do as you expect. Typically, information is provided in a packet they receive and reinforced when you review the packet materials with them. For certain events such as a phonathon, more specific training programs are necessary. This can be accomplished with written material and/or with practice sessions.

Finding, then recruiting, training, and cultivating volunteers are all critical steps toward a successful event.

Exhibit 10–4 Memo 1

MEMORANDUM

To: All Hosts and Hostesses

From: Barbara Levy

Date: June 3, 1993

Re: Gala Update

Fantasy Flight 1029 prepares for take-off!

The flight crew reports that preparations are going well for *Fantasy Flight 1029*. Since our lovely evening at the Slavin's residence, several noteworthy happenings have transpired including the following:

1. The Board of Regents have moved their October meeting to be in Tucson for the Fine Arts dedication and gala.

2. After University approval, the crew has met with Facilities Management and Risk Management regarding dancers rappelling from the rooftops for the finale.

3. Rhea gathered several artists who are hard at work painting tablecloths.

4. Annalyn and Joy are putting the finishing touches on the invitation design.

5. Carrol and Jory are locking in the many performance sites and the performers who will make our evening a real fantasy.

6. Cande and Ellen are about to descend on Tucson's finest restaurateurs to enlist their services.

As preparations proceed, we would welcome any "connections" you might offer. Please let me know if you have influence with the following:

1. any party rental businesses (if we can't get a full donation, perhaps a 50-percent discount); and

2. a business that might lend us some large decorative plants.

Finally, we want to send save-the-date cards out in just a few weeks. Please help by returning your address list by June 11. To those who have already sent them in, many thanks!

Thanks again for your help. By the way—to date, more than twenty first class tickets have been sold!! What an evening this will be. Dean Sevigny says its's O.K. with him to sell a whole flight of first class seats! If you have any questions, please call me at 555-8822.

Exhibit 10–5 Memo 2

MEMORANDUM

Memo To: Hosts and Hostesses for *Fantasy Flight 1029*

From: Maurice Sevigny, Dean of Fine Arts

Date: July 16, 1993

Re: The Latest Flight Report

I am pleased to report that wherever I go, someone is certain to mention the Gala to me. That means you are all doing your jobs and talking up this exciting event. Thank you!!

Plans and arrangements are falling into place now. Ticket dollars have even started to come in! By the way, if you have interested anyone in a $500 ticket, Barbara Levy will be glad to write to them to thank them and suggest that they may pay at their convenience. She will also write if someone commits to a contribution for the event.

I encourage you to do all you can to sell the business class and first class tickets. For your information, I have enclosed a reminder of the benefits. The first class and business class passenger list will be included in the program for the evening. *These are the sales that will determine the success of this project!*

If I can be of any help, please do not hesitate to call me at 555-1778.

Enclosed are your save-the-date cards and instructions. Thank you for the time that you are spending to help make this event a success. **We couldn't possibly do it without you!**

We know this evening will delight every appetite with extraordinary art and culinary experiences. Some examples will include the following:

- Mariachi Arizona

- Screening of a video developed by Media Arts

- A brass choir

- A jazz band

- The Rosewood Marimba Band

- A performance art presentation

- The guitar ensemble

- A scene from *The Merchant of Venice*

- The Tango

- Harp Fusion (the country's only jazz harp ensemble)

Again, we thank you for all you are doing to make this event a success.

Exhibit 10–6 Memo 3

MEMORANDUM

To: All Hosts and Hostesses

From: Barbara Levy

Date: July 16, 1993

Re: Save-the-Date Cards

At last! Our save-the-date cards are ready for your messages. Enclosed you will find the following:

• A memo from the Dean

• Your list of names and addresses

• Cards addressed and stamped for your written notes

• A reminder of the ticket prices—you will note one welcome change. The tax deductibility of the first class tickets has been revised. The deductible portion is now $410.

In case of duplication of names, we tried to sort out the most even number of prospective names. Because it is necessary to send only one card, we had to choose one person. However, *you will be given the opportunity to write notes to all of those on your list* when the invitations go out. If you have questions or problems, please do not hesitate to call me.

Thank you for your help!!!

Points to Ponder

When developing lists of possible volunteers, consider the following resources:

- major donors

- major donor prospects

- previous attendees

- volunteers for events run by other organizations

- civic and social clubs

- community leaders

- social leaders

- former members of the governing board

Summary

The committee structure varies to reflect the specifics of the event. Within the structure, develop a charge to the committee for each committee. Develop a job description for each volunteer position, one that clearly defines the role and responsibility of volunteers and of staff.

The successful recruitment of volunteers for an event parallels that of recruitment for other fundraising activities. Develop the case for the event, prepare job descriptions, and profile the ideal committee member to be recruited based on the primary goal of visibility, cultivation, or income. Recruit from the top down, beginning with the chair or chairs. Recruit the strongest person possible based on the primary need. Let the event chair be responsible for the recommendation and recruitment of subsequent levels within the structure.

Clear, defined policies are as essential to the management of a special event as they are to other portions of the development effort. Policies, preferably shared with volunteers early in the planning process, give a sense of comfort and assurance to volunteers—comfort in knowing the rules of the road and assurance that staff and administration have prepared the organization for eventualities, that the event is not being approached haphazardly and ad hoc. Policies, distributed and discussed, are protection and guidelines for all.

Be well prepared to offer and implement other standard management techniques when working with volunteers. Train those that need special attention or who feel awkward and unprepared to fulfill their roles. Communicate often and meaningfully about progress, decisions, and the building excitement. Report progress and expanding awareness. Recognize the volunteers for their involvement and acknowledge the efforts they are expending on behalf of the organization. The closer the involvement, the greater the opportunity for success.

Chapter 11

What About the Invitation? Who Should Receive It?

Your wealth is where your friends are.

Plautus

The following will be covered in this chapter:

- invitation design

- save-the-date cards

- post office requirements

- decisions about numbers

- copy issues

- fair market value and tax deductibility

- addressing invitations

- compiling the invitation list

- establishing the database

- orchestrating the note writing

- important notes to keep

Invitation Design

There are numerous options to consider when designing an invitation. The design will depend entirely on the type of event you are conducting. If it is a seminar or tour, the invitation will be much more business-oriented than if for a tea or a black-tie ball. Whatever the event, consider first the appropriateness of your invitation. These days, many invitations are of minimal materials—for example, a 5 1/2 by 8 1/2 card printed on two sides, using one color on a different colored paper. You may also have seen invitations designed on a computer, printed on colorful paper, and folded in three as a self-mailer. If, however, you're having an event requiring a return card, you'll need to consider other options.

Should your invitations be designed by a volunteer, make certain that the volunteer is educated about all the requirements. You might find yourself with a beautifully designed invitation that has no response mechanism, exceeds standard post office measurements, or has no room for host and hostess notes. Such a scenario will push your printing budget well over the edge. It will also create embarrassment for all concerned. You certainly will not want to waste your volunteer's time and effort, much less create ill will when you don't (or can't) accept the proposed design. This dilemma is fraught with potential problems. Avoid it by providing all of the information up front, and there will be much less room for misunderstanding.

The most effective approach to appropriate invitations, no matter how they are being designed, is a review of the following questions:

1. What kind of response mechanism will you use?

2. Will you be asking people to make a phone call or send a check?

3. How many confirmations or ticket orders do you anticipate mailing?

4. Would you be willing to consider additional postage for a unique and special invitation design?

5. Will the printing be donated?

6. If so, are you able to get a four-color invitation?

7. Will a fancy invitation look too expensive (or inappropriate) for your organization?

8. How will these invitations be addressed? By computer? By label? By hand?

9. Will addressing with a colored pen provide an inexpensive boost to the invitation design?

10. Do you need white space for volunteers to write notes?

11. Would you prefer enclosing a card on which notes have been written?

12. What copy do you require on the invitation?

13. Do you have a list of hosts and hostesses to include?

14. Are there sponsor or underwriter acknowledgments that must be included?

15. Do you need to include a map ?

16. Will you want to print a save-the-date postcard?

17. Will you want a printed program for your event?

Although printed programs are not discussed in this chapter, you'll want to consider printing the cover at the same time as the invitation is printed. If the same graphics and colors are being used, it may make sense and possibly save money.

The answers to all of the listed questions will guide the design of your invitation. In fact, these questions should be resolved before discussing design with anyone. Whether you are paying a designer, receiving pro bono design work, or engaging a volunteer to design your invitation, the designer will need to know all of the information you've reviewed before beginning the creative work. By the way, if you're fortunate to live in an area where there are schools of graphic arts, you may find that a class would be interested in a "competition" to design your invitation. This naturally requires that you have all the questions answered well in advance of your event. You need to allow several months for this process. Despite the time that it takes, it will definitely be to your advantage. The invitation for *Fantasy Flight 1029* came from a graphic design class, and the concepts developed for the invitation actually inspired some of the other decisions about the event.

Donated Printing

If you are asking a printer to donate the print job, you'll want to be specific from the start. In fact, this actually applies to any print job whether donated or not. However, it's more important for a donated job because the printer will need to know what you have in mind to evaluate your request.

Exhibit 11–1 lists the specifications for the print job for *FantasyFlight 1029*.

Some of the specifications include some terms used in the printing business. Full bleed means that

Exhibit 11–1 Sample Printing Specifications

PRINTING SPECIFICATIONS
UNIVERSITY OF ARIZONA
FINE ARTS GALA

All artwork will be camera-ready.

SAVE-THE-DATE POSTCARD

3,000   4 × 6

Printed two sides

Four color—some screens—
full bleed

ENVELOPES

3,000   #10   Outside envelope

Printed one side

Pantone/one color

2,500   #9   Response envelope

Colored stock

Printed one side

Pantone/one color

INVITATION

3,000   Size—Fits in #10
envelope

8 pages—printed both sides

Full bleed on cover

Screens

Some reverse type

Cover stock for outside

NOTE CARDS

1,500   3 × 2 card for personal
messages

Four color—one side only

CONFIRMATION

250   4 × 8 1/2 folded in
half—created pocket for
tickets

Medium weight stock

Four color—two sides

Full bleed and screens—one
side

TICKETS

250   3 × 7 1/2

Card stock

Four color—screens and full
bleed both sides

PROGRAM

500   Standard 8 1/2 × 5 1/2

16 pages

Cover—70# gloss paper

Cover—four color with
screens and bleed

Pages—gloss

Pages one color—Pantone

the color goes all the way to the edge of the page; there is no border. Screens are used to provide shading in the amount of ink that gets through to the page. A 50-percent screen allows less ink to pass through than a 70-percent screen. Pantone colors are special colors that are ordered by number and require that the printer clean the press and prepare it for Pantone colors instead of the standard colors used.

How Many to Print

By now you'll know how many people are on your invitation list. But, to print just exactly that number is inviting problems. There will always be last-minute additions to your list. A volunteer will call and ask you to send out an additional ten invitations or so. You'll remember some of the VIPs in your organization whose names never made it to the list. As a rule of thumb, always print more than you need. How many more is difficult to determine, but consider 10 percent more than you think you'll need. Remember that you'll want some invitations for the file. If you have underwriters, they may want some for their files. Your graphic artist may want some samples and then you'll want to have some left for those last-minute additions. It's difficult to go back and print more! And printing a little more than you need will not cost significantly more money. So, it's a good safety measure.

Save-the-Date Cards

Today, society has set the standard for sending advance notification of an event. Even if your event is a sold-out affair, sending advance notice or confirmation of the date has become a good practice. Along with ever-increasing numbers of not-for-profit organizations producing events, there is serious competition for a community member's time and money. Advance notice of a new event or a reminder of a traditional event will encourage potential benefactors to write that commitment on their calendars; this is the first step in cultivating your audience.

> As a rule of thumb, always print more than you need.

Copywriting

When writing the copy, consider some of the basics, and create a checklist for yourself. These reminders will ensure that you have covered the following information important to your guests:

- event name
- time/date/place
- fair market value/tax deductibility
- event chairs/committee
- hosts and hostesses
- honoree (if any)
- underwriters or sponsors
- directions to the event
- the address to which reservations should be sent
- information about tickets by return mail/or your check is your reservation
- a line for contributions on the response card
- payment method—checks, charge cards (if appropriate)
- relevant telephone number or address

Be certain to make clear the tax-deductible portion of your ticket price. It inevitably requires some explaining to the volunteers when your entire event is underwritten and the volunteers then tell their friends that the whole ticket price is tax deductible. Not so. Every event ticket carries a fair market value (FMV) and that value reflects the price that a person would pay for a similar experience in the marketplace. For example, if you are having a dinner dance, then you'll need to consider what a person might pay for a comparable dinner and then the cost of dancing. These two costs then constitute the FMV. The difference between your ticket price and the FMV is then the tax deductible portion that the guest may report. You may wonder then about the underwriter's contribution. Well, it's just that—a contribution that is fully tax deductible, less any value that might be received, such to keep a template nearby when designing your invitation. And if you have an artist designing for you, don't forget to remind your artist that there are some limitations regarding the size of the invitation. If you are looking for something truly out-of-the-ordinary, you may choose to pay the few cents more. But it's wise to make that decision before the fact rather than after!

Following the template in Figure 11–8 will ensure that there will be no surprises regarding additional postage or qualifying for bulk mail. The post office is always ready to answer your questions should the template not answer everything.

Event Tickets and Seating

Are tickets really necessary? There are many events today where tickets are not used. Guests check in at a table, and that's fine if the number attending is such that the irritation of queuing up is minimized. On the other hand, one advantage of mailing tickets is that doing so provides one more "contact" with your guests. Often, the event theme lends itself to tickets. For *Fantasy Flight 1029,* the boarding pass was a natural choice (Figure 11–9). The pass reconfirmed the event time and place. Your decision about the necessity of tickets will depend on such issues as whether you want to pay the additional postage for mailing, or even how you visualize your guests arriving at the event.

However you handle tickets, seating will be one of the most complex and evolving of all special event processes. As discussed in Chapter 2, cultivation is one of the primary reasons for producing a special event. Accordingly, your seating arrangements should reflect that intent. To function at your event, you'll need a seating chart that is formatted by table, with hosts and guests. Your second list is in alphabetical order with table assignments next to the names. Armed with many copies of both of these formats, your volunteers should be equipped to handle anything.

Establishing the Database/
Constructing the List

It will be easier to add information about the event if your organization has fund-raising or event

a problem because those who might consider attending may have discarded their invitations thinking that the deadline had passed. On the other hand, with no printed deadline, people may wait until the day of the event to respond. Although this may sound unrealistic, it happens and it creates a nightmare for any event planner and caterer. To avoid this dilemma, people can be motivated to make their decision in a timely manner when they read that seating is limited, or when the host couple encourages early reservations.

Figures 11–1 through 11–7 depict several styles of invitations to different types of events. Each is included to demonstrate a particular point.

Help from the Post Office

The U.S. Post Office has forms (Figure 11–8) that help to guide your decision about the size of an invitation. Those that fit the standards set by the post office will not require additional postage. Those that do not meet their standards will require varying amounts of additional postage. It's helpful

Please Join Us

The University of Arizona Faculty of Fine Arts invites you to take a journey you will never forget. Join us for:

FANTASY FLIGHT 1029
An Arts Extravaganza!

DEPARTURE DATE: October 29, 1993, 6:45 pm
DESTINATION: The University of Arizona Fine Arts Complex
ITINERARY: Journey through an exciting evening of
                      Artistic Excellence and Culinary Perfection
ATTIRE: Creative* Black Tie   (* If you choose)

Itinerary

Your exciting adventure through the new Fine Arts Complex will include a variety of fascinating stopovers. During this special evening, you will view unique exhibitions and performances in Art, Dance, Media Arts, Music and Theatre provided by the remarkable talents of students and faculty.

You will have the rare opportunity to catch a glimpse of our nation's artistic future! Fine dining for this evening's journey will be provided by the very best of Tucson's restaurateurs.

Figure 11–1 *Fantasy Flight 1029*—This unique design establishes the tone for the evening. The creative style provides an opportunity to include a significant amount of copy without creating visual overload or confusion. It is clear that the event is something out of the ordinary. The list of hosts and hostesses provides the credibility needed for the community to wish to take part. Courtesy of Jackson Boelts, Annalyn Chargualaf, Joy Solon, and the University of Arizona Department of Art, Tucson, Arizona.

Figure 11–1 continued

Ticket Fares

First Class $ 500 per person [$ 410]*

Passengers will be provided with:
A hand painted "creative" black tie and/or evening bag
A ticket hot-line for priority seating at Faculty of Fine Arts Events throughout the year
Recognition in gala program

Business Class $ 250 per person [$ 180]*

Passengers will be provided with:
A ticket hot-line for priority seating at Faculty of Fine Arts Events throughout the year
Recognition in gala program

Coach Class $ 125 per person [$ 55]*

* Tax-deductible portion of fare

For more travel information call the ticket office: 621-8824

A Benefit To Endow The Dean's Fund For Excellence

The Dean's Fund for Excellence is being established to provide discretionary funds to enhance The University of Arizona Faculty of Fine Art's mission to create and achieve excellence in education and training in the arts.

This new fund will augment Fine Arts programs in many ways:

• Assisting students with opportunities to represent The U of A at national or international events
• Providing support for students and faculty with creative projects
• Recruiting and retaining the most qualified and talented students and faculty
• Providing appropriate recognition awards for outstanding teaching, performance, creative output, research and service

Special Thanks

Honor Committee Chairs: Mr. & Mrs. Darryl Dobras   and   Mr. & Mrs. Louis Slavin

Hosts & Hostesses:

Mr. & Mrs. Jerry Alpert
Mr. & Mrs. Victor Arida
Mr. Paul Ash & Ms. Bridget Carnell
Mr. & Mrs. Rick Barrett
Ms. Joan Beigel-Kaye
Dr. & Mrs. James Blute
Mr. & Mrs. Robert Bracker
Ms. Esther Capin
Dr. & Mrs. William Casey
Ms. Shirley Chann
Mr. & Mrs. Gerrit Cormany
Dr. & Mrs. James Dalen

Mr. & Mrs. Michael DeBell
Mr. & Mrs. Donald Diamond
Chief Justice & Mrs. Stanley Feldman
Mr. Gary Gethmann & Ms. Gini Moran
Mr. & Mrs. Gregg Gibbons
Dr. Joseph Gross & Ms. Suzanne Werbelow
Mr. & Mrs. Charles Hall III
Dr. & Mrs. Ken Hatch
Mr. & Mrs. C. Donald Hatfield
Mr. & Mrs. Larry Hecker
Mr. & Mrs. Ralph Henig
Dr. & Mrs. Leonard Joffe

continued on back

Special Thanks

Hosts & Hostesses Continued:

Dr. & Mrs. Ron Kolker
Mr. & Mrs. Frank Lazarus
Mr. Bill Lundquist
Mr. & Mrs. John McLaughlin
Mr. & Mrs. John Munic
Mr. & Mrs. Douglas Nelson
Mr. Tino Ocheltree & Dr. Moira Shannon
Dr. & Mrs. Manuel Pacheco
Mr. & Mrs. Greg Papanikolas
Gen. & Mrs. Julius Parker
Mr. & Mrs. Lars Pederson
Mr. & Mrs. Louis Pozez
Mrs. Charles Putnam

Ms. Lillian Rosenzweig
Dr. & Mrs. Stephen Seltzer
Mr. & Mrs. Donald Shropshire
Dr. & Mrs. Ernest Smerdon
Mr. & Mrs. George Steele
Mr. & Mrs. Alvin Stern
Mr. & Mrs. Robert Stubbs
Dr. & Mrs. John Sullivan
Mr. & Mrs. Alfred Thomas
Dr. & Mrs. Ron Weinstein
Mr. & Mrs. Tom Weir
Mr. & Mrs. Larry Wetterschneider
Mr. & Mrs. Michael Williams

The University of Arizona Faculty of Fine Arts gratefully acknowledges the services contributed by Skyline Printing

Handmaker Jewish Services for the Aging
P.O. Box 13090 Tucson, AZ
85732-3090

Dr. and Mrs. Martin Levy

"There's No Place Like Home."

Handmaker Jewish Services for the Aging cordially invites you to the 15th Annual

Rainbow Ball

Honoring Mr. and Mrs. J.H. Handmaker

Saturday the sixth of May   Nineteen hundred and ninety-five

Skyline Country Club   Cocktails 7:30   Dinner 8:30

Casino~Fine~Jewelry Auction   Dancing to Limelight

Black Tie Optional   Valet Parking

Figure 11–2 *Rainbow Ball*—The name of this event stimulates the imagination. Further, the design permits a creative use of panels. The actual invitation was printed on an insert. This permitted the printing of additional cover pages that could be used (without the invitation insert) as thank you note cards. Courtesy of Handmaker Jewish Services for the Aging, Tucson, Arizona.

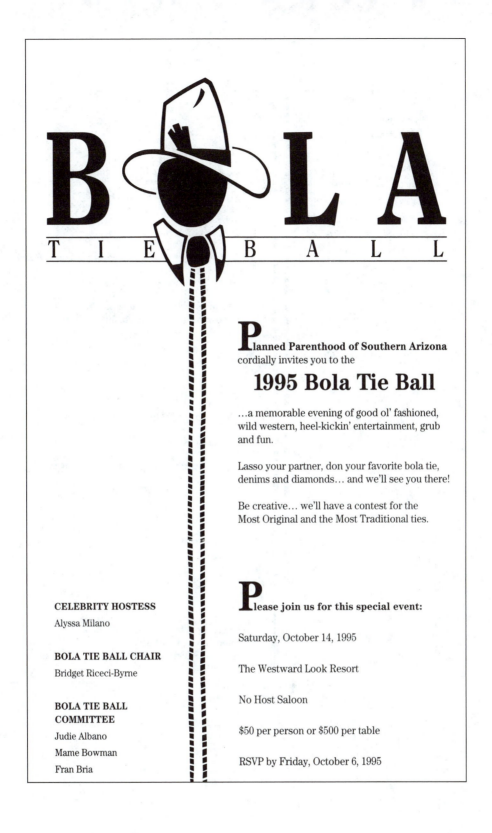

BOLA TIE BALL

Planned Parenthood of Southern Arizona
cordially invites you to the

1995 Bola Tie Ball

…a memorable evening of good ol' fashioned,
wild western, heel-kickin' entertainment, grub
and fun.

Lasso your partner, don your favorite bola tie,
denims and diamonds… and we'll see you there!

Be creative… we'll have a contest for the
Most Original and the Most Traditional ties.

Please join us for this special event:

Saturday, October 14, 1995

The Westward Look Resort

No Host Saloon

$50 per person or $500 per table

RSVP by Friday, October 6, 1995

CELEBRITY HOSTESS
Alyssa Milano

BOLA TIE BALL CHAIR
Bridget Riceci-Byrne

**BOLA TIE BALL
COMMITTEE**
Judie Albano
Mame Bowman
Fran Bria

Figure 11–3 *Bola Tie Ball*—The design of this invitation reinforces the theme of the event at little expense. The invitation simply unfolded into a long, thin format, representing bola tie strings. The event is an informal, western dance, perfect for those who have no desire to be part of another black-tie event. Courtesy of Planned Parenthood of Southern Arizona, Tucson, Arizona.

Figure 11–3 continued

Jenny Guilford
Lynda Gunn
Karen Manza
Kathie Noble
Deborah Oseran
Frances Martinez Pitts
Emily Pollack
George Rosenberg
Andrea Schindler
Trisa Schorr
Cynthia Tancer
Don Tringali
Lisa Valdivia

Special Events of the evening include:

Western Games and Mariachi Trio begins at 6:00 p.m.

Dinner at 7:00 p.m.

Dance to the music of the *Dayna Wagner Band*

Bola Tie Contest

Raffle Drawing - Grand Prize: Trip for two to Cabo San Lucas and much, much more

With special thanks to the following:

Print Expressions

The Westward Look Resort

All proceeds benefit **Quinto Education Endowment Fund of Planned Parenthood of Southern Arizona**

Figure 11–3 continued

B⬤LA
TIE BALL

☐ **YESSIREE!**
I/we will attend!

☐ Sorry, I/we will
not be able to
attend, but here's
my contribution of
$ _____ .

Enclosed is my check *for $ as follows
_____ individuals at $50   = $_____
_____ tables at $500   = $_____
_____ raffle tickets at $10   = $_____
                                    Total: $ _____
Please RSVP by Friday, October 6th

_____
NAME(S)

_____
ADDRESS

_____
CITY   STATE   ZIP   PHONE

☐ Please seat me/us at a no-host table.
☐ Please seat me/us with the following parties: (Tables seat 10 people.)

_____   _____

_____   _____

_____   _____

_____   _____

*Please make checks payable to Planned Parenthood of Southern Arizona, and note "Bola Tie Ball." Your cancelled check is your reservation. The non-deductible entertainment value of the evening is $28 per person. The balance of your contribution is tax deductible ($22).

Salud

Carondelet Foundation
cordially invites you to attend
the 19ᵗʰ annual

Carondelet Gala
Salud

Saturday, October 14, 1995

Doubletree Hotel Grand Ballroom

445 South Alvernon Way

6:00 Hosted Cocktails   7:00 Dinner

Supporting the healthcare mission of the

Sisters of St. Joseph of Carondelet

Black Tie Optional

I would like to make a gift of:

Cherubs $25 ~ $99   amount $ ____

Angels $100 ~ $499   amount $ ____

Archangels $500+   amount $ ____

All underwriters will be recognized in the Gala program

Name (PLEASE PRINT) _____

(Gifts must be received by October 2, 1995 for inclusion in program)

Tax deductible portion of each ticket is $90.

Check may be made to Carondelet Foundation

Charge to my VISA/MASTERCARD # _____

Name (PLEASE PRINT) _____ Exp date _____

Figure 11–4 *Salud*—This is a most effective and inexpensive black and white invitation. This invitation could work for most any organization. Courtesy of Carondelet Health Care Corporation, Tucson, Arizona.

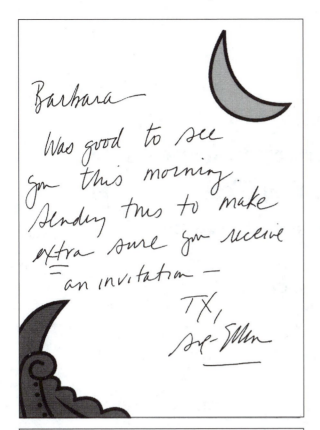

Barbara —
Was good to see
you this morning.
Sending this to make
extra sure you receive
an invitation —
TX,
Sue-Ellen

1995 Gala Committee

ROSE MOFFORD
Honorary Chair

DOROTHY FINLEY and GEORGE MIRABEN
Co-Chairs

Joan Beigel-Kaye	David and Denise McEvoy
Jim and Karin Blute, III	Judy Miller
Esther Capin	Carolyn Monjoi
Bruce and Katie Dusenberry	Marlene Musty
Slivy Edmonds	Manuel and Karen Pacheco
Joe and Laura Estes	Gregory and Lyn Papanikolas
Bob and Anita Friesen	Richard and Judith Polheber
Becky Gaspar	Herb and Emily Pollock
Donna Haskell	George and Bobbe Rosenberg
Don and Sandy Hatfield	Brenda Scott
Sharon B. Hekman	Sally Simmons
Nanette Kaneen	Craig Bradford Snow
Jan Lesher	Larry and Myrna Stern
Ron MacBain	Tom and Arlene Webster

Support for the evening has been provided by Desert Diamond Casino and MCI.

The Arizona Theatre Company Board of Trustees
and
The Gala Committee
Cordially Invite You To Attend

The 1995 Gala Celebration

Honoring Betsy Bolding
Saturday, October 7, 1995

Complimentary Wine Reception Begins at 6:00 p.m.
Program begins promptly at 6:45 p.m.

Order of the Evening

Welcome

Recognition and Presentation
ATC's Production of
A Midsummer Night's Dream
by William Shakespeare

Buffet Dinner Catered by The Dakota Cafe
Dancing to the Music of Concord Jazz Recording Artist Dennis Rowland

Temple of Music and Art
330 S. Scott
Tucson, Arizona

Black-Tie Optional   Valet Parking
                                       Cash Bar

Figure 11–5 *Arizona Theatre Company 1995 Gala*—This colorful and attractive invitation immediately engages the reader's interest. It represents a fun, lively evening with many entertaining components. This invitation also demonstrates the use of a handwritten note. Courtesy of Arizona Theatre Company, Tucson, Arizona.

for
Tucson Adult Literacy Volunteers'
Second Annual Tea.

Celebrating Literacy Month ♦ September 1995

Guy Atchley, Event Chairman

Pick up a book and a cup of tea,
And settle into your easy chair;
For if you know the pleasure of reading,
Here's an opportunity for you to share.

More than 110,000 adults in our community
Are simply unable to read;
With your gift to T.A.L.V.,
We can help those who are in need.

So while you enjoy your book and tea
In a moment of quiet relaxation,
Fill out your card with the RSVP
And send it back with your donation.

♦

Tucson Adult Literacy Volunteers, Inc., is a not-for-profit organization
of volunteer tutors and an affiliate of Laubach Literacy Action.
Since 1960, we have taught adults in Pima County to read, write, and speak English – for free.
Last year our 135 volunteer tutors taught 450 students, from beginners to high school dropouts.
Our students go on to citizenship, better jobs, college, and improved parenthood.
They need books and tutors. Please help us to help them.

Figure 11–6 *Tucson Adult Literacy Volunteers' Second Annual Tea*—Not only was this invitation inexpensive and effective, the event was even less expensive! The copy is straightforward and easy to understand. This was a good fund-raising piece for a non-event. Courtesy of Tucson Adult Literacy, Tucson, Arizona.

Figure 11–6 continued

T.A.L.V. would like to thank the following friends
for donating specialty services and items for the Tea:

Rincon Rotary Club
Positive Formulators
Cafe by Peter / Eclectic Cafe
Mayfield Florist & Plant Shop
STASH Tea Co., Tigard, Oregon
Tucson Cooperative Warehouse
Book Mark / Haunted Bookshop
Arizona Inn / Gas light Theatre
LEAVES Pure Teas, San Francisco – at finer stores

This invitation was printed through the generous support of
QUIET GRAPHICS

RSVP

Yes, I will join T.A.L.V. for Tea!

◆

Enclosed is my contribution for
$25 __ $50 __ $100 __ Other $ __

Name _____
Address _____
_____

◆

Your donation makes you eligible for a drawing
which will be held November 1st.
Winners will be notified by mail

Please make checks payable to:
Tucson Adult Literacy Volunteers.
Contributions are tax-deductible.

The Board of Directors of

Most Holy Redeemer AIDS Support Group

invites you to join them

for a cocktail buffet reception

on Saturday, the twenty-first of September

Nineteen hundred and ninety-six

from seven o'clock to ten o'clock

at the home of Dr. Raul A. Hernandez and Mr. David C. Heitz

Through the generosity of
Dr. Hayden Klaeveman & Mr. Gregory Dendler,
Mr. George E. McBride & Mr. Alberto Pelaez, Bro. George Cherrie, OFM, Conv.,
Dr. Louis S. Coloia and Dr. Raul A. Hernandez & Mr. David C. Heitz,
100% of all event receipts will benefit direct client services of
Most Holy Redeemer AIDS Support Group

Figure 11–7 Most Holy Redeemer AIDS Support Group—This invitation was simple and elegant. The return card effectively used the front to list the board and the back as the response card. The card clearly designates the fair market value of the event price. Courtesy of Most Holy Redeemer AIDS Support Group, San Francisco, California.

Figure 11–7 continued

Most Holy Redeemer
AIDS SUPPORT GROUP

Officers

Jessica Anne Clarke, MD, Ph.D., President
Raul A. Hernandez, MD, First Vice President
Natalie Smith, Second Vice President
Nanette Lee Miller, CPA, Treasurer
David B. Lloyd, Esq., Secretary

Members

Georgette M. Beainy   Harry M. Johnson, Jr.
Rabbi Allen B. Bennett   George E. McBride
John L. Boland   Rev. Zachary J. Shore
Louis S. Coloia, Ph.D.   Allen M. Sowle, Jr., LL.M.
Roger W. Dickson   Wayne A. Strei
Mark A. Hickey   Senator Art Torres (Ret.)
Frank C. Hudson

Executive Director
Louis S. Coloia, Ph.D.

Please reserve for Saturday, September 21, 1996:
_____ Ticket(s) at $125 each *

Name(s) _____

_____

Address _____

City _____ State _____ Zip _____

Daytime Phone _____

Evening Phone _____

○ Enclosed is my check
   in the amount of _____

○ I regret that I am unable to attend but
   I wish to contribute _____

○ Please charge my Visa/Mastercard
   in the amount of _____

Visa/Mastercard No. _____

Exp. Date _____

Signature _____

Please make your check payable to
Most Holy Redeemer AIDS Support Group
and return in the enclosed envelope by September 13.
For further information, please call (415) 863-1581.

* The fair market value of each ticket is $25. All
contributions exceeding this value are tax deductible.
No tickets will be mailed; reservations will be held at
the door.

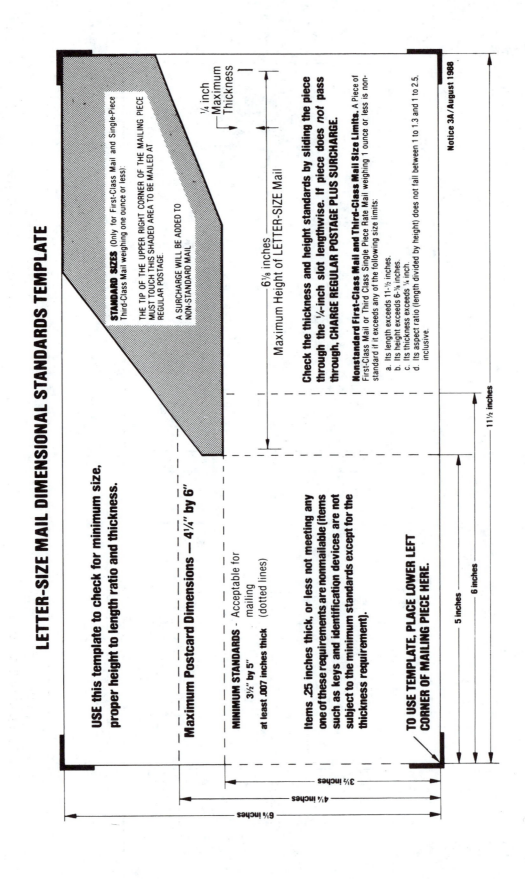

Figure 11-8 Courtesy of U.S. Post Office.

Figure 11–8 continued

EXAMPLES OF USING TEMPLATE

PROCEDURE FOR USE OF TEMPLATE:

1. Align the mailing piece with the lower left corner of this template (just inside the lines).

2. The upper and right side of the pieces must touch or extend past BOTH the top and right-hand minimum lines. Otherwise, the piece cannot be accepted for mailing.

3. If the piece meets the minimum size, but the upper right corner falls outside the shaded area of the template, or is larger than the template, the piece may be mailed. CHARGE REGULAR POSTAGE PLUS SURCHARGE.

4. If the piece meets all other criteria, check the thickness. If the piece exceeds ¼ inch in thickness, CHARGE THE REGULAR POSTAGE PLUS SURCHARGE.

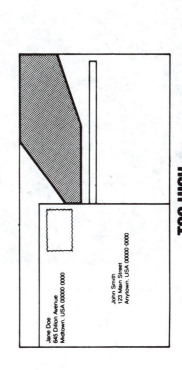

WITHIN RATIO

TOO HIGH
(Subject to Surcharge)

TOO LONG
(Subject to Surcharge)

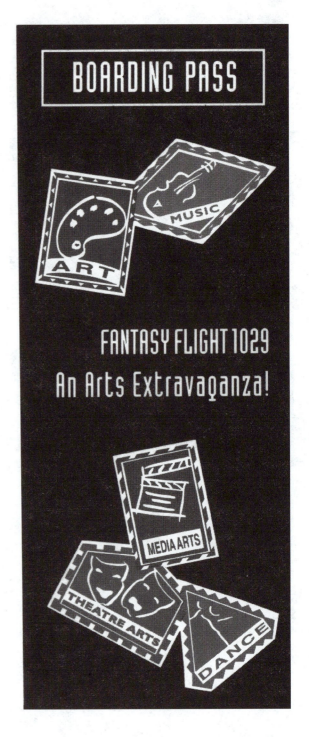

Figure 11–9 Boarding Passes for *Fantasy Flight 1029.* Courtesy of Jackson Boelts, Annalyn Chargualaf, Joy Solon, and the University of Arizona Department of Art, Tucson, Arizona.

software. There are software products that have a module just for special events. There are also free-standing special events software packages. If your organization produces events as a regular part of its development program, it may be worthwhile to invest in specialized software. No matter how the information is manipulated within a computer, consider capturing the following bits of information that will keep you up-to-date on progress, ease the ticketing and seating functions, facilitate reporting after the event, and aid in the post-event evaluation process.

- Name and address

- Nick name (for name tag, etc.)

- Phone number

- Spouse name, if appropriate

- Company name, if appropriate

- Telephone number

- Volunteer/contact person (who suggested the name)

- Host name

- Date of ticket purchase

    Number of tickets

    Total amount

    Amount that constitutes the charitable gift

- Additional gift amount

- Tickets purchased but not attending

    Tickets routed to:

- Date tickets mailed, if appropriate

- Table assignment

- Gift level designation (angel, benefactor, sponsor, etc.), if appropriate

- Gifts-in-kind

- Participation in event extras (auction, raffles, etc.)

- Other comments

Capturing the Names

When your volunteers indicate that they have no new names to give you, suggest their Christmas card lists; their church group lists; and their bridge club, golf club, racquet club, social, or business club lists. Many people don't think that their bridge group or church group would have interest in other events, when, in fact, these lists are excellent sources for prospective guests.

Exhibit 11–2 depicts an example of a form used to gather names from hosts and hostesses.

As these lists are returned to staff, they should be entered into the database with as much information as is available. That might include names of husband and wife (or date), telephone, address, who submitted the name, and any additional information that you might happen to know. For example, if you know that couple A does not mix well with couple B, then you might enter that information on your list with a note, "do not seat with couple A." Or, if you know that one or more individuals prefer vegetarian meals, that would be helpful to add in a special note section of the database. If one of the guests has a handicap that will require special attention, it would be helpful to note this information. For *Fantasy Flight 1029*, there were several guests with such requirements. It was important to be certain that those guests were assigned a route that they were physically able to follow. Because several such routes were planned, there was no problem in assigning those guests. Finally, when one or more of your guests are prospects for significant cultivation, you'll want to be aware of where you seat them. It will be important to seat them with the right people who are aware of their role in the cultivation process. The more information you gather, the easier your future tasks will be, such as seating, ordering, etc.

Exhibit 11–2 Invitation Guest List Form

NAME:_____PHONE:_____

Please print names (husband and wife), title, address, zip, and phone number for the guests you would like to invite.

When to Build Your Invitation List

The timing of your list construction can be critical. If you are planning to send a save-the-date card, you'll need that list at least six months before the event. This may sound like a long time, but if you are in the typical development office, and especially if you are a volunteer, it will take you at least two months to collect, enter, and delete duplications. If it is to be effective, your save-the-date card should be sent out at least three months before the event. Suddenly, there isn't much time left!

When you enter this list into your database, whether computerized or on handwritten cards, be sure to enter the name of the person who gave you the information. There may be instances when you'll want to call up your list by the names of the volunteers *and* the names they submitted. This effort will prove enormously helpful when making calls to engage people in attending your event. If more than one person submits a name, enter *all* of the people who submitted that name. When sending a save-the-date card, you'll want to send only one to each person. But, when sending invitations out, many notes can accompany the same invitation. Think about receiving an invitation and finding notes in it from several of your friends. What a motivating message!

Your list will also provide a resource to use when recording ticket sales. By using your existing list, you won't have to re-enter information; simply mark it so that it can be selected for a report. Finally, when you are ready, you'll be able to print up a list of only those who are attending the event; in fact, you may even be able to list their table assignment at the same time.

Duplication and Other Problems

These are an inevitable part of list building. You'll want to spend some time reviewing your list with at least two people. Looking at names is a surprisingly hypnotic activity; it is easy to overlook duplications, especially when you have both a business and a home address. You might flag these for future review by the board members who submitted them.

Additional caution is advised when using old lists such as country club or organization lists. These often can be outdated, especially when divorces, marriages, and deaths occur. Nothing is so offending as sending an invitation to a couple who are no longer a couple. You will also find that many married couples use two names. Here again, mail addressed to Mr. & Mrs. is not warmly received.

Remember when you're printing the invitation that you may want to consider printing a part of the program as well. For example, because the outside of the invitation for *Fantasy Flight 1029* and the cover of the program were the same design, both were printed at the same time. This saved the printer considerable expense. The next chapter will guide you through the construction of a program for your event.

Orchestrating the Note Writing

Now that you have your list prepared and your invitations designed, it's time to determine how to get the note writing accomplished. It's evident that you aren't going to be able to get all of your hosts and hostesses together for a note-writing session. That would, of course, be ideal. But given the busy schedule of most of those involved, you'll find it necessary to figure out how best to distribute the invitations (or insert cards) and how to orchestrate their return.

Points to Ponder

The most compelling reason for anyone to attend an event is to be with the other people who are going to be there. People naturally want to attend events that draw their friends, attract socialites, or feature people who are celebrities. To see and be seen are an essential appeal of events, especially high-end events.

The best resource to obtain the names of new attendees is those who have previously attended an event and enjoyed themselves. Consider asking previous attendees to recommend someone for the invitation list.

Those invited should reflect the goal, the event, and the program. If cultivation is the goal, invite the target market plus individuals the market trusts and believes. If visibility is the goal, invite people of power, influence, and access. If income is the goal, invite actual and potential major donors; all the invitees should be prospects. If the event is high-end social, invite people of means. If the event is a golf tournament, invite golfers and golf-associated people. If the program honors a physician, invite individuals from the medical community and bio-medical company executives. If the program is to include an auction, invite people that would be interested in and have the means to competitively bid for the offerings.

Consider sending different invitations. Previous attendees could be reminded about earlier events. New attendees could get more in-depth information. Sponsors could get information about the target audience.

Generally speaking, it is unwise to sell tickets at the door or to hold unpaid tickets for pickup at the door. Last-minute changes of plans are less likely for individuals who have paid in advance, and it is less likely that you will have to cover guarantees from net proceeds if you have money in hand.

A word about ticket pricing: avoid under-pricing and avoid establishing the price by what the committee or the board believes to be the level at which they can sell to friends and associates. Set the price according to what the target market will pay for the value received. Test market the price months before the event by steadily increasing the amount being tested until people voice opposition.

If the event is a repeat, consider an early mailing to previous attendees, offering a reduced (last year's) ticket price if paid in advance.

One method could involve sending the addressed and stamped invitations to the host and hostess who submitted names. They will then write notes to their prospective guests and put the invitations in the mail. Two problems exist with this method. First, you personally are not placing those invitations in the mail. They might sit on someone's desk for a week or more, or worse, get buried, never to surface again. The second problem is that for many prospective guests, there will be several of your hosts and hostesses who would want to write a note.

The most effective way to avoid these problems is to provide each host and hostess with a separate matching note card to be written to their friend and then included in the invitation. To initiate this process, you'll send each host and hostess a packet including the following:

- the list of the guests whom they are inviting

- enough cards for a note to each guest (including some extras for mistakes)

- instructions about writing the note and returning all the cards by a specified date

- a stamped, addressed envelope for returning the cards

Using this method, you'll know when the cards are written, you'll insert them into the appropriate invitations, and then all of the invitations will be mailed at the same time. Some invitations will contain many notes and will be all the more effective. Most importantly, you'll know that all the invitations have been mailed at the same time.

Is this worth the hours of effort and the cost? Absolutely! The more personal an invitation is, the more likely it is to evoke a positive response. Even though you may have asked your hosts and hostesses to call the people they are inviting, the previous method is the only way you have to guarantee that a personal message will be received.

Perhaps your organization is small, and your invitation list not too lengthy. You may be able to get enough people together to write notes directly on the invitations. Although this would be effective, usually someone is unable to attend. The previous method will ensure that everyone is able to write notes.

Summary

The design of the invitation should reflect the event, establish the tone of the activities, and heighten the expectations of the invitees. It should be considered as the key marketing device to elicit interest in the target group.

The invitation should give necessary information in an attractive, eye-catching format that is appropriate to the event and to the target market.

The invitation should meet the requirements of both the Internal Revenue Service and the United States Post Office.

Copy should be checked, double-checked, and triple-checked by more than one individual for accuracy and completeness,

The invitation list is a critical piece of the process. Getting invitations into the hands of the target market is the first step in getting the right people to attend the event. Event volunteers, board members, staff, and others all play a key role in developing the list of invitees, but the bulk of the names should come from the event volunteers. Encourage these volunteers, early and often, to share

> **Arranging to have handwritten notes on the invitations is a powerful tool in increasing attendance.**

names and addresses with staff for the purpose of expanding the invitation list.

Arranging to have handwritten notes on the invitations is a powerful tool in increasing attendance. Volunteers who submitted names should be asked to write such notes for the invitees from the volunteers' lists. The personal attention and endorsement of the event can be just the thing to encourage the invitee to attend.

Chapter 12

What Goes in the Program?

Our wanderings to guide.

Lewis Carroll

In this chapter you'll find the reasons why you might want to print a program for your event and what you might want to include. There is the possibility that a program won't be necessary for your event. At the end of this chapter, you'll find examples of various types of event programs.

Do You Want or Need a Program?

Some events do not need a printed program. A press conference, for example, requires other printed information to be distributed, but not a program. Most conferences or workshops call for a packet of materials of which a program is only one part. In this case, the program might be a one-page piece with the schedule and location of presentations. A car wash or bake sale does not call for a program. But let's look at the many purposes that a printed program can serve.

Programs are helpful when you wish to identify the following:

- event schedule

- performers—photos and/or biographic information may be included

- speakers—photos or bios also may be included

- hosts and hostesses

- chair, cochairs, or honorees

- board members

- key staff members

- underwriters and sponsors

- donors

- information about your organization

- philosophy of your organization or program

- message from the president or CEO

- menu

If for no other reason, the opportunity to tell your audience about your organization is a key point. This is your chance to highlight that part of your organization that you most want this audience to understand. It may mean just including your mission statement. Or, it may mean a letter from the CEO. It's your program to be whatever you want it to be.

The program for *Fantasy Flight 1029* was lengthy. The four-color cover for the program was printed at the same time as the invitation. This saved considerable printing expense (in this case, for the printer who donated the work) and simply meant that the covers were finished well in advance of the time when they would be needed. In fact, the printing of the inside pages of the program was donated by a different printer. The inside pages could be a one-color print job, and the second printer could stitch the program pages to the cover as part of the contribution.

As you'll see from the following examples, programs come in many forms and are as simple or complex as you wish to make them. Whatever your decision, remember that the program is another ideal cultivation opportunity. If you wish to provide recognition, help to position your volunteers, or explain your organization, the program is the perfect vehicle. Further, the program is something people can take home. Often, it serves as a memento and a reminder of an event.

When organizations are producing an event for an honoree, they often use their programs to provide ongoing recognition of recipients of past awards. In so doing, they provide an opportunity for further cultivation of those individuals.

Often, a colorful or elegant program, placed on the table, contributes to the table decor, an aspect to consider when designing your program. Certainly, the program provides an opportunity to reinforce a thematic design of an event. In the program for *Fantasy Flight 1029*, the travel theme for the evening was reinforced throughout (Figure 12–1).

The cover:
Repeated the theme of the invitation using the same colors and design.

The Title Page:
Repeated the title of the event and defined it as An Arts Extravaganza!

Named the sponsoring organization.

Listed the Fine Arts department heads.

The Table of Contents:
Provided easy access to the contents of the program by using page numbers.

> Remember that the program is an ideal cultivation opportunity.

The Itinerary:
Provided a list of events and times and gave guests an overview of their evening. This was especially helpful because of the unusual nature of this unpredictable experience.

Fantasy Flight 1029 Performances:
Provided the opportunity to recognize all of the performers who were contributing their talents to the evening.

The Flight Manifest:
Fulfilled the visibility promise to those who purchased the more expensive tickets. Both business class *and* first class passengers were listed in the program.

From the Galley:
Recognized all the restaurants and suppliers.

Hosts & Hostesses:
Recognized the many hosts and hostesses for the evening, because it was this group of people who made this particular event a smashing financial success.

The Flight Crew:
Acknowledged the group that made the technical part of the evening happen. They ran lights, sound, and wiring, and also included media arts students who filmed the activities of the evening.

Without this group, this event would never have happened!

Acknowledgments:
Recognized those who had donated cash, products, talent, or services.

The thank you section on the last page promised yet another list of volunteers that would be published in a newsletter at a later date. The newsletter was later published, and the names of the many students and other volunteers were included.

Selling Program Ads

Some organizations find that selling ads is another income-generating activity. If you have the volunteers (or paid staff) who will go out into the community to sell advertising, and if you want your program to include some commercial types of ads, then it is a good way to generate a little more income. If, however, you don't have a group of people (or even one staff member dedicated to this task),

FANTASY FLIGHT 1029

An Arts Extravaganza!

The University of Arizona
Faculty of Fine Arts
Opening Gala
October 29, 1993

DEAN - Maurice J. Sevigny, Ph.D.

DEPARTMENT OF ART - Jon W. Meyer, M.F.A.
COMMITTEE ON DANCE - Jory L. Hancock, M.S.
DEPARTMENT OF MEDIA ARTS - Caren J. Deming, Ph.D.
SCHOOL OF MUSIC - Dorothy K. Payne, Ph.D.
DEPARTMENT OF THEATRE ARTS - Albert D. Tucci, M.F.A.

Figure 12–1 Program for *Fantasy Flight 1029.* Courtesy of Jackson Boelts, Annalyn Chargualaf, Joy Solon, and the University of Arizona Department of Art, Tucson, Arizona.

Figure 12–1 continued

3

Itinerary

Event	Time
PRE-BOARDING	6:45-7:30
FLIGHT DEPARTURE	7:30
IN FLIGHT VIGNETTE	7:35-7:45
Follow your color designated guide to sites for Special Performances	
PERFORMANCE FEASTS - will be held in five sites designated by the colored dots you received	
PURPLE - New Lab Theatre	
TURQUOISE - Crowder Hall	
GREEN - Joseph Gross Gallery	
PINK - Marroney Theatre	
YELLOW - Orchestra Rehearsal Room	
FIRST PERFORMANCE FEAST	7:55-8:40
Follow your guide to your designated site	
IN FLIGHT VIGNETTE	8:45-8:55
Follow your guide	
SECOND PERFORMANCE FEAST	9:05-9:50
Follow your guide	
FLIGHT FINALE	10:00-10:15
Courtyard	
DESSERT & HARPFUSION	10:15-11:15
Museum of Art	
DESSERT & DANCING	10:15-midnight
On Deck in Courtyard	

Table of Contents

Figure 12–1 continued

Fantasy Flight 1029 Performances

Pre-Boarding

PRIDE OF ARIZONA MARCHING BAND   PARKING GARAGE
Enrique C. Feldman, director

PRIDE OF ARIZONA MARCHING BAND AUXILIARIES   SPEEDWAY UNDERPASS

CREATIVE MOVEMENT CLASS   HOLSCLAW RECITAL HALL ENTRANCE
Melissa Lowe, director
Charles Spaulding, assistant

Final Call

LISA LEMAY TRIO   FINE ARTS COURTYARD

On the Runway

THE BUILDING OF POEMS   FINE ARTS COURTYARD
written and performed by C. Nicholas Johnson
with the Lisa Lemay Trio

Take-Off

TROIS CHANSONS   FINE ARTS COURTYARD
by Claude Debussy
choreography by Nathan Montoya
performed by Melissa Lowe
with the Symphonic Choir, Josef Knott, conductor

In Flight Vignette

KONZERT FOR 4 VIOLINS   LIBRARY UNDERPASS
by G.P. Telemann
performed by UA Graduate Guitar Quartet

THE SEVENTEEN-YEAR DREAM   FIBER STUDIO
Gayle Wimmer, with students of the Art Department

VIENNA PHILHARMONIC FANFARE   CCP PATIO
by R. Strauss
performed by the UA Brass & Percussion Choir
Enrique C. Feldman, director

MEDIA FLIGHT   FOUNDATIONS ROOM
produced by Phillip G. Buckner

4

First Course

MUSICA "A LA CARTE"   NEW LAB THEATRE
performed by Mariachi Arizona, Richard Obregón, director

DAWN'S ATTIC   NEW LAB THEATRE
choreography by Ellen Bromberg
music by Patrick Neher, lighting design by Julie Mack
performed by UA Dance Ensemble and the AZ Double Bass Ensemble

SOMETHING WONDERFUL (EXCERPTS)   JOSEPH GROSS GALLERY
by Rodgers & Hammerstein
devised, directed & choreographed by Daniel Yurgaitis
performed by Encore, AZ Repertory Theatre Ensemble

MY FATHER'S SHOES   JOSEPH GROSS GALLERY
conceived & performed by Herb Stratford, Art Department

DUETS FOR SPANISH & CLASSICAL GUITAR   MARRONEY THEATRE
performed by Pastrana/Rijos Guitar Duo

NINE (EXCERPTS)   MARRONEY THEATRE
by Arthur Kopit & Maury Yeston
directed by Richard Hanson
performed by AZ Repertory Theatre Ensemble

MUSIC TO CHEW BY   ORCHESTRA REHEARSAL ROOM
performed by the Rosewood Marimba Band, Gary Cook, coordinator

THE CONSUL (EXCERPT)   ORCHESTRA REHEARSAL ROOM
by Gian-Carlo Menotti
Charles Roe & Josef Knott, directors
set design by Tyler Herring
piano accompaniment by Elizabeth Chadwick
performed by UA Opera Theatre students

TRES TANGOS   CROWDER HALL
choreographed & performed by Mara Carlson and John Dahlstrand, UA Dance
music by Astor Piazzola

MEDIA ARTS' FINEST   CROWDER HALL
produced by Phillip G. Buckner

In Flight Vignette

RACHMANINOV SONGS   MUSIC ROOM
performed by Grayson Hirst, tenor & Paula Fan, piano

UNFORGETTABLE   VOICE & MOVEMENT STUDIO
By Irving Gordon
performed by the Choraliers, Jeffrey Haskell, conductor

5

Figure 12–1 continued

Flight Manifest

With special appreciation, the Faculty of Fine Arts gratefully recognizes those passengers whose generous gifts are helping to create the Endowment for the Dean's Fund for Excellence. This list recognizes ticketed passengers as of October 15.

First Class Passengers

Mr. & Mrs. Frank Barret
Mr. & Mrs. Rick Barrett
Ms. Joan Beigel-Kaye
Mr. & Mrs. Dale Birtch
Ms. Esther Capin
Ms. Shirley Chann
Ginny & Bill Clements/
Golden Eagle Distributors, Inc.
Mr. & Mrs. Gerrit Cormany
Mr. & Mrs. Edward Cuming, Jr.
Dr. & Mrs. James Dalen
Mr. & Mrs. Darryl Dobras
Mr. & Mrs. Edward Farmilant
Ms. Lisa Frank & Mr. James Green
Dr. Joseph Gross & Ms. Suzanne Werbelow
Mr. & Mrs. Michael Hard
Dr. & Mrs. Kenneth Hatch
Mr. & Mrs. C. Donald Hatfield
Mr. & Mrs. William G. Hillenbrand
Dr. & Mrs. Henry Koffler
Dr. & Mrs. Martin Levy
Mr. Bill Lundquist
Mr. & Mrs. Douglas Nelson
Mr. & Mrs. Lars Pederson
Mr. & Mrs. Louis Pozez
Mr. & Mrs. Shaol Pozez
Mrs. Charles Putnam
Dean Maurice J. Sevigny
Mr. & Mrs. David Sherwood
Mr. & Mrs. Donald Shropshire
Mr. & Mrs. Louis Slavin
University Medical Center
Mr. & Mrs. John Westman

Business Class Passengers

Mr. & Mrs. Victor Arida
Mr. Bill Arms
Dr. Allan Beigel & Ms. Nancy Sher
Mr. Tom Black
Dr. & Mrs. James Blute III
Bobby & Roberta Bracker
Mr. & Mrs. Donald Diamond
Dr. & Mrs. Robert Dzioba
Chief Justice & Mrs. Stanley Feldman
Ms. Rowena Foster
Mr. & Mrs. James Garrett
Mr. & Mrs. Ralph Henig
Mr. & Mrs. Frank Lazarus
Mr. & Mrs. Humberto Lopez
Mr. & Mrs. John Munic
Mr. & Mrs. Gregory Papanikolas
Drs. William Penn & Dorothy Payne
Mr. & Mrs. James Rodolph
Ms. Lillian Rosenzweig
Mr. & Mrs. Russ Russo
Mr. & Mrs. Tom Sanders
Drs. John & Helen Schaefer
Mr. & Mrs. William C. Scott
Dr. & Mrs. Gary Simpson
Mr. Paul Speyer
Dr. & Mrs. John Spizizen
Dr. & Mrs. John Sullivan, Jr.
University Medical Center
Ms. Deedee Walden & Mr. Bruce Caruth
Dr. & Mrs. Ronald Weinstein
Mr. David L. Windsor
Dr. Rachael Yocom

7

TWO CIRANDAS   FINE ARTS COURTYARD
by Heitor Villa-Lobos
performed by Ingrid Barancoski, School of Music

MERCHANT OF VENICE (EXCERPT)   ACTING STUDIO
by William Shakespeare
directed by Harold Dixon
performed by AZ Repertory Theatre Ensemble

3-D EXPERIENCE   MUSIC GREEN ROOM
coordinated by Dennis Jones
featuring students of the Art Department

MY OLD ROCKIN' CHAIR   MARRONEY THEATRE ENTRANCE
choreography by Nina Janik, music by Jay McShann
costumes, furniture & props courtesy of Theatre Arts
performed by Tina Curran & Thom Lewis, UA Dance Ensemble

THREEFOLD BLESSINGS DANCE   HOLSCLAW RECITAL HALL
Gods of the Himalayas Come to Holsclaw Hall!
choreography by John M. Wilson, music by Mickey Hart
performed by members of the UA Dance Ensemble

GERSHWIN CONCERTO   CHORAL REHEARSAL ROOM
performed by 3 Grand Piano Trio

Second Course

Please refer to your first course flight plan

Final Destination

FIREWORKS FOR FINE ARTS   FINE ARTS COURTYARD
choreography by Michael Williams
music by Dr. Alban
music mixed by Wiley Ross, School of Music
performed by UA Dance Ensemble

CAPTAIN'S DANCE   FINE ARTS COURTYARD
Dean Maurice J. Sevigny

Passenger's Choice

DESSERT WITH HARPFUSION   MUSEUM OF ART
Carrol McLaughlin, director

DANCING & DESSERT   FINE ARTS COURTYARD
UA Studio Jazz Ensemble, Neal Finn, conductor
with Jeffrey Haskell

REFLECTIONS OF THE NIGHT
TV wall supervised by Phillip G. Buckner, Media Arts

6

Figure 12–1 continued

Hosts & Hostesses for Fantasy Flight 1029

Sincere appreciation to this energetic group of supporters who have given their time and effort this summer to ensure the success of Fantasy Flight 1029:

Chairs

Mr. & Mrs. Darryl Dobras
Mr. & Mrs. Louis Slavin

Committee

Mr. & Mrs. Jerry Alpert
Mr. & Mrs. Victor Arida
Mr. Paul Ash & Ms. Bridget Carnell
Mr. & Mrs. Rick Barrett
Ms. Joan Beigel-Kaye
Dr. & Mrs. James Blute III
Mr. & Mrs. Robert Bracker
Ms. Esther Capin
Dr. & Mrs. William Casey
Ms. Shirley Chann
Mr. & Mrs. Gerrit Cormany
Dr. & Mrs. James Dalen
Mr. & Mrs. Michael DeBell
Mr. & Mrs. Donald Diamond
Chief Justice & Mrs. Stanley Feldman
Ms. Rowena Foster
Mr. Gary Gethmann & Ms. Gini Moran
Mr. & Mrs. Greg Gibbons
Dr. Joseph Gross & Ms. Suzanne Werbelow
Mr. & Mrs. Jack Gumbin
Mr. & Mrs. Charles Hall III
Dr. & Mrs. Kenneth Hatch
Mr. & Mrs. C. Donald Hatfield
Mr. & Mrs. Larry Hecker
Mr. & Mrs. Joseph Heller
Mr. & Mrs. Ralph Henig
Dr. & Mrs. Leonard Joffe

Dr. & Mrs. Ron Kolker
Mr. & Mrs. Frank Lazarus
Mr. Bill Lundquist
Mr. & Mrs. John McLaughlin
Mr. & Mrs. John Munic
Mr. & Mrs. Douglas Nelson
Mr. Tino Ocheltree & Dr. Moira Shannon
Dr. & Mrs. Manuel Pacheco
Mr. & Mrs. Gregory Papanikolas
Gen. & Mrs. Julius Parker, Jr.
Mr. & Mrs. Lars Pederson
Mr. & Mrs. Louis Pozez
Mrs. Charles Putnam
Ms. Lillian Rosenzweig
Dr. & Mrs. Stephen Seltzer
Dean Maurice J. Sevigny
Mr. & Mrs. Donald Shropshire
Dr. & Mrs. Ernest Smerdon
Mr. & Mrs. George Steele
Mr. & Mrs. Alvin Stern
Mr. & Mrs. Robert Stubbs
Dr. & Mrs. John Sullivan, Jr.
Mr. & Mrs. Alfred Thomas
Dr. & Mrs. Ron Weinstein
Mr. & Mrs. Tom Weir
Mr. & Mrs. Larry Wetterschneider
Mr. & Mrs. Michael Williams

9

From the Galley

Special thanks for the galley preparations for this benefit evening. The following restaurants and vendors have made this gourmet experience possible with their generous contributions:

Restaurants & Caterers

Boccata
Cafe Terra Cotta
Cucina Contenta (Catering by Daniel's)
Dakota Cafe
El Saguarito
Eric's Ice Cream
La Joyeux
Le Bistro
Ovens Restaurant
Pronto Cucina
Presidio Grill
Sheraton El Conquistador
Sweet & Savory Cravings
Vivace Restaurant
Westin La Paloma

Purveyors

City Meats
John Dough Bread Company
Kodiak Produce
S.E. Rykoff

Beverages

Arbuckle Coffee
Arizona Vinyards
Cactus Beverage
Common Grounds Espresso Co.
O'Malleys
Southern Wine & Spirits
United Beverage

Ice Sculptures

Ramada Downtown

Hospitality Room for Fantasy Flight 1029 Volunteers

Blue J's
Carl's Jr.
Dunkin' Donuts
Gentle Ben's Brewing Company
The Great Impasta Express
Jack in the Box
Kippy's
Mike's Place
Radisson Suites Hotel
Two Pesos
7-Eleven/Lavicio's

8

Figure 12–1 continued

Acknowledgements

Thank you to the following donors whose contributions have helped to make this evening possible:

Donors

Drs. Joseph Alpert & Helle Mathiasen	Drs. Bruce Jarrell & Leslie Robinson
Mr. & Mrs. Nicholas D. Badami	Dr. & Mrs. Leonard Joffe
Ms. Joan Beigel-Kaye	Mr. & Mrs Robert Kovitz
Dr. & Mrs. Reidar Bjorhovde	Dr. & Mrs. Herbert J. Langen
Ms. Esther Capin	Mr. Bill Lundquist
Mr. & Mrs. John Carter	Mr. & Mrs. John McLaughlin
Mr. & Mrs. Michael DeBell	Dr. & Mrs. James Newell
Mr. & Mrs. Darryl Dobras	Mr. & Mrs. Nicholas O'Keeffe
Chief Justice & Mrs. Stanley Feldman	Ms. Barbara Rogers
Mr. & Mrs. Randall Fisher	Dr. & Mrs. Ken Ryan
Mr. & Mrs. Richard Flynn	Mr. & Mrs. James N. Schmidt
Ms. Pamela Grissom	Mr. & Mrs. Louis Slavin
Mr. & Mrs. Charles W. Hall III	Drs. Alvin Goldman and Holly Smith
Dr. & Mrs. Kenneth Hatch	Dr. & Mrs Robert Snyder
Dr. & Mrs. Robert Hirsch	Mr. & Mrs. David White

Invitation and Program

Design :	Annalyn Chargualaf
	Joy Solon
Art Direction :	Jackson Boelts and Eric Boelts
Digital Output :	Andresen's Graphic Services
Printing - Covers :	Arizona Lithographers
Inside Pages :	Skyline Printing
Program Design :	Phil Corbin

Environment

Art Work :	Barbara Rogers
	Bruce McGrew
	Turner Davis/Karen Medley/Beata Wehr/Audrey Mosaghin/Terry Moody/Stephanie Sheppard/Ana Amavisca-Gaines/Grace Rodriquez/Jay George Zanios/ Renee Koehler
	Maurice J. Sevigny
	Keith McElroy
	Rhea Hatch
	Moira Geoffrion
	The Plantsman
	Plants of Distinction
	Krzyzanowski & Co.
Greenery/Flowers:	Villa Feliz Flowers

Flight Crew

Honorary Captains	Mary Ann & Darryl Dobras
	Marjory & Louis Slavin
Captain	Dean Maurice J. Sevigny
Pilot	Barbara Levy
Navigator	Pat Bjorhovde
Flight Environment	
Performance Venues	Rhea Hatch
Out-of-doors	Keith McElroy
Performance Captains	Jory Hancock
	Carrol McLaughlin
Flight Technical Directors	Deon Hill
	Jeff Warburton
	J. Michael Gillette
Galley Captains	Cande Grogan - Ovens Restaurant
	Ellen Burke Van Slyke - Boccata
Flight Arrangements	Judy Bassnett
Chief Steward	Lisa Ferguson
Stewards	Brett Bendickson
	Darlene Lizarraga

Figure 12–1 continued

Signage

Painting : J! Randall Morris & Peter Vlk
Supplies : Posner's Art Store
Grumbacher Paints, Inc.

First Class Favors

Maurice J. Sevigny
Margo Dutton
Rhea Hatch

Equipment

Roh's Inc.
Party Concepts

Lighting

Snellstrum

Rapelling Advisor

Bruce Rischar

Pre-event Performance Artists

Paul Groves   Naomi Bartholomew
Douglas James   Kimberly Houser
Carrol McLaughlin   Melissa Lowe
Maria Banks

Lanterns & Standards

Keith McElroy

THANK YOU !!!

The talented and generous individuals who have made this evening possible number in the hundreds. In order to recognize all the performers, volunteers, technical people, and many others whose names could not be included in the program, a newsletter will be printed following this event. Until then, <u>thank you</u> one and all for your work and dedication which have been the foundation for the Dean's Fund for Excellence.

12

it can become a burdensome activity. It is also wise to consider the prospect pool before deciding to sell advertising. Are these businesses that might be underwriters for your event? Which would be more valuable to you: an advertiser (whose requirements you must meet) or a donor who is helping to underwrite your event?

Is your event one that will attract businesses to purchase advertising? If it is a large event reaching a significant number of people, or if the people invited will represent just the right market for certain businesses, then it is a viable activity. If, however, the numbers you will reach are small, and if the prospect pool includes some of those businesses that might have made contributions to underwrite your event, then the effort is not worthwhile.

Selling ads also takes a considerable amount of time and people power. You'll have to prepare the specifics of your program at least six or seven months before your event to have adequate time to sell advertising.

The Program and the Timeline

Where does the program fit in the timeline of activity? You don't want it to be a last-minute affair, when you'll wonder if the ink will dry in time to fold it. But, the program typically includes some last-minute information. You may want the opportunity to add another contributor to the program. You may decide to change the order of part of the evening. And you certainly don't want to have to announce that the program is incorrect. This means that you and your printer need to figure out just how "last minute" this program can be. It saves wear and tear if you will complete as much of the program in advance as possible. In fact, in Chapter 11, the suggestion was made that printing the program cover at the same time as the invitations is a good practice from the perspective of the printer.

It may even save you some money. If your cover is more than one color, but your inside pages will be just one color, then it makes sense to get that multi-color job done while the ink is on the press rather than sustain charges for more than one ink at a later date, when all you need is one color for the inside pages.

The program for the Arizona Children's Home *Deck the Halls* is simple (Figure 12–2). This two-page program folds to provide eight half-pages of copy. The program recognizes the sponsors and the entertainment. It provides guests with the order of the evening and the donors. The words to some of the more familiar carols are included because during the entertainment portion of the evening, the audience is invited to sing along. Finally, the lists of the Board of Directors of the Agency and the Board of Trustees of the Foundation are included on the back page.

Another simple program was used for an event for the *Medici Circle* membership (Figure 12–3). This group was the outgrowth of *Fantasy Flight 1029*. These annual donors of $1,000 provide ongoing funding for the Dean's Fund for Excellence. The 1995 Cocktail Cabaret program provided donors with a list of the recipients of funding from the Dean's Fund for Excellence and how they used the money. The program for the evening included acknowledgments and a list of the members. This two-page program, designed on computer and printed on inexpensive paper, was made more glamorous with a light glitter spray.

Summary

Consider the following: First, do you want or need a program? Is there a purpose? Second, think about how to produce it. Should you sell ads? Third, watch your timeline when printing a program. Fourth, consider many different program styles.

American Home Furnishings

Arizona Bank

Tucson Newspapers

present

DECK THE HALLS

to benefit

The Arizona Children's Home Association

For your musical entertainment

Harp Fusion

Nancy Davis Booth

The Festival Bell Ringers

The Rosewood Marimba Band

The Catalina Carolers

The Arizona Children's Home Association is a non-profit, state-wide agency that has provided a treatment resource for troubled Arizona children and their families since 1914. Your support tonight will help the Arizona Children's Home continue to provide needed services to over 8,000 children and their families in the coming year.

Deck the Halls
1995

Figure 12–2 Program for *Deck the Halls*.

Figure 12–2 continued

A special thank you from the Children of the Arizona Children's Home to all those who have made significant contributions to this evening

Presenting Sponsors:

American Home Furnishings
Arizona Bank
Tucson Newspapers

Other Donors:

Alonzo Berry
Regina Brandt and Hank Brandt Associates
Esther N Capin
Mr. and Mrs. Thomas Chagaris
Eric Chandor
Alice F. Chang
Swain Chapman
Cecilia Cusimann
Mr. and Mrs. Robert Friesen
Gregg and Dee Anne Gibbons
Carrie Hall
Dr. and Mrs. Gary L. Henderson
Buzz & Barbara Isaacson
Frances McClelland
Hon. Lou-Ann Preble and Col. (Ret.) Wm. F. Preble
Jack Roberts (Addison, Roberts & Ludwig)
Mr. and Mrs. Golden Smith
Drs. Lisa and Steven Strober
Shirley W. Struthers
Deedee Walden

Table centerpieces were donated by
Bloomers
Casas Adobes Flower Shop
Fiesta Flowers
Flowers For You
Galleria Florist
Inglis
Mayfield Florist
The Plantsman

Favors were donated by
Country Estate Pecans

Invitations and printed materials were donated by
Spectrum Printing

Thank you for coming tonight, and for your support of

The Arizona Children's Home
Association

Deck the Halls

Program

6:00 p.m.   Hors d'oeuvres and no-host cocktails
            Rosewood Marimba Band

7:00 p.m.   Deck the Halls Holiday Buffet
            Festival Bell Ringers
            Catalina Carolers

8:00 p.m.   Acknowledgements
            Fred Chaffee
            Presentation
            Jim Welter

8:15 p.m.   Harp Fusion
            Nancy Davis Booth

Figure 12–2 continued

THE ARIZONA CHILDREN'S HOME
"It Shouldn't Hurt To Be A Child"

The Arizona Children's Home Association
Board of Directors

Jim Welter, President
Brenda Even, 1st V.P.
Blake Down, 2nd V.P.
Robert L. Shaff, Secretary
Paul Zucarelli, Past President

Betsy Bolding
Richard Bratt
Ben R. Buehler-Garcia
Elizabeth F. Claiborne
Wesley Colvin
Diane Costantino
Ted Doe
Ponce Duran
Doris Ellis
Dorothy H. Finley
George Garcia
Elizabeth Howell
Stephen Jewett
Robert J. Kurtin
Rebecca Lefferts
Troy Richards
Jim Ronstadt
Christina Tanaka
Alice Udall
Thomas K. Wilson
Linda Yocum

The Arizona Children's Home Foundation
Board of Trustees

Dorothy H. Finley, President
Dick Fitzgerald, 1st V.P.
Pamela Barbey, 2nd V.P.
Dr. Francine Hardaway, Secretary
Fred Chaffee, Treasurer

Larry Adamson
Thomas P. Ambrose
Diana Balich
Lee Blaugrund
Philip Connors
Carrie Hall
Patrick Hoog
Barbara R. Levy
Michelle Monserez
Tanya Pepper
Ople Sorich
Ann Symington
Perri Touché
Jim Welter
Mary Beth Zanes
Paul Zucarelli

Arizona Children's Home
Chief Executive Officer
Fred J. Chaffee, M.A., M.S.W.

Arizona Children's Home Foundation
Executive Director
Barbara R. Levy, ACFRE

The University of Arizona
College of Fine Arts
Medici Circle

1995 Cocktail Cabaret

Sunday, the seventh of May

Loews Ventana Canyon Resort

Figure 12–3 Medici Circle 1995 Cocktail Cabaret. Courtesy of the University of Arizona College of Fine Arts, Tucson, Arizona.

Figure 12–3 continued

DEAN'S FUND FOR EXCELLENCE RECIPIENTS
July 1994-April 1995

Students

Mark Baldwin, *Art*, recognition for college holiday card design

Pia Cuneo, *Art*, catalogue for graduate student art history exhibition at University of Arizona Museum of Art

Elizabeth Ferguson, *Art*, recognition for invitation to participate in American Photography Institution Seminar in New York

Mark Gray, *Art*, attendance at public art conference

Mark Gray, *Art*, construction of a sculpture to be placed at Holsclaw Hall

Gary Lim, *Art*, recognition for invitation to participate in American Photography Institution Seminar in New York

Gigi Schroeder, *Art*, scholarships for the Wildcat Art Program

Jory Hancock, *Dance*, support for UA Dance Ensemble to accept invitation to represent US at International Jazz Dance Congress

William Dietz, *Music*, support for student UA Bassoon Trio to compete in National Association of Chamber Music Finals in Albuquerque

Neal Finn, *Music*, support to enable UA Studio Jazz Ensemble and Jazz Combo to compete in the 28th Annual Reno International Jazz Festival

Mark Miceli, *Treistman Center*, travel support to enable him to accept an invitation to present a paper he co-authored with Tim Kolosick at the International Conference on Acoustics and Musical Research held in Italy

UA Student Showcase, research expo on UA Mall during Homecoming Weekend

Faculty

Jackson Boelts, *Art*, 20% matching grant towards a design computer system upgrade

Craig Caldwell, *Art*, computer equipment for graphic design

Craig Caldwell, *Art*, career advancement attendance at Art, Culture & the National Information Infrastructure Conference

Michael Croft, *Art*, faculty development training

Michael Croft, *Art*, guest artist/scholar in Japanese metalsmithing

Mickelle Smith Omari, *Art*, printing of African Art exhibit catalogue

Barbara Rogers, *Art*, printing of faculty exhibit announcements

Staci Widdifield, *Art*, support to create prototype imagery course

Nina Janik, *Dance*, technique redevelopment training grant

Caren Deming, Media Arts, support for guest lecture/reception

Mary Beth Haralovich/Michael Gillette, *Media Arts*, high tech classroom/demonstration

Alfonso Moises, *Media Arts*, support for multi-media Mesoamerican Cultural Code project

Beverly Seckinger, *Media Arts*, support for spring film and video series

Elizabeth Ervin, *Music*, support to attend MacAcademy, 2-day computer workshop/training session

Nohema Fernandez, *Music*, guest artist cellist for master classes

Tim Kolosick, *Music*, support for Orchestra Nova which was invited to attend international conference

Patrick Neher, *Music*, guest artist for bass symposium

Peter Beaudert, *Theatre Arts*, support for creation of a theatre props database

Julia DeHesus, *Theatre Arts*, support for research on new box office management system

Brent Gibbs, *Theatre Arts*, support of accreditation in fight directing

Richard Hanson, *Theatre Arts*, rehearsals for orchestral score taping

Karen Husted, *Theatre Arts*, support to attend induction into Educational Theatre Association Hall of Fame

Al Tucci, *Theatre Arts*, guest scholars for Literature into Drama outreach series

Staff

Barbara Myers, *Art*, training on self-directed work teams

Deon Hill, *Music*, workshop on technology in performance halls

Figure 12–3 continued

- Program of Artists Funded by
Dean's Fund for Excellence -

Welcome   Don Shropshire
               Chair, Dean's Board
Remarks   *Maurice Sevigny, Dean*

Set I

Mark Gray's "Body of the Buddha"
by Andy Polk
  - Department of Art

Fight scene, freely adapted from
Design for Living by Noel Coward
Brent Gibbs
Matt Lincoln
  - Department of Theatre Arts

Divertissement by Eugene Bozza
allegro giocosa
Trios for Bassoon by Julius Weissenborn
polka
Turkish march
University of Arizona Bassoon Trio
John Rising
Pat Nelson
Chris Mayor
  - School of Music & Dance

Acknowledgments   Maurice Sevigny

Set II

Muted Instrument
four mutes for trumpets
1. Dark Blues
2. Hormones
3. Now what does it mean??

concept/choreography   Michael Williams
original score/arrangements   Neal Finn
musical consultant   Greg Hanson
costumes   Michael Williams

dancers	trumpets	bass
Beth Benites	Kevin Christensen	Lee Gardner
Elena Fillmore	Matthew Rhaldi	understudies
Tiffany Hansen	Chad Shoopman	Coutney Combs
Celena Leal	Jeffrey Stoff	Claire Hancock
	- School of Music & Dance	

Figure 12–3 continued

FOUNDING MEMBERS OF THE MEDICI CIRCLE

Pennie & Gary Abramson
William S. Arms
Joan Beigel-Kaye*
Pat & Reidar Bjorhovde
Esther N. Capin*
Gerrit & Carla* Cormany
James & Priscilla Dalen
Sally S. Drachman
Sandra & Kenneth* Greenblatt
Joseph F. Gross & Suzanne P. Werbelow
Louise & Jack Gumbin
Al & Dorothy Hampel
Vivian Hanson
Michael & Kathy Hard
Rhea & Ken Hatch
Bill & Doby Hillenbrand
Susan & Dick Imwalle
Anonymous
Jana B. Kooi
Barbara* & Martin Levy
Dorothy & Wayne Mackin
Ann & David Meltzer
Anne E. Nelson
Craig T. Nelson
Linda & Stuart Nelson
Kenneth J. Orms
Gregory & Lyn* Papanikolas
Lynn & Greg Pivirotto
Mrs. Charles M. Putnam, Jr.*
Lillian R. Rosenzweig
Drs. Helen & John Schaefer
Dr. & Mrs. Gulshan Sethi
Shirley & Maurice* Sevigny
Mary Ruth & Don* Shropshire
Marjory & Louis Slavin
Paul R. Speyer
Margaret & George* Steele
Kay & John* Sullivan
Dr. Susan Sullivan & E. Thomas Sullivan
Deedee* Walden
Larry* & Laurie Wetterschneider
David L. Windsor

*Member, Dean's Board

Dean's Board
Special Events Committee

Lyn Papanikolas, *Chair*
Carla Cormany
Norma Feldman
Irene Putnam

Acknowledgments

Loews Ventana Canyon Ranch
Joan Beigel-Kaye

The Medici Circle consists of a group of individuals who, through contributions, support excellence in the arts at The University of Arizona College of Fine Arts. Medici Circle funds support the Dean's Fund for Excellence and are used to:

Support study or travel for students
Support visiting artists or scholars
Promote excellence in teaching through support of faculty enrichment
Support artists' resources of excellence
Support research grants
Support new initiatives

If you would like to invite someone to join the Medici Circle or if you wish information about renewing your own membership, please call Pat Bjorhovde at 621-9057.

Chapter 13

What About Decor?

Imagination is the true magic carpet.

Norman Vincent Peale

How important is the decor? Who can help to make it happen? What will it cost? Can it be done for less? The extent of decor necessary to your event depends on the size, location, and theme of your event. This chapter will offer some suggestions and possibilities for decor, plus an evaluation tool that will help guide your decisions.

Possibilities for Decor

Decorations can provide a special addition to your event, and may range from the use of contrasting linens on the tables to elaborate centerpieces with matching hangings on the walls. When thinking about the places that one would like to decorate, consider the following:

- Arrival path

  –lanterns on the ground

  –streamers in the trees

  –lights in the trees

- Entrance, registration, and welcome

  –flowers

  –colored banners

  –colored linens

- Room

  –walls

  –trees

  –lights

  –podium

- Tables

  –linens

  –streamers

  –mirror plates

  –flowers

  –fruit

  –party favors

  –place cards

–decorative programs

- Buffet Tables

  –ice sculptures

  –flowers

  –plants in cachepots

  –sculpture

- Staff/Volunteers

  –name tags

  –costumes

  –uniforms

  –flowers

Design and the Budget

Reality dictates that the budget will control the extent and quality of the design. However, here lie significant opportunities for contributed services and goods. Naturally, florists are one of the first to be suggested as a contributor. In response to that phenomenon, florists do give generously. But other possibilities exist when it comes to flowers. One possibility is asking a wholesale florist for flowers, and then asking a designer or a volunteer for help in arranging them. You may choose to engage a florist to help suggest alternatives to flowers. Many effects can be achieved by "suggestion." Often, an artist can provide inspiration regarding centerpiece and/or other decor ideas. And sometimes these are ideas that can be easily implemented by volunteers. A single carnation or rose at each place at the table provides elegant decor.

Large potted plants add significantly to the atmosphere in a room. Consider requesting the loan of such plants for an evening. Typically, the audience at a benefit is the very market to which a plantsman seeks exposure.

When asked to lend expertise to the out-of-doors entrance to a courtyard for *Fantasy Flight 1029*, an artist borrowed some white twinkle lights and framed the sidewalk with lights, thus provid-

ing a "runway" for the passengers to travel as they entered the courtyard for the cocktail hour. This same artist initiated the concept of fluttering silver strips to line the underpass from the parking garage to the complex, providing a festive and exciting atmosphere for little money. Talking with artists and designers can open up some amazingly simple and inexpensive ideas.

Installing Your Design

There are many varied ideas and concepts, but remember that the installation of ideas may require some out-of-the-ordinary equipment. Hanging lights, fabrics, streamers, or flats (large "walls" from a painted theater set), can provide fabulous atmosphere for your event. In fact, you may even have the volunteers install them. But, do they require additional equipment? A cherry picker or lift, for example, is essential to the volunteer who must reach high ceilings to hang things or adjust lighting instruments.

Availability of electrical power is important. When planning *Fantasy Flight 1029*, an in-depth study of available power in the whole complex was needed. The power required for outdoor lighting, sound systems, food warmers, and coffee makers added up, and the limited outlets were not sufficient to support all those needs. In this case, the university physical plant staff had to be called in to review the requirements. In one area, there were no outlets and the only lights available were halogen work lights that give a most unflattering hue to everything and everyone. Masking those lights proved to be the best solution and the least expensive option.

Time

You've thought about what you have to do to be ready. And you've thought about how many people you'll need to make it happen. But have you thought about how much time it will take? It could be that you'll be able to set up your event in just a few hours. But it's more than likely that it will take much longer than you expect. If you are doing extensive decorations, you'll need extensive time in which to do them! And you'll be much happier to be finished early than if you are finishing the last flower arrangement when the first guests arrive. Remember, the first guests are *always* earlier than you expect them! This is especially true if you have an older audience.

Once it is up, who will take it down? Will decorations need to be removed as soon as the event is over, or can they be left until the next day? And will the decorations require storage for another year? If so, where? By whom?

It doesn't usually take as long to dismantle an event as it took to put it together. However, many of the larger events will require coming back the next day to finish the take-down/clean-up job. If it's an especially large event, you'll be glad if you've planned to pay for a clean-up crew. This is particularly true if the event site is not a hotel or a place where there is a clean-up crew on staff and the cost is part of the rental fee. Bear in mind, too, that cleaning up is much less fun and seems to take even more energy. If your committee is part of the clean-up crew, plan a fun activity such as taking them out to lunch or some reward for the more difficult, less glamorous work. By all means, do consider the time that it will take to dismantle your event and plan accordingly.

Decorations Provide an Opportunity for Additional Income

Table centerpieces provide a special ambiance during your meal, but what happens when the event is over? If you are conducting a formal event, you may want to find a means to allow one person at the table to win the centerpiece. The winner could be the person with the birthday closest to the date of the event. It could be the person who has known the organization for the shortest, or longest, period. There are other methods of determining the winner, such as the penny or label under the saucer or under the chair. Use your imagination and creative juices.

In a less formal event, you could use the opportunity to offer it to the highest bidder, thus earning a few more dollars. If you are planning to provide the means for a guest to win the centerpiece, it's wise to announce this early in the event. Otherwise, you will find that the centerpieces are leaving with guests before you have the opportunity to share your plan.

Party Favors

Favors can provide interesting, unique gifts as a thank you to your guests. Sometimes these favors are inscribed with the name of the organization. Gifts such as paperweights, pens, or other such memorabilia are effective marketing instruments because they are typically placed in sight in someone's office. It's important to remember that if you provide an item that has a fair market value of more than a few dollars, the cost must be figured into the total fair market value of the event. It should be included in the amount stated on the invitation as the fair market value, and that amount is *not* tax deductible. You also may want to issue receipts for the donation.

Points to Ponder

Consider using centerpieces as a link to the program or to the organization's mission.

Program linkage could be creations of students or clients that get auctioned off. Clothing on mannequins can line the entryway and grace the stage of a fashion show.

Fund-raising campaign linkages could be bricks on which guests paint their names, with the names to be later engraved on pavers or stepping stones in the new building, garden, or walkway.

Meaningful artifacts such as a broken gargoyle from a museum or a design from a yard bench from a school can be a centerpiece that gets auctioned off.

Centerpieces created by merchants—florists, chefs, silk flower shops, confectioners—can be raffled or auctioned. Consider charging the merchant for the right to design the centerpieces.

> If your committee is part of the clean-up crew, plan a fun activity such as taking them out to lunch or some reward for the more difficult, less glamorous work.

One successful event included gingerbread replicas of local historical buildings. Architectural firms were invited to pay an entrance fee, team up with bakeries, and compete for the prize. The results were displayed in a downtown plaza during the week before Christmas. The winners of the competition, selected by a panel of experts, were announced at the event, the gingerbread castles—which were now centerpieces—were auctioned off, and the event and the winners received great press coverage the next day.

Favors can become a vehicle by which the event, and thereby the organization, is remembered with warmth and pleasure. Favors that reflect the theme, the honoree, or the mission can be especially evocative.

Summary

Decisions about decor are dictated by the site, theme, and budget for each event. Site requirements are what determine where to hold the event. The choices of type of decor are driven by the theme. The decision regarding how much you can do is driven by the budget.

Of the three, budget may be the most flexible if there are opportunities to seek contributed, at-cost, or low-cost decorations from local vendors and merchants. Creativity can play a key role in keeping decoration costs low while presenting an exciting and attractive setting.

Creativity in turning the decor into an income opportunity can enable you to do more than your budget might have permitted. Decorations that have special qualities or special meaning to event guests are often a source of revenue.

Favors can become a vehicle by which the event, and thereby the organization, is remembered with warmth and pleasure. Favors that reflect the theme, the honoree, or the mission can be an especially treasured memento.

Chapter 14

What About Public Relations?

A bell is not a bell until you ring it. A song is not a song until you sing it.

Oscar Hammerstein

Media exposure is something to be earned, not automatically granted. Volunteers often expect exposure for the events they are producing, but rarely do they understand that media exposure stems from media relations. This chapter offers ideas about how to think about and plan for media interest in your event.

The Public Interest

Why should the public be interested in your event? If you are planning an expensive, formal event, the newspapers generally will not provide advance coverage because they contend that they can't publicize something that is not accessible for everyone. If, however, you are producing a walk, a run, or some other athletic endeavor, it's generally a less expensive event and more accessible to the general public. But, if you are proposing to benefit a charity that provides free services, impacting a significant number of people, the live media (radio and television) may be interested and willing to run some public service announcements (PSAs). If, as in the case of *Fantasy Flight 1029*, something unusual is occurring like the ballet dancers rappelling from the theatre roof, the media have something visual to present, and will cooperate. When the TV cameraman came to tape the rehearsal, he also chose to interview someone about the event.

The media are interested in the unusual or anything with a human interest angle. This does not include simply publishing the fact that your organization is sponsoring a benefit. If you can provide information that tells a story, the media may pick up on it. There is never a guarantee that your story will generate interest, but a story will have a much better chance than just the facts about your event or your organization. Of course, the calendar section of a paper or magazine will print the date of the event and how to get tickets if the event meets their criteria and does not cost more than a nor-

> **If you can provide information that tells a story, the media may pick up on it.**

mally pre-established amount (pre-established by the media).

Having stated all of that, if one of your volunteers knows a reporter or editor, that individual may be able to generate some interest in your event. Just as in any fund-raising experience, it is much more effective to have a personal contact.

Knowing the type of publication or station that might be interested in your event will also help. Local magazines and neighborhood or community papers will be much more interested in an event taking place in their area or involving the people living in their area. The same applies to a television or radio station with local interest segments. Talk show hosts, for example, will be interested in interviewing a volunteer, an artist, or star of an event. They may even be interested in your organization's story.

Building Relationships

If you expect media coverage at any time in your organizational life, the sooner you get acquainted with your media representatives, the sooner the coverage will start. These are the reporters who typically cover your organization or subject. Although this news person may not always accept your story ideas, it's possible that you might be referred to another reporter or interviewer. Such relationships cannot begin too soon.

If your organization has someone on staff (a public relations person) whose responsibility it is to work with the media, by all means, talk to your staff member and request guidance about the best way to obtain coverage.

Who Should Speak for Your Event?

Typically, there is one person who provides "the public voice" for your organization or event. This person might be on staff or be a volunteer. Whoever it is should be knowledgeable and well informed about the entire organization. You'll be most effective when your organization and committee understand who that spokesperson is and know that should they personally be approached by the media, they should immediately recommend the designated spokesperson. When more than one person speaks about an issue, there is room for contradiction or confusion. When one person speaks, there is only one story and much less room for misunderstanding.

You may have other offerings that would interest reporters. If your event is to benefit a certain activity or program, perhaps there are people who have received such services that have significantly changed their lives. These people can make excellent spokespersons for your event. A story about their experiences might catch a reporter's interest, and then you have an article.

The circumstance you want to avoid at all costs is that of having several different people talking with the media and providing different information. And this is not an unusual scenario. Remember those job descriptions discussed in Chapter 10? If you have designated the appropriate person to speak with the media, there will be much less room for confusion or error.

The Society Column

As you know, the society column reports on what has already taken place; this is an important concept to remember. Although you aren't likely to get coverage before your event, it is possible that a pre-event happening might be mentioned. Suppose that you have a small event for your hosts and hostesses, and suppose that you have some interesting announcement or story to unveil at that event; these facts would certainly provide a potential for interest from the media. If your guest of honor is an important local, state, or national figure, it is possible that his or her arrival in town, or any pre-event happenings, might receive press interest. If you have done your homework and have strong ties to the media, there should be no problem in attracting interest in your pre-event happening.

> If you expect media coverage at any time in your organizational life, the sooner you get acquainted with your media representatives, the sooner the coverage will start.

In spite of the fact that it won't sell tickets in advance, society page coverage is an important part of your event. The fact that the coverage will be printed after the event doesn't diminish its importance, but does change the objective of the coverage. The cultivation begins when you make certain that you have included the society reporters on your complimentary ticket list. Some reporters will have budgets with which to pay for their own tickets, but many will accept your invitation to be a guest. When they attend the event, they should be treated like any other VIP. Their impression of your event will come across loud and clear when it's printed and you want to be certain that it is favorable. Help them with photo opportunities. Make certain that the most influential guests are photographed. If you can afford to provide a staff person to guide the photographer, it will ease your mind considerably. Despite your intentions, you simply can't be everywhere at once!

If your event is particularly large or spread out, you will want to think through your photography plan well beforehand. The photographs may or may not be used with event coverage by the media, but they certainly can be used with your own coverage; you'll want to have photographs of your events for your own newsletters or publications.

When you have effectively dealt with the press, they are much more responsive the next time you come to them with an event. So, the seeds of interest that you plant now are more than likely to bear fruit when you return sometime in the future.

Ties to Community News or Trends

If you are celebrating the opening of a community institution and your event will raise dollars to fund a problem that has received widespread community coverage, then you may expect to receive more than the typical amount of media coverage. Your event is then part of the "news" and you should be prepared to deal with it accordingly.

> **Despite your intentions, you simply can't be everywhere at once!**

In a large city, you'll then be part of the local news, and in a smaller community you'll be *the* news.

Trends are typically short term. However, knowing that and making the best use of them, you may possibly be able to mount an event that will meet all of your criteria as well as attract significant media attention. Such trends might be general in nature, such as a focus and interest in health and activities that promote well-being. The plethora of marathons has attested to this widespread interest. Other such trends might include a new focus on education due to the concern in the community about the lack of updated schools for their children. Special events that raise dollars for new equipment or programs in schools will undoubtedly attract media attention in that community, whereas there may be no interest at all in a more affluent community where schools are new and well-equipped. If your event is dependent on a trend, be advised that the longevity of this event should be seriously considered on a regular basis. When the trend changes, you won't want to be producing the old event because it will no longer stimulate the same interest that it has previously enjoyed.

Your placement in the newspaper will determine the market you'll reach. Society, of course, will read the society column, but the business community will read business and local news first. This suggests that it's worth considering what market you wish to reach before making your pitch for coverage.

Talk Shows

Both radio and television offer the opportunity to be featured on talk shows. These are generally fifteen to thirty minutes in length and provide an opportunity to tell your story to the market served by that station. The common practice is to ask the interviewee for a list of questions that will help the interviewer direct the conversation. When you construct the questions, then you obviously have the opportunity to make the points you wish to make.

Here again is an opportunity to plan ahead so you'll be sure to include the five Ws about your event—who, what, when, where, and why. And if your event is supporting a special project, be sure to discuss that as well. Take every opportunity to spread the news. However, you cannot be certain that your interviewer will stick to your list! There will be times when one thing or another will catch his or her interest and you'll be swept along with the tide. You can only be prepared for this.

Talk shows reach varying markets depending upon when they are broadcast. Those radio shows airing during drive time have a dedicated audience with ten to fifteen minutes of listening. Television talk shows that air during the weekday will reach homemakers. Those that air on weekend mornings will reach a broader and less well-defined market. Knowing the listening and viewing habits of the people you want to reach will help you determine where you need to put your energies.

Development has been likened to a puzzle. Finding the right piece to fit in the right space at the right time is much like finding the right prospect to be asked by the right person at the right time. So, too, is public relations like a puzzle. It requires as much in research skills as the development process.

Other Coverage

Magazine coverage is entirely different from any other venue used for public relations. In this genre, information should be provided many weeks, even months, before your event. In discussions with the editor, you may wish to request a special sponsorship that will include pre-event coverage. Many community magazines will dedicate a cover and several pages to an event if they are recognized sponsors. With such a sponsorship, you'll probably be asked to arrange for a photo shoot to provide pictures to be published in advance. For large events, a magazine might include maps and other such material as a special insert. This is some of the best publicity you could wish for.

Magazine editors are also able to identify their markets distinctly. You just have to ask. Find out who reads a publication before you ask that publication to do a two-page spread about your event or organization.

Fliers or brochures distributed to a specific market provide excellent visibility. This is especially true of athletic events. Walks, runs, and triathlons all invite a specific market. People interested in this kind of event can be found in health clubs, gyms, and sporting goods stores, and sometimes they frequent certain restaurants.

Fliers are especially effective for events that involve food or tastings. Think about where your potential patrons might be shopping, eating, or playing. Use those places for your handout information.

Drop-in promotional spots in newspaper advertising offer opportunities for major advertisers in the community to provide some exposure for your organization or event. A little box providing the date, time, and cost of the event can be dropped into a larger ad and can be helpful. The cost of typesetting the drop-in will probably be your only cost.

Media Sponsorships

As previously mentioned, magazines will commit to significant exposure when they are recognized as sponsors. Radio and television stations will also commit to significant public service announcement times, as well as interviews. The only catch is that they may request exclusive sponsorship. In the event that such a proposal is made to you, consider the following:

- Does "exclusive" mean no other media at all, or does it impose a limit only on the same media?

- If you are limited within the same media, does this station, paper, or magazine reach the market you need to reach, or will you restrict yourself too much with this agreement?

- How many mentions does it include? For how long? At what times?

- Does the sponsorship include a cash gift along with the promised coverage?

- Does this particular business have a track record with sponsorships in the community?

When you are satisfied with your answers, you will make the right decision for your circumstance.

It's tempting to leap at the first offer. But it's important to look at the ratings for live media and the circulation rate for print media. Aim to reach your market, and your event will be a success. Be careful not to accept the first offer just because it's a sure thing. It may limit your other possibilities.

Exhibits 14–1 and 14–2 present examples of press releases for various kinds of events.

For a Press Conference

If there had been a press conference for *Fantasy Flight 1029*, the additional information in the press kits would have included information about each of the departments in the College of Fine Arts. Further description of the event is optional. If you wish to build interest in your event, yet be able to surprise the participants with the unfolding of the evening, then you wouldn't choose to provide the full program for the evening. On the other hand, if you want to offer just a few teasers, that's a good way to engage media representatives and possibly your audience. For *Fantasy Flight 1029,* such a teaser might include a photo of one of the performing groups in costume.

The following material was prepared for a different kind of press conference, one that was intended to be educational in nature. The Arizona Children's Home Association and CODAC Behavioral Health Services held a joint press conference to inform the public and the legislative and political leadership of five counties about the substance-abuse group home that was funded by tobacco tax dollars, a controversial issue in Arizona. La Cañada is a cooperative effort between the two agencies. Exhibit 14–3 presents the invitation to this educational press conference.

Exhibit 14–4 presents the materials used in this educational press conference. It includes information about each agency, identifies the problem with some fact sheets, and provides statements from participants in the program. This press conference was not intended to generate a blitz of media coverage, but rather to inform press, media, and politicians from the counties involved about the results of this project. The interest generated some significant publicity and raised a decided interest on the part of many politicians, some of whom could not attend, but requested that materials be sent to them.

Brainstorming Public Relations Ideas

Exhibit 14–5 provides a chart of media ideas for *Fantasy Flight 1029*.

Exhibits 14–6 through 14–8 provide examples of three different kinds of press releases. The first, in Exhibit 14–6, is a news release designed for newspapers as well as radio and television news spots.

The next example, found in Exhibit 14–7, is a media alert designed to attract media to come to the site of the walk and possibly shoot footage or photographs of any of the activities listed. This is also a way to possibly attract interest when the first news release may not have been as interesting. The technique of what, when, where, and why makes it easy for a reporter to see at a glance what is happening. It's also a good way to format so that if a reporter is looking up the site, it is easily spotted. The information about the event and the sponsoring organization is brief and to the point.

The last example, Exhibit 14–8, is an in-depth release providing more detail that will lend credibility and possibly generate interest in the event. This detail pulls out all the stops on names and sponsors to provide as much information as possible to attract attention.

Points to Ponder

In large measure, the timing of public relations and media exposure can be determined by the size of the event, its goal, and its target market. When the event is seeking large numbers of attendees and has a relatively small ticket price, advance exposure can be essential. The media is a vehicle for ticket sales and the exposure is part of the visibility. When the event is marketed to a select group and has a high ticket price, media exposure for the attendees after the event can be more advantageous. Personal contact is the vehicle for ticket sales, and the exposure is part of the cultivation.

Consider having a photographer at the event taking candid shots of the guests. The photos can become part of the effort to build ongoing relationships with the attendees. Photos can become an additional contact as part of the "thank you for attending" or they can be used as part of the invitation for the next event—as sort of a "remember

Exhibit 14–1 Sample Press Release

PHOTO OP: DANCERS JUMP OFF ROOF FOR THEIR ART

(From Rich Amada, 555-1877)   (Sent Oct. 22, 1993)

PHOTO EVENT: *UA DANCERS RAPPEL FROM THE ROOF TO THE BASE OF THE NEW FINE ARTS COMPLEX IN REHEARSAL FOR UPCOMING GALA PERFORMANCE*

An event organized by the Faculty of Fine Arts at The University of Arizona in Tucson

DATE/TIME: Tuesday, Oct. 26, 5 p.m.

PLACE: Courtyard of the new Fine Arts Complex behind Marroney Theatre on the UA campus—located at the south end of the pedestrian underpass on Speedway Boulevard, east of Park Avenue.

CONTACT: Pat Bjorhovde, assistant director for development of fine arts, 555-9057

Members of the media are invited to attend and shoot photographs/video of a dance rehearsal in which the dancers will jump off the roof of the new UA Fine Arts Complex and rappel down to the ground in a choreographed routine that will be an exciting visual highlight of the upcoming fine arts gala.

The gala (which takes place Friday evening) commemorates the new additions to the Fine Arts Complex—an $18.7 million construction project that is nearing completion. The rappelling dancers are just one of several arts events planned for that evening. It is an invitational event that will serve as a fund raiser for the Dean's Fund for Excellence.

Courtesy of the University of Arizona News Services, Inc., Tucson, Arizona.

Exhibit 14–2 Sample Press Release

NEWS RELEASE:

GALA FEAST AND PERFORMANCES TO COMMEMORATE OPENING OF NEW UA FINE ARTS COMPLEX OCT. 29

(From Rich Amada, 555-1877)   (Sent Sept. 24, 1993)

The Faculty of Fine Arts at The University of Arizona was on the verge of bursting its seams—so to speak—when the UA began is first major construction project in that area in more than 30 years. Now, the newly expanded Fine Arts Complex is going to be commemorated in a fine style with a gala event on October 29.

Fantasy Flight 1029 is the theme of the gala, and guests will partake of a moveable feast as they "travel" about the new complex, dining on food from some of Tucson's finest restaurants, seeing the new fine arts facilities, and enjoying exhibits and entertainment provided by the five fine arts departments (art, dance, media arts, music, and theatre arts). The festivities will begin at 6:45 p.m. Guests who park their cars in the parking garage on the northeast corner of Speedway Boulevard and Park Avenue will be greeted by members of the Pride of Arizona Marching Band and treated to a variety of performances and exhibits as they make the short walk through the underpass to the Fine Arts Complex, where the bulk of the evening's activities will take place.

The much anticipated opening of the new $18.7 million facility more than doubles the UA Fine Arts work space and offers the community, as a whole, even greater opportunities to enjoy the arts. Among the new facility's benefits will be:

• Holsclaw Recital Hall—a hall built especially to house a new $300,000 pipe organ that was donated to the University

• A newly remodeled and expanded Marroney Theatre to facilitate greater technical ability in theatre productions

• Gross Gallery—a new student art gallery

• An expanded Crowder Hall

• An expanded photography section with a student photography display area

• A new studio lab theatre with multi-arrangement seating that will allow for optional staging techniques such as theatre in the round.

The gala is an invitational event to benefit the establishment of the Dean's Fund for Excellence. The goal is to raise $50,000 for the endowment, which will be used to enhance Fine Arts' mission to create and achieve excellence in education and training in the arts. Members of the public who are interested in attending may contact Lisa Ferguson at 555-8824. Tickets start at $125.

VISUAL HIGHLIGHT: Among the evening's visual highlights will be The Courtyard Finale, featuring dancers rappelling off the rooftops in a choreographed plunge to the ground.

For more information, Call Barbara Levy, UA Foundation.

Courtesy of the University of Arizona News Services, Inc., Tucson Arizona.

Exhibit 14–3 Press Conference Invitation

ARIZONA CHILDREN'S HOME

2700 SOUTH 8TH AVENUE • POST OFFICE BOX 7277 • TUCSON, ARIZONA 85725 • 520-622-7611

**Arizona Children's Home Association
&
CODAC Behavioral Health Services, Inc.**

Present

An Informational Press Conference

about

La Cañada: A Therapeutic Substance Abuse Group Home

Thursday, October 17, 1996

10:00–10:45 a.m.

5312 N. La Cañada

Learn how tobacco tax dollars are working for notch-group adolescents in your community. This is an opportunity to learn about a program that is addressing the increasing problem of substance abuse.

Please join

Fred Chaffee, CEO
Arizona Children's Home Association

&

Neal Cash, Executive Director
CODAC Behavioral Health Services, Inc.

Learn about the scope of the problem and this partnership's success in addressing it.

Courtesy of CODAC Behavioral Health Services, Inc., Tucson, Arizona.

Exhibit 14–4 Press Conference Materials

ARIZONA CHILDREN'S HOME
ASSOCIATION

Serving Arizona's Children and Families Since 1914

HISTORY

The Arizona Children's Home was founded by a group of women who wanted to stop the flow of Arizona Children to the California Children's Aid Society. In the early 1920s the orphanage was built on the South Tucson site where the 7 1/2 acre campus is still located. This site houses the Residential Treatment Center serving the state and the state administrative headquarters of the agency.

To meet the changing needs of Arizona, it was necessary to create an Association with multiple services. It wasn't long before the agency had evolved into a child welfare/behavioral health agency. Today, as Arizona Children's Home Association (ACHA), 90% of its services are delivered in the homes of children and families.

The primary focus of ACHA is early intervention, breaking the cycle of child abuse, and providing a safe, permanent home for every child. Arizona Children's Home, in collaboration with CODAC Behavioral Health Services, Inc., offers a program called La Cañada. The following is a description of program services:

JOINT PARTNERSHIP WITH CODAC LA CAÑADA

• La Cañada provides services for male and female youth who have a substance abuse problem. La Cañada offers a 3-phase program. Phase I is a residential program for 30 days. During this period, clients and their families receive individual, family, and group therapy, as well as psychoeducation and case management. During Phase II and III, CODAC continues to offer case management, therapy, and increased involvement in self-help activities referred to as Growth Activities and Self-Help.

PROGRAM DETAILS

• La Cañada provides services for male and female youth who have a substance abuse problem. La Cañada offers a 3-phase program. The program addresses educational and lifestyle needs through activities that build self awareness, self-esteem, create and improve problem-solving skills and teach these youths simply how to have fun. These activities are accomplished through using the G.A.S.H. system (Growth Activities & Self-Help.)

• **Admission Criteria:** Males/Females ages 12–17. Children in the CPSA and SEABHS catchment areas. Children who have a primary Axis I diagnosis of substance abuse and are not Title XIX eligible.

• **Referral Information:** Referrals can be made by parents, therapists, teachers, C.P.S., J.P.O., and courts.

SUPPORTED BY

Funded by tobacco tax dollars

CONTACTS

Chief Executive Officer, Fred Chaffee

La Cañada is a collaborative effort between Arizona Children's Home, CODAC Behavioral Health Services, and SEABHS, meeting the needs of children in the geographic CPSA area.

continues

Exhibit 14–4 continued

CODAC Behavioral Health Services, Inc.

HISTORY

CODAC was founded in 1970 as an umbrella organization to create a network of treatment and prevention programs to combat the growing problem of drug abuse in Pima County. In 1972, CODAC secured an eight-year grant from the National Institute on Drug Abuse for the establishment and ongoing operation of a coordinated network of drug abuse treatment and prevention programs in Pima County. Upon the expiration of the NIDA grant in 1980, CODAC secured funding from federal, state, and local sources for the continued operation of the network.

By 1983, the organization had evolved into CODAC Behavioral Health Services, Inc., and expanded its scope into the broader range of behavioral health, and the role of umbrella was abandoned in favor of direct provision of services. Today, CODAC is a comprehensive, nonprofit community behavioral health agency bringing the highest level of professional expertise to the field. CODAC offers the La Cañada Program in collaboration with Arizona Children's Home Association. The following is a description of the joint venture:

JOINT PARTNERSHIP WITH ARIZONA CHILDREN'S HOME

La Cañada provides services for male and female youth who have a substance abuse problem. La Cañada offers a 3-phase program. Phase I is a residential program for 30 days. During this period, clients and their families receive individual, family, and group therapy, as well as psychoeducation and case management. During Phase II and III, CODAC continues to offer case management, therapy, and increased involvement in self-help activities referred to as Growth Activities and Self-Help.

PROGRAM DETAILS

• The partnership provides a 9-bed facility for male and female youths: 6 males reside at La Cañada and 3 females reside at Arizona Children's Home Association.

• During Phase I, the La Cañada program provides clients and their families individual, family, and group therapy, as well as psychoeducation and case management. During Phase II and III, CODAC continues to offer case management, therapy, and increased involvement in self-help activities referred to as Growth Activities and Self-Help.

• **Admission Criteria:** Males/Females ages 12–17. Children in the CPSA and SEABHS catchment areas. Children who have a primary Axis I diagnosis of substance abuse and are not Title XIX eligible.

• **Referral Information:** Referrals can be made by parents, therapists, teachers, C.P.S., J.P.O., and courts.

SUPPORTED BY

Funded by tobacco tax dollars

CONTACTS

Executive Director, Neal Cash,   555/555-4505
Clinical Coordinator, Dale Pilson, MA, CSAC   555/555-4234 ext. 133
Office Hours: 8:00 a.m.–5:00 p.m. Administration/Residential, 24 hours/7 days a week

> La Cañada is a collaborative effort between Arizona Children's Home, CODAC Behavioral Health Services, and SEABHS, meeting the needs of children in the geographic CPSA area.

continues

Exhibit 14–4 continued

ARIZONA CHILDREN'S HOME ASSOCIATION
CODAC Behavioral Health Services, Inc.

PARTNERSHIP

How Community Partnership of Southern
Arizona Works With La Cañada

The Community Partnership of Southern Arizona, Inc., (CPSA) was formed to provide an alternative to the existing Regional Behavioral Health Authority (RBHA) system in Pima County and to integrate RBHA functions across two Geographic Service Areas (GSAs)—Pima County, designated as GSA 5, and Graham, Greenlee, Cochise, and Santa Cruz Counties, the four Southeastern Arizona counties which comprise GSA 3. Although these service areas are different in many respects, their history is interwoven and they share the richness of cultural diversity and the traditions of the American West.

There is extensive "overlap" between the behavioral health service provider network in the four Southeastern Arizona counties and Pima County. More specifically, GSA 3 has a shortage of "within area" providers and is reliant on specialty services and providers based in Pima County. By contrast, Pima County has no shortage of inpatient, residential, and other specialty services and/or "within area" providers. Given the "overlap" in the service provider network within the five (5) county areas and the lack of "within area" services in GSA 3, essentially any improvement, enhancement, or expansion of the provider network within Pima County ultimately benefits the four Southeast Arizona counties as well.

An example is the Tobacco Tax funded Substance Abuse Residential Treatment Program, La Cañada, which is a result of a partnership between the Arizona Children's Home, CODAC Behavioral Health Services, Inc., and Southeastern Arizona Behavioral Health Services. The program serves Non-Title XIX underinsured or uninsured youth, ages 12 through 17 years, who have a primary diagnosis of substance abuse and who have demonstrated an inability to achieve desired treatment goals in a lower level of care. The program is located in Pima County (GSA 5), but is available to youth from both GSA 5 and GSA 3. Admission to the program is based on the age range specified, as well as demonstrated medical necessity. Comprehensive substance abuse services are provided with both intensive short-term residential treatment and strong aftercare components. *It is this type of partnering that will ensure greater accessibility to medically necessary behavioral health treatment across the five counties.*

continues

Exhibit 14–4 continued

ARIZONA CHILDREN'S HOME ASSOCIATION
CODAC Behavioral Health Services, Inc.

PARTNERSHIP

FAST FACTS

• La Cañada: A Therapeutic Substance Abuse Group Home partnership between Arizona Children's Home Association, CODAC Behavioral Health Services, Inc., and SEABHS.

• Phase I: 30-day residential treatment program

   Phase II: 60 days case management and therapy support

   Phase III: 60 days continued case management with integration into the community and self-help activities referred to as Growth Activities and Self-Help

• La Cañada opened: April, 1996

• Youths Treated to Date: 53

• Number of recurring clients: 0

• Success rate: 100%, not one youth has tested positive for substance or alcohol use while in the program.

• Program service area: Pima, Graham, Greenlee, Cochise, and Santa Cruz counties.

• 9-bed facility: La Cañada has 6 for male residents, and Arizona Children's Home has 3 for female residents.

• Average age: 15 1/2

• The program reflects the county's demographics.

• Serves youths ages 12–17 who are in the CPSA and SEABHS catchment areas who have a primary Axis I diagnosis of substance abuse and are not Title XIX.

• The program serves as a pilot for other programs in the U.S.

• La Cañada continually runs a full program of 9 youths.

   The waiting length of time is 3–4 weeks for females and 1 week for males.

• The majority of the youths are referred by the Pima County Juvenile Court system.

• The drug of choice: Marijuana and alcohol are the basic drugs of choice. If unavailable, then crystal methanal, cocaine, and acid.

continues

Exhibit 14–4 continued

ARIZONA CHILDREN'S HOME ASSOCIATION
CODAC Behavioral Health Services, Inc.

PARTNERSHIP

DATA RELEVANT TO YOUTH AND SUBSTANCE ABUSE

National

- Number of 12–17 year olds using marijuana nearly doubled between 1992 and 1994[1]

- 28% of 1994 high school seniors said they had binged on alcohol recently[1]

- 18% of students in junior and senior high say they use illegal drugs every month[2]

- Costs of alcohol, drug abuse and mental health problems are high in terms of health, productivity and crime—$314 billion in 1990. 34% from loss of productivity due to injury or illness, 26% from health care costs, and 22% from crime, criminal justice costs and property damage.[3]

- About 20 million people ages 15–54 have a substance abuse problem[3]

- Preliminary results from CSAT's National Treatment Improvement Study show that criminal activity decreased significantly after treatment[4]

Arizona

- The percentage of Arizona juveniles killed in 1995 dramatically increased over the previous year—drugs often involved.[5]

- Almost 25% of Arizona's children lived in poverty in 1994[6]

- Teen homicides increased 161% between 1990–1994[6]

- Juvenile arrests for drug crimes increased 212% between 1990–1994[6]

- Although substance abuse is evident among 26.2% of Arizona behavioral health clients, only 7.9% of funding is devoted to this problem[7]

- Since 1990, lifetime use of marijuana has more than quadrupled among Arizona junior high students[7]

- Within Arizona elementary schools, 31.1% of all children reported having tried alcohol[7]

- The number-one killer of teens and young adults in the U.S. is alcohol-related highway death[7]

- Savings to taxpayers over seven times the cost associated with treatment (for every dollar spent on treatment $7 are saved due to loss in productivity, crime, and health care costs)[7]

- National Center on Addiction and Substance Abuse reports that alcohol is implicated in up to 75% of rapes and 70% of domestic violence[8]

[1] National Household Survey on Drug Abuse, in *The State of America's Children Yearbook*, 1996.
[2] *Tucson Citizen*, 9/26/96, quoting National Parents' Resource Institute for Drug Education survey.
[3] Rouse, B.A. (1995) *Substance Abuse and Mental Health Statistics Sourcebook*. U.S. Department of Health and Human Services.
[4] National Treatment Improvement Evaluation Study, conducted for SAMHSA/CSAT by the National Opinion Research Center at the University of Chicago in collaboration with The Research Triangle Institute, 1996.
[5] *Tucson Citizen*, 9/23/96.
[6] Children's Action Alliance, *The State of Arizona's Children*, 1996.
[7] MacFarlane, Steve. (1994). *Arizona Alarming Trends 1994*.
[8] *Tucson Citizen*, 6/6/96.

continues

Exhibit 14–4 continued

CODAC Behavioral Health Services, Inc.

La Cañada provides services for males and females ages 12–17 who have a substance abuse problem. La Cañada offers a 3-phase program funded by tobacco tax dollars. Phase I is a residential program for 30 days. During this period, clients and their families receive individual, family, and group therapy, as well as psychoeducation and case management. During Phases II and III, CODAC continues to offer case management, therapy, and increased involvement in self-help activities referred to as Growth Activities and Self-Help.

Substance abuse is a challenge for millions and millions of Americans who try to overcome this obstacle every year. The following is an example of the trials and tribulations a teenager goes through when entering the La Cañada Program.

The thoughts of a teen in La Cañada and the services he/she receives in the 30 day program.

1. "This isn't hap'in'. This is lame!"

   —Am I gonna fit in. The staff better be cool.
   - Nurse visit
   - Confidence-building course—ropes, trapeze
   - Narcotics Anonymous (NA) and/or Alcoholics Anonymous (AA)
   - Urinalysis or drop test
   - Orientation to the facility: program expectations, dress code, rules, privileges

2. "It's cool."

   —This is OK. This place is pretty real. Staff is all right, too.
   - Individual Therapy
   - Family Therapy
   - Substance Abuse Therapy
   - Psychoeducational Groups
   - Case Management
   - Analysis of lifestyle needs and changes
   - Urinalysis/drop test

3. "I gotta make some changes."

   —I'm tired of being tired. I gotta find my life again. I don't wanna go back.
   - Testing for HIV and STDs
   - Continue all group and one-on-one therapy
   - Set court dates
   - Resume communication with families
   - Register for school
   - Seek employment
   - Schedule community service
   - Urinalysis/drop test

continues

Exhibit 14–4 continued

4. "I know what I gotta do now."

—I'm on track and gonna stay there.
- Continue reconciliation with family
- Continue all group and one-on-one therapy
- Practice job applications
- Prepare for school
- Final urinalysis/drop test

Courtesy of CODAC Behavioral Health Services, Inc., Tucson, Arizona.

Exhibit 14–5 Public Relations Chart

Media	Idea	Responsible Person	Contact/Date
Local magazine	Hand-painted tablecloths Artistic dining Hosts and hostesses Dining on art		
Newspapers	UA art class in Mexico -painting for event		
Television	Rappelling from roof Media Arts clip Computerized tour of complex		
Radio	Arts journal		
Other options	Antiphonal brass choir Sculpture installation Toddlers in tutus		

Exhibit 14–6 Press Release

NEWS

"WALK AMONG THE STARS"

FOR ARIZONA'S ABUSED KIDS AND FAMILIES IN CRISIS

Phoenix, Ariz. (September 16, 1996)—The Arizona Children's Home Association (ACHA) is currently registering walkers and volunteers to join the group's annual 6-mile charity walk.

Scheduled for Saturday evening, September 28, in the historic Biltmore neighborhood, "Walk Among The Stars" will raise funds to aid Arizona's abused children and families in crisis. Registration begins at 4:30 p.m., the walk starts at 5:30 p.m. with a mid-route food-taste sponsored by several Biltmore Fashion Park restaurants including Bamboo Club, California Pizza Kitchen, Che Bella, Coffee Plantation, Hops, Nola's, and Sam's Cafe.

"Walk Among The Stars" will start and end at the Anchor Centre Plaza, 2231 E. Camelback. Autographed footprints from more than 250 big-name stars such as Harrison Ford, Rosie O'Donnell, and Christian Slater will decorate the finish-line pizza party. Other exciting happenings include free massages and live entertainment by two special performers—The Rave and C.C. Jones.

Walkers, sponsors, and event volunteers should call 555-3733 to register. Minimum fund-raising goal is $25. Walkers can participate individually or as a team, with top fund raisers winning prizes. First prize is a trip for two to Costa Rica.

Arizona Children's Home Association, founded in 1912, is a nonprofit community mental health agency that provides a wide array of services to abused children and families in crisis. More than 11,000 children and families are served each year.

###

CONTACT: Christie Davis, Development Associate

Courtesy of Arizona Children's Foundation, Phoenix, Arizona.

Exhibit 14–7 Press Release

MEDIA ALERT

LEGENDS RALLY BEHIND ARIZONA'S TROUBLED KIDS
Danny Ainge, Wesley Person, A.C. Greene, and Frank Johnson
Latest to Lend Support

WHAT: "Walk Among The Stars" is an exciting 6-mile evening walk through the historic Biltmore area featuring the autographed footprints of more than 275 local and national celebrities.

WHEN: Saturday evening, September 28, 1996
Registration begins: 4:30 p.m.   Walk begins: 5:30 p.m.

WHERE: Starting location: Anchor Centre Plaza, 2231 E. Camelback
(22nd Street & Camelback in the Plaza behind Ruths' Chris Steakhouse)

WHY: The Walk will benefit Arizona Children's Home Association. It's purpose is to raise awareness and dollars for Arizona's abused and emotionally troubled children and families.

WHO CAN PARTICIPATE: The Walk is designed for people of all ages and fitness levels. Each walker must collect pledges or donate a minimum of $25 to participate. Walkers are eligible for prizes based on the money they raise.

THEME: "Walk Among The Stars" offers participants a unique evening walking event which has attracted the participation of both local and national celebrities. Over 275 autographed footprints will be displayed along the route including: Muhammad Ali, Gena Davis, Harrison Ford, Whoopi Goldberg, Meg Ryan, Barbara Streisand, James Taylor, and many others.

EVENT HAPPENINGS:

* Warm-Up Exercises
* Free flashlight to "Light Up The Night" for Arizona's Children
* Food Sampling by exclusive Biltmore Fashion Park Restaurants
* Finish-Line Pizza Party
* Massages
* Live entertainment by two special performers: The Rave and C.C. Jones

ARIZONA CHILDREN'S HOME ASSOCIATION (ACHA): Arizona Children's Home Association is dedicated to preventing child abuse and providing early treatment of behavioral disorders in children. Established in 1912, the private, nonprofit child welfare organization offers services throughout Arizona. More than 11,000 Arizona children and families are served each year.

FOR MORE INFORMATION: Contact Christie Powell Davis.

Courtesy of Arizona Children's Foundation, Phoenix, Arizona.

Exhibit 14–8 Press Release

DATE: August 15, 1996

CONTACT: Christie Powell Davis, Development Associate,
Arizona Children's Home Association, 555-3733

FOR IMMEDIATE RELEASE

"WALK AMONG THE STARS"
FOR ARIZONA'S KIDS

Phoenix, AZ — Saturday evening, September 28, caring Arizonans will join over 200 local and national celebrities in lighting up the night for Arizona's troubled children.

The occasion is a six-mile evening walk benefitting Arizona Children's Home and themed "Walk Among The Stars." The event will start and end at the Anchor Centre Plaza, 22nd Street and Camelback. Participants will be routed through historic Biltmore estate neighborhoods and Biltmore Fashion Park. Registration begins at 4:30 p.m. and the Walk at 5:30 p.m.

The Walk aims to raise awareness levels as well as dollars for Arizona's abused children and families in crisis. How badly do our kids need the help? Arizona ranks in the bottom third of our states in providing care for them in their critical years.

A NEW KIND OF WALK

Walks aren't new. But "Walk Among The Stars" is an innovative and fun idea that has attracted the participation of celebrities, both here at home and nationwide.

As walkers make their way through the fashionable Biltmore area, they'll spot the autographed footprints of such living legends as **Muhammad Ali, Kathy Bates, Candace Bergen, Dick Clark, Cotton Fitzsimmons, Harrison Ford, Whoopi Goldberg, Bob Hope, The Judds, Meg Ryan, Hewey Lewis, Al McCoy, Randy Travis, Barbara Streisand,** and many more.

STARLITE SNACKS, LIVE ENTERTAINMENT AND MASSAGES

The walk will begin with an energizing warm-up by valley aerobics instructors. Along the route, participants will enjoy rest stops and food stations set up by the Bamboo Club, California Pizza Kitchen, Che Bella, Coffee Plantation, Crown Sterling Suites Hotel, Hop's, Nola's, and Sam's Cafe.

The walk will conclude with a finish-line celebration featuring a starlite dinner and cold beverages. There'll be live music and, for those walkers who need some help relaxing after the walk, free massages will be provided by professionals from the Phoenix Therapeutic Massage College.

TEAM UP UNDER THE STARS

Walkers can participate individually and as a team. Prizes will be based on the amount of money walkers raise and each person must raise at least $25 to participate. The top fundraiser will win an exciting trip for two to exciting Costa Rica, courtesy of American Airlines.

Teams of 8 or more may be made up of friends, family, fellow employees, or group members. Team members are eligible for individual prizes as well as team prizes.

continues

Exhibit 14-8 continued

SPONSORS RALLY IN SUPPORT

The list of sponsors grows almost daily. It includes: **A**BC Channel 15, **A**MC Theaters, **A**irtouch Cellular, **A**lphagraphics, **A**merica West Airlines, **A**merican Airlines, **A**rizona Biltmore Estate Villages Association, **A**rizona Biltmore Hotel, **A**rizona Repeaters Association, **B**amboo Club, **B**artlett Homeowners Association, **B**ear Essential News For Kids, **B**est Western International, **B**iltmore Fashion Park, **B**iltmore Publishing Company, **B**ull Worldwide Information Systems, **C**alifornia Pizza Kitchen, **C**he Bella, **C**igna, **C**offee Plantation, **C**ontinental Homes, **C**oopers & Lybrand, **C**ox Communications, **C**rown Sterling Suites, **C**rystal Bottled Water, **G**reat Western Publishing, **H**oneywell Go Club, **H**ops, **I**mpact for Enterprising Women, **J**ohn C. Lincoln Hospital, **K**ID740 AM, **M**aricopa County Sheriff's Posse, **M**ohr, Hackett, Pederson, Blakley, Randolph, & Haga, **N**ola's, **O**'Connor, Cavanagh, **O**utdoor Systems, **P**hoenix Emergency Rescue, **P**hoenix Suns, **P**hoenix Therapeutic Massage College, **Q** The Sports Club, **R**ed Baron Pizza, The **RR**EEF Funds, **R**ural Metro, **R**uss Dopke and Bruce for Creative Materials, **S**am's Cafe, **S**terling Institutional Food Service, **T**aliverde Homeowners Association, and **V**alley Rentals.

Arizona Children's Home Association (ACHA) is a non-profit, nonsectarian community mental health agency. For 80 years, ACHA has provided a wide array of professional services and special education to abused children and families in crisis.

If you'd like to join us as a sponsor or walker, or be an event volunteer, there's still time. "It's your night to shine!" For more information call 555-3733.

Courtesy of Arizona Children's Foundation, Phoenix, Arizona.

how much you enjoyed yourself last time." If you are going to use photographers, plan to have one for every 100 guests.

A similar approach would be to videotape the event. It could be broadcast during the festivities and then sold to both attendees and nonattendees. Or, as with the still photographs, it could be sent as a thank you for attending or as an inducement to attend the next event.

Summary

Media coverage can be difficult to obtain unless the event is highly unusual, has broad public appeal, or involves an extraordinary number of participants. Often, the organization with coverage is the organization that has cultivated the media over time, establishing good relationships that predate the event.

Coverage within the society pages is a possibility when the participants are newsworthy to the society editor. Most society coverage occurs post-

> Often, the organization with coverage is the organization that has cultivated the media over time, establishing good relationships that predate the event.

event. Although post-event coverage does not encourage attendance, it has great value when the goal of the event was cultivation or visibility. Also, when the event was to honor one or more individuals or a corporation, post-event coverage continues the recognition process.

Community magazines often cover events that show the unique qualities of the community or spotlight activities of special interest within the community. This coverage, which can be linked to sponsorship of the event by the magazine, may appear either before or after the event, depending on the slant of the article and the interests of the author or the publisher.

Chapter 15

How Do You Handle Logistics?

I am only one, but I am one. I cannot do everything, but I can do something. And I will not let what I cannot do interfere with what I can do.

Edward Everett Hale

Logistics is everyone's nightmare but is critically important. This chapter discusses event management and the checklists that are sure to save you from possible disasters. In addition, you'll find a discussion of the event walk-through, another potential lifesaver! The key to success is finding pitfalls before they trip someone!

Event Management—Tools of the Trade

Relationships

Relationships are important to event management, and your relationship with on-site staff is critically important. When you know the right person to call, and that person knows you and your event, any problem can be resolved promptly. Or, conversely, if you do not know the right person to call, you'll waste precious time and experience great frustration until the problem is ultimately resolved.

Written Confirmation

Written confirmation should be made for all arrangements involving delivery times and places. Names and phone numbers should be at your fingertips. When armed with this information, you are in much better control of potential problems. Another security blanket is a list of alternative sources for the equipment you need.

During the event, keep at hand all *lists* of names and phone numbers of volunteers (or paid help) who are participating in the event production. Your list should include emergency telephone numbers in case of accident, illness, or fire.

Back-Up Plans for Emergencies

Back-up plans for emergencies are not typically something you like to think about; but, without them, you are at significant risk. It's wise to have one knowledgeable, unflappable person who is prepared to deal with emergencies. Chances are, you won't experience a significant emergency at a press conference or an annual meeting, but it makes sense to be prepared. A simple first-aid kit should be a must at every special event.

Keys or Access to Keys

Keys or access to keys can assume a vital function in event management should an emergency arise. For example, finding a broom to sweep up a broken glass can be a problem when you are without access to the right closet.

Basic Supplies and Equipment

Basic supplies and equipment including such basics as needle and thread, scissors, tape, and paper and pen can make life a lot easier when the need arises.

Communication Tools

Communication tools are essential. The more territory covered by your event, the more critical the communication. Walkie talkies are well worth the small rental charge, especially when one site must coordinate with another. During *Fantasy Flight 1029*, workers at each of the five food and performance venues had to be in contact with each other so that when guests were moved from one place to the other, workers at the next site were ready to receive them. Event setup and clean up would have been infinitely more complicated without these remarkable conveniences.

Practices That Prevent Problems

Checking Deliveries

Checking deliveries is very important. When the truck arrives, someone with the list of items ordered should be checking the items off before moving them to another site. This step will help alert you to mistakes in the order *before* the need arises for that particular piece of equipment.

Reviewing Plans

Review plans with key staff. You have a plan, and everyone has a copy, but don't assume that everyone has read it or understood it. Take the necessary time to meet with everyone and review the entire event schedule as well as the plan for emergencies. It's a good idea, during this process, to acknowledge the people responsible for the various parts of the schedule.

Reviewing Responsibilities

Review people responsibilities with volunteers and staff. Who will be available for the guests who arrive early? Is someone assigned to each VIP guest? Who will meet the performers and help them find the person to whom they must report? Who will ensure that the CEO meets all the VIPs? Who will be visible to answer questions after guests are seated? Will someone be at the door to thank departing guests? If your event moves from place to place, is there someone to look for the lost or straggling guests? Who is meeting the media representatives and escorting them through the crowd?

The Event Walk-Through

Take your clipboard along and pretend you are a guest—do what the guests will do, step by step. You'll be amazed at some of the issues that will surface. For example, what about outdoor lighting for an evening event? For guests who have to walk any distance to arrive at the site, is there adequate lighting? Don't just look for light fixtures, turn them on and make certain that they work!

Time your experience as you walk from the car to the location(s) of the event. Will it take longer to walk than you planned? It helps to take someone along with you so you can compare notes. Will people know where they are supposed to go when they arrive on the site? Note where you will need to post signs. Are the restrooms well marked and easy to access? Do you have trash cans where they are needed and are they large enough? If you are having an all-day event, have you made arrangements for them to be emptied periodically during the day? What about ice? Soap and water?

Walk-Through for Key Leadership

Walk key leadership through. Typically, these are people whose names have been affiliated with the event; many of the guests will ask them questions, and the key leadership will feel good *only* if they have ready answers. They would benefit from having a copy of the event plan before the event itself. Few staff members think to do that. It can make a significant difference in the comfort level of your volunteers.

Walk-Through for Volunteers

Have a walk-through for the volunteers who will accompany the photographer. The volunteers assigned to the photographer should be familiar with the guest list as well as the site. If certain photographs should be taken, the photographer will need a guide. In fact, the photographer may even want to join you for the walk-through, but if not, at least there will be a volunteer who knows the schedule, the people, and the site.

Walk-Through for Service People

Walk service people through. When developing the concept for *Fantasy Flight 1029*, the restaurant owners involved in the food sites were invited to a walk-through designed especially for them. This enabled those involved to walk through and to see what everyone else was doing. Many had suggestions for their personal areas, especially the behind the scenes prep rooms where dishes and food were stored and processed. When the day of the event arrived, each worker knew where to go and no one required any special attention in the midst of other preparations.

Observing Things Normally Not Noticed

Look at the things you don't normally notice. As you conduct your walk-throughs, be sure to look at *everything* you pass. Suddenly, the paint sprayed on the sidewalk is noticeable. Look at the site with the eyes of someone who has never seen it before. Be certain that you walk through at the same time of day as your event will be held. This is particularly important if it is an outside event. If it's a daytime event, will the sun be in people's eyes? Will it be hot, cold, breezy, or uncomfortable? A walk-through such as this may inspire you to add a tent to your rental list. If you are having a buffet table,

> **Look at the site with the eyes of someone who has never seen it before.**

will it be in the sun? When the crowds of people are present, will there be access to the table for the staff who are keeping it stocked?

If you're planning an event on someone's patio, has the owner checked with neighbors to see if they have anything planned for the same time? A neighborhood swimming party with loud music and raucous laughter can have a negative impact on a cultivation event at which the chairperson of the board is scheduled to speak.

Listen for sounds you might not have heard before. The College of Fine Arts happens to lie in the flight path of the air force base. During the day, there are times when a plane flying low overhead makes it impossible for a speaker to be heard. Although *Fantasy Flight 1029* was an evening event, the formal dedication of the complex was scheduled for late morning when most guests would be able to attend. There was no way to stop the planes overhead, but it was a consideration when planning the type of sound system needed. It would not have been possible to get by with a small podium microphone. Listen for traffic, trains, school playgrounds, and other such generators of sound.

Walk-throughs help you refine your timeline for the day of the event, what will be done, and when. What can be done ahead of time? What must wait until the last moment? Will you have time to go home and dress for the event? Or, will it be better to plan your shower and clothing change for someplace near the event site? This is the kind of thing that can throw you for a loop at the last moment, and it is just the kind of experience that a walk-through can help you to avoid.

The Staff

In the case of *Fantasy Flight 1029*, the entire staff was curious about how the planning and preparation for this event had consumed the time of so many people for over a year. Although many of the staff were invited to participate as guests and volunteers, there were those who could do neither.

> When your event requires that people be moved from place to place, it's useful to foresee the flow of traffic.

So the evening before the event, when the dress rehearsal was held, those staff members were invited to attend. This gesture of goodwill enabled those who would be stationed in only one area to observe areas they would not see the night of the event; it helped everyone feel a part of the whole event.

Moving People

When your event requires that people be moved from place to place, it's useful to foresee the flow of traffic. Will everyone be moving at the same time? If so, will the space accommodate them? The movement of guests at *Fantasy Flight 1029* was so complex that a walk-through was used to trace the path of each and every group. Maps were drawn depicting the traffic pattern for each group using the color of the dots guests would be given when they signed in at the ticket counter. Each of the five color groups would have a different traffic pattern for the evening to avoid the mass confusion that would have resulted had they all chosen to walk through the same hallways. This walk-through was scheduled earlier than the more public walk-through. Each of the traffic patterns was timed and then evaluated. Several modifications were made. When the routes were initially assigned, two of the five routes had to be handicapped-accessible. The walk-through for those routes required assurance that there were no stairs or other problems that would require special assistance for guests.

When It Is Not Possible to Schedule a Walk-Through

There will be times when it's simply not possible to have access to a site long enough to schedule for all of the people you wish to join you for a walk-through. Usually, the sites are hotels or other commercial sites where other events are regularly scheduled. In these circumstances, you are not usu-

ally dependent on as many volunteers as you are when using a noncommercial site; nor is it necessary to involve the paid staff who receive their instructions from the catering managers. However, the catering manager must be informed about your activities and your plans, both in conversation and with a written confirmation.

When a Walk-Through Becomes Cultivation

There were many people involved in *Fantasy Flight 1029* and many who either contributed financially or provided other help. Although it certainly wasn't necessary to take these people on a walk-through, several were invited to arrive early so that a volunteer could take them around to see all five venues. This special treatment cost nothing, but generated considerable good feelings.

The Walk-Through as a Mini-Event

The walk-through obviously serves many useful purposes. You're encouraged to make use of as many of them as possible. You may even choose to create a simple invitation to this event, but only if you can really handle all the implications!

Organizing by Chart

The chart in Exhibit 15–1 illustrates a combination of functions. First of all, it identifies tasks, clarifies who will execute those tasks, provides space to enter the appropriate contact, and recommends a timeline.

Volunteer Instructions

When you have volunteers working on an event, it is important that they not only feel comfortable with their assignment, but that they have something in writing to which they can refer when you are nowhere in sight. Written instructions, distributed before the event (sometimes at the walk-

> This special treatment costs nothing, but generates considerable good feelings.

Exhibit 15–1 Organization Chart

Task	Volunteers	Foundation	Vendor/Point Person	Timeline
California Pacific Medical Center Foundation **Special Events/Public Relations Committee** **Special Event Volunteer's Worksheet**				
Location				9 months prior
Contract	✓			
Confirmation	✓			
Send deposit		✓		
Underwriting				
Generate list*	✓			
Approval and coordination of underwriting prospects		✓Lee Ann M.		
Request letter approved by foundation		✓Lee Ann M.		
Foundation letterhead		✓		
Letter production and mailing			✓Lee Ann M.	
Follow up	✓			
Processing gifts		✓		
Acknowledgment letters		✓		
Invitations				3 months prior
Printing	✓			
CPMCF approval		✓Lee Ann M.		
Mail lists*		✓Elizabeth H.		
		Joan D.		
Addressing/ mailing	✓			

continues

Exhibit 15–1 continued

Task	Volunteers	Foundation	Vendor/Point Person	Timeline
Catering				
Contact		✓		
Coordination	✓			
Confirmation	✓			
Program				
Coordination of information	✓			
CPMCF* approval		✓		
Printing	✓			
Decorations				
Party favors	✓			
Valet Parking				
Confirmation	✓			
Music	✓			
Flowers	✓			

*CPMFC will generate the appropriate lists for special events invitations; however, staff will not provide updating and merging of new information.

Courtesy of California Pacific Medical Center Foundation, San Francisco, California.

through), serve as a confirmation of everything you have shared with them up to that time.

Exhibit 15–2 provides an example of an instruction sheet for one of the guides at *Fantasy Flight 1029*.

Although this schedule appears to be incredibly detailed and impossibly close in timing, it was the result of having strolled through the routes while timing them. Lengthy planning took into consideration people in conversation, seeing and being distracted by friends, as well as other obstacles. This complicated evening was dependent upon timing, and guides with walkie talkies connected with one another, making certain that the pathways were clear and that guests were finished at each dining site before moving them to their next site. Remember, each guest was assigned to an itinerary designated by colored dots numbered 1 and 2. They would visit two dining sites and stop by one vignette on their way to each site.

The guides were not the only people directing traffic. Guests were instructed at each site how to follow their itineraries and once the initial large group of people was on their way, the groups then were separated into smaller and more manageable groups. This was critical because the narrow hallways simply wouldn't accommodate large numbers of people all moving in the same direction.

Although it is highly unlikely that you'll ever be producing this type of event, the illustration is intended to point out the need for serious traffic control of your event, including the planning of how you intend to move people from place to place if that is your event design. The same thought must be given to accommodating a large group of people who are trying to check into an event being held at one site. Will the space permit this? Should you consider staggering the arrival times? What will make your guests' experience a pleasant one?

Even an apparently simple event such as a car wash demands careful planning. Where will drivers be notified of the opportunity? Will there be time to pull over? How many cars will the site accommodate at one time and how many washers? How long will it take for a driver to take a car through the process?

There cannot be too much planning in the logistics arena. Even if your plans do not come to

pass exactly as you have planned, you will have thought through some alternatives and will be prepared for modifications.

There are many ways to handle logistics, and Exhibit 15–3 illustrates how one organization handled the logistics for their event. This method is slightly different, but incorporates the same concepts.

The Logistics of Rentals

Although your event may be limited to one site, Exhibit 15–4 demonstrates some advance thinking about what will go where. If you have any such logistics to consider, planning for them before the delivery of rentals will save everyone problems. In this situation, the rental company was provided with this list so that they could pack their trucks accordingly. Someone was on hand at the loading dock at the appointed time to guide the trucks to the appropriate sites. The special delivery of forks and napkins was to provide time for volunteers to wrap the forks in the napkins and tie them with ribbons. There was a high number of dishware, glassware, and utensils because there would be two seatings for each guest.

Points to Ponder

The scary part of logistics is spending money. As the event date draws closer, the decisions being made involve spending money—money to solve problems and to cover unexpected opportunities. As time shortens, anxiety increases, and with anxiety comes the opportunity for faulty decision making.

David Nelson, a noted consultant, in his one-day seminars, "Getting the Payoff From Special Events," maintains that event management is the riskiest form of fund raising. The way to manage the risk is to share the risk, preferably by pre-selling everything before the final go/no-go decision must be made. Mr. Nelson has developed a series of "Nelson's Laws." His Law of Financial Accountability states, "The person with the most to lose should make the final logistical decisions," which usually means staff. Volunteers often make decisions based on personal preference or agendas or to appeal to their circle of friends and acquaintan-

Exhibit 15–2 Volunteer Instructions

FANTASY FLIGHT 1029—FACULTY OF FINE ARTS GALA
INSTRUCTIONS FOR GUIDES

Name: Susan Quinn Williams

Route: Turquoise/Purple (TRQ/PRP)

Dining Site: Crowder Hall/Lab Theatre

Thank you for agreeing to be a Guide Captain for the Fine Arts Gala, *Fantasy Flight 1029*. Your role in this event is critical, because it will be your responsibility to (a) train and supervise the TRQ guides and (b) guide your group of guests (all guests who have selected the TRQ/PRP itinerary) through their itinerary in a timely and entertaining manner. The most critical aspect of this event is the schedule, so please make sure you have A RELIABLE WATCH and that you arrive at every designated point at least 10 MINUTES EARLY.

Dress: Costume, watch, TURQUOISE LANTERN

Date: Friday, October 29

Arrival Time: On-site at **6:00 p.m.**
                   Personal belongings may be left in Room 122

Schedule:

6:15	In place in Courtyard: Greet guests, assist in locating cocktail service tables and getting their drinks; until 7:00.
7:00	All TRQ guides (6) in Room 110 to pick up lanterns and staves
7:15	All TRQ guides to be at SE corner of Courtyard near main entrance
7:25	At end of Chorus/Melissa Lowe dance, hold up lantern and staves and help gather all TRQ 1 passengers (112 people) into group
7:30	Walk TRQ-1 group east on music sidewalk to general area in front of Holsclaw Hall to view Brass Choir on porch of Center for Creative Photography
7:45	When choir finishes, walk back through main lobby entrance to Music Building, turn left to east hallway, south to backstage Crowder corridor, turn right, and first half go to west backstage door, other half through east backstage door; guide guests into buffet lines; until 8:10
8:10–8:20	Check passageway between check-in and Crowder Hall for lost and/or late-arriving guests
8:20	Return turquoise lantern to room 110 and pick up **PURPLE LANTERN**
8:30	Be at stage right rear door with TRQ/PRP-1

continues

Exhibit 15–2 continued

8:40	Exit with PRP-2 passengers (56 people) out stage right rear, left to east hallway, left to end of hall, left across front of Crowder to end of hall, right then left to NW corner courtyard door to area around grand piano
8:45–8:55	When piano finishes, walk across courtyard to Theatre Arts lobby doors and into main Lab Theatre doors; guide guests into buffet lines
9:10–9:30	Free to visit hospitality suite Room 39A
9:30	Be inside Lab Theatre at doorways to assist
9:40	Guests exit to Finale in Courtyard
9:50	FINALE
10:05–10:25	Mingle in courtyard, help guests find desserts and coffee, explain dancing in courtyard and performance in Museum, get to Museum, and thank guests who are leaving, etc.
10:30	You are free! THANK YOU, THANK YOU, THANK YOU!

Courtesy of the University of Arizona, College of Fine Arts, Tucson, Arizona.

Exhibit 15–3 Lobster Landing

Description: This event raises money for the organization by selling lobsters, fresh fruit and vegetables, and freshly baked bread to area residents.

Special features/attractions: The availability of fresh lobsters is not common in Arizona. The event is held in conjunction with the organization's farmers' market.

Revenue raised: $18,000 to $25,000 from the sale of lobsters, produce, and other items.

Cost estimate of hosting the event: $2,500. All lobsters, produce, and bread are prepaid by those who place orders. The only expense is the initial mailing announcing the event, a reminder mailing, and follow-up "thank you."

Net funds from event: $15,500 to $22,500.

Expenses covered or underwritten by sponsors/companies: $2,000 to $3,000. Occasionally, area farmers donate produce. Also, tents at the farmer's market and the refrigerated trucks that pick up and deliver the lobsters to Tucson are underwritten or donated as in-kind services.

Time needed to coordinate the event: Three months.

Number of staff involved: Two. Staff members help coordinate the mailings, order lobsters and produce, and line up baked goods.

Number of volunteers involved: 40 to 50. Volunteers take orders prior to the event. On the day of the event, they help hand out orders and sell produce and bread at the various booths in the farmers' market.

Number of participants needed to make the event successful: 1,800 to 2,000.

Size of constituency needed to make the event successful: The mailing list includes 7,000 names and addresses.

Tips to maximize event effectiveness: Get 100% board commitment because all board members play a role in the success of the event. They sell lobsters and inform the public about the event. Also, publicize the lobster/produce/bread sale and date as much as possible in area newspapers, the organization's newsletter, etc. Rent out produce booths at farmers' market for increased revenue.

Pitfalls to avoid: The price of lobsters varies seasonally. If you take orders at $12 each and the price of lobsters goes up considerably, you may lose money on the event. Cushion yourself. Don't sell too cheaply.

Additional information. . .

"We've held our Lobster Landing fund raiser for five years," says the administrator of the Tucson Association for Child Care. "Last year, we sold 2,000 lobsters and netted $15,500. We hope to sell 3,000 this year!"

The key to the event's success is offering a complete "menu" of items in addition to lobsters. What started out as a simple "pick up your lobsters and take them home" has turned into a major food event in the community. Two years ago, the organization's board members added a farmer's market, complete with locally-grown fresh fruit and vegetables.

This past year, they featured freshly baked bread from a nearby bakery, lobster recipes from local restaurants, and bibs from a Red Lobster restaurant! "We also tripled the amount of produce available for sale and still sold out," the administrator says. "To add some fun to the event, board members were also available to cook lobsters on request!

"For our next Lobster Landing, we plan to raffle off a gourmet dinner prepared by a local chef right in the winner's home," the administrator tells me.

Editor's Note: Take a look at how this strategy might work in your community. If your organization is on either coast where seafood is plentiful, consider selling steaks from the Heartland to people who've been asking, "Where's the beef?"

Contact: Tucson Association for Child Care

continues

Exhibit 15–3 continued

Planning List

Three months prior:

❏ Meet with board to discuss special event and develop a plan of action
❏ Set date of lobster sale/farmers' market
❏ Contact a restaurant association to get list of lobster wholesalers
❏ Contact refrigerated trucking company to contract for pick up and delivery of lobsters (ask if transportation could be donated in-kind)
❏ Advertise the farmers' market to coincide with the lobster delivery (those interested in selling produce at the farmers' market should contact you within one month
❏ Contact company for renting tents, tables, chairs, etc., for farmers' market

Two months prior:

❏ Set deadline date for taking lobster orders
❏ Send letters to community residents informing them of the lobster sale (note that proceeds from the sale may be considered charitable contributions)
❏ Continue advertising the sale and farmers' market to generate orders
❏ Start taking prepaid lobster orders

One month prior:

❏ Order lobsters from wholesaler
❏ Verify the rental of tents
❏ Verify and contract with trucking company to transport lobsters
❏ Give trucking company instructions as to where and when lobsters can be picked up and where to deliver them

Two weeks prior:

❏ Send reminder notices to those who ordered lobsters that they can pick them up at the farmers' market
❏ Send reminder notices to those who showed interest in having a produce stand at the farmers' market

Three days prior:

❏ Contact trucking company to confirm that truck is en route and will deliver lobsters on schedule to the farmers' market

One day prior:

❏ Clean up farmers' market area and put up signs to direct traffic, etc.
❏ Set up tents
❏ Set up stands/booths for farmers' market
❏ Set up lobster stands

Day of:

❏ Complete all last-minute setup items
❏ Hold the event

Follow up:

❏ Prepare cost analysis
❏ Report results of Lobster Landing to board
❏ Send "thank yous" to sponsors and buyers

Source: Reprinted from C. Elliot, *Aspen's Guide to 60 Successful Special Events: How to Plan, Organize & Conduct Outstanding Fund Raisers*, pp. 19–22, © 1996, Aspen Publishers, Inc.

Exhibit 15–4 Logistics Planning

RENTALS BY ROOM

NOTE: 918 forks and napkins to be delivered to Marjory Slavin by 9:00 a.m.

Napkins by Room

Crowder Hall	39 grape	39 royal blue	39 magenta	39 orange
(Total 234)	39 lime	39 lemon yellow		
Orchestra Rehearsal Room	218 black			
Lab Theatre	36 yellow	36 orange	36 turquoise	36 kelly green
(Total 218)		36 red	38 magenta	
Marroney Theatre	124 ivory			
Gross Gallery	124 charcoal			

THEATRE LOADING DOCK DELIVERY

Courtyard (deliver all to New Lab Theatre)

12 card tables

100 white wooden chairs

50 gold chairs

650 wine glasses

400 salad plates

300 cups and saucers

400 salad forks

150 teaspoons

8 standing heaters	10 turquoise banquet cloths	22 bus tubs
25 aisle stands	8 fuchsia (#28) skirts	
200 ft. chain	__ Velcro clips	
2 purple banquet cloths	1 skirt	

continues

Exhibit 15–4 continued

New Lab Theatre—13 tables, 104 people per seating

2	36" round tables
13	48" round tables
218	white plates
125	wine glasses

Round table cloths—2 red / 2 yellow / 3 turquoise / 2 orange / 2 magenta / 3 green

       add 1 yellow and 1 red smaller round (or square)

2	red banquet
2	red skirt
52	Velcro clips

Gross Gallery—7 tables, 56 people per seating

1	36" round table
7	48" round tables
124	white plates
124	wine glasses

Tablecloths

7	ivory round
2	ivory banquet
2	grey skirting
52	Velcro clips

Museum (Deliver to Lab Theatre)

50	gold chairs
100	dessert plates
100	dessert forks

continues

Exhibit 15–4 continued

50	spoons
75	cups and saucers

MUSIC LOADING DOCK DELIVERY

Crowder Hall—14 tables, 112 people per seating, 122 music chairs

2	36" round tables
14	48" round tables
230	white plates
224	wine glasses

Tablecloths

2	grape round
3	magenta round
2	orange round
2	lemon yellow round
2	lime round
3	royal blue round
2	blue skirting
2	damaged cloths
52	Velcro clips

Orchestra Rehearsal Room—13 tables, 104 people per seating, 114 music chairs

13	48" round tables
214	black plates
214	black-stem wine glasses

continues

Exhibit 15–4 continued

Tablecloths

13	round black
2	white banquet
2	black skirting
52	Velcro clips

TABLE SETUP (8 ft. serving tables)

Gazebo	2
Courtyard	11
Lab Theatre	3
Prop Room	3
Marroney Theatre	3
Prep Area	2
Crowder Hall	3
Orchestra Rehearsal Room	3
Scene Shop	4
Music Room 106	3
Total Tables	37

ces. Staff members make decisions based on the resources and needs of the organization. Volunteers tend to view the event as though it is their personal party. Staff members tend to see the event in terms of its goals of cultivation, visibility, or income.

Summary

Event management demands attention to detail, availability, and authority to make decisions. The responsibility to manage the event is best placed in the hands of staff. The role requires reviewing, checking, deciding, troubleshooting, replacing, substituting, cajoling, and other skills supported by intimate knowledge of the plan and all its details as well as the people involved—a daunting task made large and complex by the size and complexity of the event itself.

Dress rehearsals in the guise of a walk-through will identify potential problems and create a degree of comfort for the various stakeholders such as key leadership, volunteers with important roles, staff, entertainers, and service providers. There is great value in identifying trouble spots and devising alternatives before they become problems.

> **Event management demands attention to detail, availability, and authority to make decisions.**

Chapter 16

What About Legal and Insurance Requirements?

We are so busy doing the urgent that we don't have time to do the important.

Confucius

Chapter Outline

- Insurance, Licenses, and Permits

- Current IRS Regulations

- Accounting Practices for Special Events

- Special Event Policies

- Points to Ponder

When you invite the public to an event produced by your organization, there is no doubt that you have opened your organization to risk. This chapter contains important information on types of insurance and IRS regulations in place at the time of publication of this book. You'll want to be certain that these regulations are still in effect, and that your event is in compliance with all regulations.

Insurance, Licenses, and Permits

Insurance Riders

Insurance riders are simple to get and are generally inexpensive. They extend the insurance coverage for your organization to cover a venue that is not your own, and depending upon what your guests will be doing, it is a simple procedure. This is particularly important if you are not in your own facility *and* if liquor is being served. If you are in a hotel or other public meeting place, your organization may not need a rider. It's best to check, however, with your insurance agent before making that rider decision.

Specialty Insurance

Specialty insurance may be necessary for events such as a trip or tour, or a golf tournament. You may want to recommend specialty insurance to patrons who have signed up for a trip. Typically, this is available through any travel agent. It protects the investment made in the downpayment. It's easier for the organization not to get involved with this insurance matter and let each person traveling deal with his or her own needs.

Hole-in-One Insurance

Hole-in-one insurance is not inexpensive. However, if you are offering expensive prizes such as a car or a Rolex watch for a hole-in-one at your golf tournament event, it may be worth consideration to purchase the insurance. If you do, be prepared for the requirement that there must be one or more witnesses on site at the specified hole for the duration of the tournament. Any hole-in-one must be witnessed by an independent person before the insurance company will pay. In many circumstances, a valuable prize may be offered. If, for example, you offered a Rolex watch for a hole-in-one, the jeweler may choose to lend you the watch for display purposes. Should someone win the watch, the insurance then covers the expense of purchasing the watch. There are several national hole-in-one insurance companies. These businesses may offer other benefits to their customers. You'll want to evaluate the advantage of such a purchase after checking with your own insurance agent.

The Liquor License

The liquor license may require some advance planning. You need to find out when and where the state liquor board meets and submit your application well in advance of that time. Most boards meet on a monthly basis, but it's wise to be certain that you leave enough time to satisfy any additional requirements they might have. For example, a typical question relates to the food being served with the alcohol. If you don't have that information, your application will not be passed at that meeting. So it's important to apply enough in advance to cover any last-minute unforeseen issues. The application will require that you identify who is buying the liquor, who is serving the liquor, whether it's being sold at the event, and, importantly, who will ensure that there will be no underage drinkers.

For the record, if you are serving wine or liquor at an event for which a guest has purchased a ticket, you are considered to be "selling" that wine or liquor. This could result in complications if your event is being held at a private restaurant, hotel, or club. In some states, if you intend to use the facility's bar for purchasing drinks during the cocktail hour, you will not be able to obtain a special liquor license to serve donated wine. There can be only one liquor permit per event, and either it's your license or the license held by the venue. In this circumstance, your only other option is to underwrite the cost of the wine.

Health Permits

Health permits may be required if you are preparing and selling food. If it is being prepared by a caterer, then it may be only your organization that has any requirements. For example, at the University of Arizona, off-site caterers were required to be licensed. Therefore, it was not permissible for a generous, talented person to bake or serve for an event unless that individual was licensed.

The Fire Marshall

The fire marshall will need to inspect your event site if you are having something other than the normal dinner or luncheon. In most communities, an event scheduled in a large public place requires inspection by the fire marshall. This is especially true if you plan to use candles or other open flame or cooking equipment. Materials will need to be fire retardant-treated and nonflammable, and there will be other requirements. It's a good idea to check these conditions before purchasing or even renting equipment and materials.

Current IRS Regulations

Because these regulations have an impact on the special events that your organization may choose to conduct, it is important to understand them in their entirety. The following regulations reflect the law at the time of the publication of this book. Please check for any changes that may have occurred since that time.

Event Tickets and the Fair Market Value

FMV or Fair Market Value has become an issue that is currently being enforced by the IRS. Although this regulation has been in effect for many years, it has been an enforcement issue only for the past five or six years. The FMV of an event is the price that a person would pay if that person purchased the same goods and/or services outside the event. For example, a black-tie dinner with entertainment has a fair market value within the community that it is being produced. The FMV will be based on what it would cost a patron to purchase these same services at a comparable place or a ticket to a performance in the community. A star attraction would naturally have a more expensive ticket than more community-based entertainment. It is the responsibility of the producing organization to competently evaluate and estimate this cost. The remainder of the ticket price is then the contributed portion. If an event ticket is $200 and the FMV is $125, then $75 is the contributed portion. It is mandatory that an organization inform its patrons about the tax-deductible portion. Most commonly, this is done on the invitation. However, it's possible that an organization might choose to inform its patrons through a statement that accompanies a ticket sent in the mail. Some patrons will determine their attendance at an event by the amounts stated on the invitation. If a person believes that the organization is not receiving enough of the ticket price, that person may elect not to attend an event. So, it's important to consider carefully when establishing the ticket price and its FMV.

Gifts of Real Estate or Tangible Property

All donors of real estate or tangible personal property shall receive notification of their contribution including the following:

- date possession of the property and the benefits and burdens of ownership are transferred (usually by executed deed)

- purpose of the gift

- description of the property but not the value

- whether the organization provided any goods or services to the donor in exchange for all or part of the contribution, and if so, a description and good faith estimate of the fair market value of the goods and services provided

If the value of an item or group of like items exceeds $5,000, the donor must (a) obtain a qualified appraisal and (b) submit an appraisal summary with the return claiming the deduction.

Gifts of Tangible Personal Property Created by the Donor

The tax deduction to individuals who contribute property they created or constructed is limited to the cost (materials, etc.) of creation or construction, not the value of the property.

All donors of personal property shall receive notification of their contribution, including the following:

- date

- purpose of the gift

- description of the created property but not the value, whether the organization provided any goods or services to the donor in exchange for all or part of the contribution, and if so, a description and a good-faith estimate of the fair market value of the goods and services provided

Special Events or "Quid Pro Quo" Contributions

All invitations, tickets, solicitations to attend, or receipts for special events that seek contributions of $75 or more shall carry the following information:

- the amount required to attend the event

- notice stating that the amount that is deductible for federal income tax purposes is limited to the excess contributed by the donor over the fair market value of the goods or services provided by the organization to the donor

- a good-faith estimate of the fair market value of the goods or services provided

If an individual purchases ticket(s) and takes constructive possession, the tax deductible portion is that which is in excess of the FMV, even if the individual does not attend the event.

If the individual purchases ticket(s) and instructs the organization to give away the tickets (never having taken possession), the tax deduction is the full amount because the individual surrendered an economic right without receiving anything of value in return.

Underwriting/Sponsorship of Special Events

All donors of underwriting or sponsorship of special events shall receive notification of their contribution, including the following:

- date

- purpose of gift

- amount of the cost of underwriting, based on actual receipts submitted to the organization *OR,* in the event the donor chooses to not submit receipts, description of the event (number of guests, meal and beverage description, etc.) but not the value

- whether the organization provided any goods or services to the donor in exchange for all or part of the contribution, and if so, a description and good-faith estimate of the FMV of the goods and services provided

Auction or Sale of Contributed Property

The organization shall determine the FMV of contributed items before the auction date. Such FMV shall be established by the contributing entity or by surveying the marketplace.

The fair market value of items to be sold at auction shall be disclosed to bidders before bidding begins, either in printed brochures, through announcement by the auctioneer, or, in the case of silent auction, by printing on the bid sheet.

Successful bidders on items auctioned by the organization shall receive notification of their transaction, including the following:

- date

- description of item

- amount received

- date amount received if different than auction date

- FMV

- tax-deductible portion of the amount (which shall be the difference between the FMV of the item and the amount received

Raffles

The following information pertains to raffles:

- Winnings of any amount, either in cash or goods, are considered income to the winner.

- If the prize has a FMV of $600 or more, the organization will have the winner complete an IRS Form W–9.

- If the prize has a FMV of $5,000 or more, the organization will withhold 28 percent of the FMV of the prize (minus the cost of the raffle ticket), which will be submitted to the IRS along with employee payroll taxes at the close of the next reporting period.

- The organization will provide the winner with an IRS W–2g form (report of certain gambling winnings) at the same time and manner as providing W–2 forms.

In addition to the IRS regulations, this fund-raising practice generally has specific state laws and regulations governing the tax deductibility of tickets and the required communication surrounding the winning of a raffle item. Although the IRS has some rulings regarding raffles, the state laws tend to be unpredictable and vary state by state. In one state, an organization raffling a house was using groups of volunteers from other organizations to sell their tickets. At that point in time, the law specifically required that raffle tickets may be sold only by members of the organization sponsoring the raffle. Members are usually defined in an organization's bylaws. And if that definition doesn't fit, you may be conducting an illegal activity in your state. Further, organizations were required to fill out a ticket for anyone who requested it, whether or not that individual had made a donation. The organization in question had to refund the money raised and reorganize the entire effort from scratch.

In some states, it is illegal to conduct a raffle through the mail. Please check with your state attorney general and city officials before deciding to do a raffle.

By now, most fund-raising staffs know that raffle tickets are not tax deductible. However, it is not uncommon for a board member to take his or her assigned tickets and tell people that they should buy a ticket because it's a tax-deductible donation to the organization. It's of vital importance that your board, staff, and volunteers be informed about the law and regulations regarding raffles.

Accounting Practices for Special Events

The income generated for special events, whether contributed or from ticket sales, is considered a liability until the event is produced. After the event, the income may move over to the asset side of the statement of financial position. If the timing of the cash flow involves two fiscal years, it is legitimate to book the expenses as prepaid expenses and the income as anticipated revenue.

Although many people prefer to net out the income and expense of a special event, it is much more advantageous to record all of the expense and all of the income. This is true even if the event was not included in the annual budget. Why? Because it's important to know the *real cost* of an event. If you choose to produce the event again in the future, you will want to know what all of the expenses were, and it won't help you to know that the printing was contributed if you don't know how much it would have cost had you paid for it

Special Event Policies

Such policies will be helpful to you when you are working with volunteers. They may even be important when another not-for-profit organization proposes doing a joint event. Questions to ask when determining such policies include the following:

1. Does the organization wish to limit relationships with individuals, corporations, or organizations whose philosophies may differ from your own? Many health organizations will not affiliate with or accept money from companies that produce alcohol or tobacco.

2. Do you want to consider limitations on food or beverages to be served at an event? Again, health-related organizations may choose to evaluate the type of food and beverage served

at their events. They are apt to use this event to promote the kind of healthful eating that their organization promotes. Some institutions (such as schools) prohibit the use of alcohol on their premises.

3. Are board members required to sell or purchase a certain number of tickets? When stated in the board-approved policies, it is easy to say that every board member must purchase or sell one table or its equivalent.

4. Is approval needed to proceed with any event using the name of the organization? If so, this will help control the number of groups who choose to mount an event to "support" your organization. When you have no control, then you have nothing to fall back on if you need to tell this group that you don't like the way they have chosen to advertise or conduct the event being produced for your benefit. You also have no control over the dollars raised versus the dollars spent to mount such an event.

5. Must an event budget project a minimum net profit? Some organizations limit their events to those that will net at least $20,000. While these are generally large organizations, smaller groups may select a more realistic lower net figure. The most effective way to limit the number and type of events recommended by the board is to develop policy. Then there are no exceptions, and everyone understands that policy is policy. It simply isn't acceptable to make exceptions.

Finally, the matter of contracting is one that has been mentioned earlier (in Chapter 5), where the contract referred to is with a hotel or other site. Contracts also must be considered when you are engaging artists or speakers. Your best approach will be to identify the following:

- date

- time

- place

- performance (exactly what you expect to be done)

- travel (if appropriate)

- lodging (if appropriate)

- additional information concerning the engagement such as meals, other people to be included, complimentary tickets, or any other special arrangements

When sending such a contract, the widely accepted practice is to send two and request that the individual being engaged sign and return one copy.

You'll find it helpful to review all of the previous requirements as they relate to your organization and your event.

Points to Ponder

One of the more sensitive insurance and liability concerns for events centers around the issue of the sale and consumption of alcohol. If your organization has no reason to exclude alcohol and the market expects alcohol to be available, develop clear policies and a plan. It is prudent, for reasons of liability, to avoid free drinks. At most, include two drink coupons with the price of the ticket.

Ask the hotel or restaurant about its policies on liquor and overconsumption. Consider having a cash bar but charge a high price for the drinks, perhaps four or five times the going rate. Announce that the increased portion will help support the cause. This technique keeps consumption low and generates additional income.

If alcohol is being served, consider advance arrangements for taxi service that could be available to guests who want or need to be transported.

Summary

Prudence demands that staff be diligent in meeting whatever legal, regulatory, and insurance requirements affect the event.

Insurance should be arranged to cover the event according to the activity, the location, and the exposure to liability presented by the event itself. The organization's insurance provider should be informed at an early date about the plan and be asked to recommend adequate coverage for the activities and the location. No organization should enter into an event without coverage.

State and local law may require specific licenses, permits, and inspections. These may require weeks or months to secure. In addition, state and local law may prohibit certain activities such as lotteries and raffles.

IRS regulation requires close attention to compliance in matters of quid-pro-quo contributions, auctions, raffles, sponsorship, and underwriting.

Establishing policy on special-event accounting before the event can prevent misunderstandings while facilitating early and reliable reporting to volunteers, governing body, and interested regulators. It has further value as data for evaluation and for the historical record.

Chapter 17

What Are the Checkpoints? How to Avoid Disaster

It is the little things that count. You can sit on top of a mountain, but you can't sit on a tack.

Unknown

Chapter Outline

- The Psychology of Special Events

- The Three-Month Checkpoint

- The One-Month Checkpoint

- The Two-Week Checkpoint

- One Week and Holding

- The Week of the Event

- Other Checklists

You have a thorough plan. You've had volunteers and other staff members discuss it and amend it if necessary. How can checkpoints help you ensure the perfect event?

Somehow, no matter how solid the plan, there is room for misunderstanding, misinterpretation, or simply forgetfulness. How many times have you said to yourself, "Why didn't I check on this arrangement?" This chapter explores the psychological aspects of special events, four checkpoints, and what to examine at each one of them. Included will be a recommended list for the three-month, one-month, two-week, and one-week periods. Each will explore areas requiring your personal hands-on review. When you've finished this review, you'll be grateful, because your bit of effort now will prevent unpleasant last-minute surprises and will en-

sure your success. You may even find that this event is one that you'll actually enjoy!

The Psychology of Special Events

This is as good a place as any to introduce the concept of psychology. Working with volunteers requires a genuine understanding of people, their feelings, and the problems associated with control. It's helpful to understand that special events are a breeding ground not only for misunderstanding, but for perceived lack of appreciation, matters of control, and even the disaster of volunteers getting out of hand! When working with volunteers, it's important always to be in tune with their experience, their feelings, and their understanding of their roles. These issues reflect back to the job descriptions presented in Chapter 10. If you have done a thorough job in this area, you'll have considerably less to worry about. Nonetheless, even in the best of all possible worlds, at least two perceived realities exist for every situation—how your volunteer understands something and how you understand the same thing.

Consider the circumstance when volunteers who have been talking among themselves decide that they would prefer to do things in a manner different from that discussed at the last meeting and then proceed to do so—without your knowledge. It could be a shock when you finally learn what they have done. Your first reaction must be to keep your cool. Do not become defensive. Try to understand their concerns and thoughts behind

> When working with volunteers, it's important always to be in tune with their experience, their feelings, and their understanding of their roles.

their decision. It could well be that it was a good decision. It might however, seriously impact other committees and the general flow of the event.

Here psychology plays its most important role. Criticizing the volunteers will have only a negative impact on your relationship with them. Before you even address the issue, you should spend time evaluating the consequences of their decision. Will it create problems? If so, is there someone in particular with whom you can talk, someone who will not take offense or feel unappreciated? Most appropriately, that person can be the chair of the committee. Talk through the situation together and if you can, help that person understand the difficulties that might arise and discuss how to bring the situation to the attention of others. It is most likely that you will find that an open discussion will improve the climate and that volunteers will then be receptive to your legitimate concerns. This is sure to happen if you share a strong relationship with them, and more importantly, if you have helped each of them to feel appreciated throughout the process. This groundwork, laid at the beginning, will facilitate dealing with difficulties that may occur at a later time.

The Three-Month Checkpoint

Review Progress with the Committee Chair

This review will not only help you to become current on the progress of each committee, it will provide the opportunity to catch some of those plans that may have fallen between the cracks. It's essential to do this, particularly if this event has been a long time in its planning period. If you catch something not completed at this stage of the event, there still will be time to correct the situation. Possibly, you can take your committee chair out to lunch and together review the circumstances. Such

an approach will be considered supportive rather than negative (appearing as though you are checking up because you lack faith in your chair). If you've done your job preparing for the event, the committee chair will probably be expecting this opportunity to review whatever progress has been made. As long as you're aware that this checkpoint might be construed in more than one way, you'll undoubtedly treat this review with careful consideration and appreciation for what has already been accomplished, and decisions can be made about the area that needs attention.

Review the Confirmation Letters

Have all of the confirmation letters come in? Are there circumstances that require change in any plans? This is a perfect time to confirm any arranged deliveries. Businesses often have a change in personnel and someone new may be handling your order. It doesn't hurt to touch base and be assured that plans remain the same.

Review the Checklist and Timeline

Is everything on schedule? The timeline, created in Chapter 6, helps take you through what still needs to be done and by when. The checklist in Chapter 15 provides the crutch for those things that can be done only at the last minute. Do both these lists still make sense, or are there necessary changes to be made and communicated? These chores may seem annoying, but they are not trivial and certainly are not to be ignored.

Look for Trouble Spots

This is the time to think ahead. Just like your walk-through will help bring problems to light, this process can alert you to possible problems. During this period in preparing for *Fantasy Flight 1029*, the discovery was made that the orchestra would be using the chairs during the afternoon. According to the plan, someone had already checked out the availability of the orchestra rehearsal room to be used as one of the eating/performance venues. But, alas, it was learned that the musicians, practicing in another studio, still needed their chairs! Arrangements were quickly altered to deliver the chairs back to the room for dinner that evening. This kind of situation could have created genuine havoc had it not come to light before the day of the event.

Time the Critical Parts of the Event

Determine activities with forethought so that you have a concrete idea of how long each part of the evening will require. Finding out at the last minute that your performers are planning a half-hour performance when you had allotted fifteen minutes could precipitate a disaster. Ironing out such dilemmas well in advance should bring everyone back into focus.

Check the Budget

Be positive that you are still on track. If you aren't, now is the time to adjust your expenses so that your final figures are within the projected budget. If you do find that your expenses will be significantly over budget, you must, at this point, determine what can be done on the income side that will improve the net profit. Caution here may forestall a potential shortfall.

The One-Month Checkpoint

The Walk-Through

The walk-through discussed in Chapter 15 takes place at this point in time. This is your opportunity to review with the entire staff their step-by-step participation. Once completed, you're ready to take your volunteers on the walk-through.

Finding out at the last minute that your performers are planning a half-hour performance when you had allotted fifteen minutes could precipitate a disaster.

Review the Checklist

Review the checklist; now you may find new items that should be added. No matter how many times you review this list, never consider it a waste of time.

Check the Seating Arrangements

Although you may not yet have received all your reservations, this is an appropriate time (if your event is a seated one) to review the seating, making certain that arrangements have been made for the VIPs.

Run Through the Arrival of Your Guests

Who will greet them? Who will usher them into the area where you've planned for them to gather? Who will accompany the photographer to make sure that the proper people have their photos taken? Who will introduce the CEO to VIP guests? And who will keep an eye out for a board member or guest who is standing alone, or worse, is trapped in a corner with someone from whom they would like to escape gracefully?

Review the Ticket Sales and Call Volunteers

Be certain that they are current on ticket availability. Must people be encouraged to sell more tickets or can you tell them they have a sold-out event? Whatever the circumstance, it is important to let your volunteers know exactly where things stand. A volunteer who is out of the loop cannot possibly maintain the desired enthusiasm and drive to make this event a success.

Check with the Media Representatives You've Invited

Check with all of the media who have been invited to participate in your event. This is especially true of the society magazines. In fact, you'll need to ascertain whether their representative is coming. Will they be bringing someone else? Are they planning to come, take photos, and leave? Or are they planning to stay for the entire event? What are their names? Will they need to be seated? Better to discover any surprises now rather than on the day of your event!

The Two-Week Checkpoint

Review the Delivery Schedule and Confirmations

Make telephone calls. Delivery people and others providing services can be, in fact should be, reminded of their commitments.

Touch Base with Your Volunteers

A diplomatic reminder of volunteer responsibility and commitment is appropriate here. They will be openly grateful for a review at this point. They are just as invested in success as you are.

Review your back-up plan. This is the plan for how to handle "no-shows" among your volunteers. How will you cover the essential responsibilities? Is the staff able to cover this work, or do you need to reassign some of the volunteers? It doesn't hurt to think about this. Although it may seem unnecessary at the time, this step can save you true embarrassment at the time of your event.

One Week and Holding

Call Your Committee Chairs

This check will let you know if everything is under control. Your volunteers will perceive this call as a caring one. There should be little to check at this point, hence it becomes a good opportunity for you to say "thank you."

Check Volunteers' "Temperatures"

This check will help to get everyone on an even keel. Remember, people work differently. For those who have done a good job, some additional recognition is appropriate. At this point, the better you can make your volunteers feel about what they have done, the more energy and enthusiasm they will bring to the actual event. When they feel good

about what they have made possible, their energy will carry over to the guests they have invited and the event begins with *everyone* feeling good about being there. You can't buy that kind of energy, nor can you predict it. It simply must emanate from the people involved and from your recognition of their efforts.

The Week of the Event

Everything that you have put into this event will come back to reward you at this point. This is when the adrenaline rush begins, and now that the countdown has begun, you may even have time to think about what life will be like when your event is over.

There shouldn't be much to do this week. The program should be at the printer, tickets sold, and volunteers and staff well versed in their roles. You've checked on the deliveries and the volunteers have their assignments, so what's left?

It's checklist time! Now comes the hour to create the checklist of things you might not have thought about before. The following is a list including information, items, and miscellany, all of which serve to guarantee that you'll probably never need them, except for "sense of humor," which you've needed and put to use from day one. Keep it there!

- emergency telephone numbers
- change for the phone
- public relations materials
- poster board, pens, tape, paper, and paper clips
- first aid kit and someone who knows how to use it
- portable sound system
- needle, thread, and safety pins
- names and numbers of volunteers, caterers, rentals, etc.
- copies of contracts and receipts
- copies of insurance and licenses

Exhibit 17–1 Sample Events Checklist

(Subject to Special Events Subcommittee approval)

Event: _____

Date/Time: _____ **Location:** _____

Activity: _____

Date	Item Needed	Person Responsible	Projected Budget	Actual Budget	Conf. ✓
	FACILITIES				
	Rental of room, arena, or site				
	Addition of equipment specify:_____ _____				
	Concessions				
	Coat check				
	Parking				
	Directional signage, marquee				
	Clean-up, pre-event				
	Clean-up, post-event				
	Public address system, lighting				
	Decorations				
	Notification of authorities				
	Other specify:_____ _____ _____				
	PERSONNEL Ticket sellers, box office				

continues

Exhibit 17–1 continued

Date	Item Needed	Person Responsible	Projected Budget	Actual Budget	Conf. ✓
	Ticket takers, door workers, house management				
	Money control				
	Workers' entrance guard				
	Security Specify:_____ _____ _____				
	Medical Specify:_____ _____ _____				
	Ushers, guidance, information, lost and found				
	Other Specify:_____ _____ _____				
	PARTICIPANTS				
	Invitations				
	Entry, registration forms				
	Entry, registration location(s)				
	Confirmation, reminder(s)				
	Acquisition of players				
	Biographical information, photos				
	Transportation to event				

continues

Exhibit 17–1 continued

Date	Item Needed	Person Responsible	Projected Budget	Actual Budget	Conf. ✓
	Escorts				
	Accommodations				
	Master of ceremonies, announcer				
	Entertainment Specify:_____ _____ _____				
	TICKETS				
	General admission printing				
	Marketed seating, printing (reserved seats)				
	Ticket distribution Specify:_____ _____ _____				
	Complimentary tickets arranged				
	Badges: Specify description_____ _____				
	Other identification Specify:_____ _____				
	PROMOTION				
	Paid advertising				
	Posters				

continues

Exhibit 17–1 continued

Date	Item Needed	Person Responsible	Projected Budget	Actual Budget	Conf. ✓
	Other materials Specify:_____ _____				
	PSAs, radio, and/or television				
	Special Specify:_____ _____				
	Direct mail				
	PRESS/PUBLICITY **(Pre-event)**				
	News releases, fact sheets				
	Press packets				
	Press briefing, conference				
	Press room, vehicle				
	Press passes				
	Special seating				
	Reminder before event				
	PRESS/PUBLICITY **(Post event)**				
	Event photography				
	Follow-up releases				
	Post interviews				
	Clipping services				
	EVENT PRESENTATION				
	Special decorations				
	Program				

continues

Exhibit 17–1 continued

Date	Item Needed	Person Responsible	Projected Budget	Actual Budget	Conf. ✓
	Brochure/playbill				
	Distribution of printed material				
	Script, agenda				
	Trophies, prizes, awards				
	Site banners, posters				
	Special needs Specify:_____ _____				
	CATERING/FOOD				
	Catering bids: _____ _____ _____				
	Beverages				
	SPECIAL FUNCTION(S) Describe				
	Location Specify:_____ _____				
	Catering Specify:_____ _____				
	Beverages:_____ _____				
	Activities, presentations Specify:_____ _____				

continues

Exhibit 17–1 continued

Date	Item Needed	Person Responsible	Projected Budget	Actual Budget	Conf. ✓
	Invitations, guest lists _____ _____				
	Script, program, agenda _____ _____				
	MISC. ITEMS				
	Special gifts_____ _____				
	Special activities_____ _____				
Courtesy of California Pacific Medical Center Foundation, San Francisco, California.					

- copies of event schedule for all volunteers

- sense of humor!

Armed with these essentials, a great team of volunteers, and an eager group of guests, you are off to a very special event—one you, too, will be able to enjoy!

Other Checklists

The checklist presented in Exhibit 17–1, used by LeeAnn Monfredini at California Pacific Medical Center Foundation, is all-encompassing. The list may be modified to fit your event and will serve as a combination checklist and budget-control instrument. Note the detail included in this list. It might well be used for a special event that is sports-related or a large, big-name benefit to be held in an arena. It might also be used for a smaller event held in a private facility. The general format of the list makes it a valuable tool when trying to keep volunteers and staff considering a plan.

The Celebrity Waiter/Waitress Event uses a different type of checklist. Exhibit 17–2 provides a description of the event and an example of the planning list used to produce the event.

Summary

Working with and through volunteers has the benefit of multiplying the human and creative resources available to the organization—the basic "many hands make light work" concept. In the absence of financial reward, volunteers require and deserve other considerations such as appreciation, understanding, and cooperation. Although recognition is important, the value and benefit of using volunteers can have other costs. These costs can be minimized by establishing early both a chain of command and the limits of the volunteer's decision-making role. The volunteer chair and staff must agree on the boundaries of decisions as well as the route and frequency of communication.

The plan for the event should include checkpoints at appropriate intervals but no less than three months before, one month before, two weeks before, one week before, and the week of the event. These checkpoints should include a review of progress, discussion of detail, confirmation of budget, and general awareness of potential trouble areas. The process should result in a written report that covers the status, the decisions, the responsibilities, and the objectives for the next period.

Exhibit 17–2 Celebrity Waiter/Waitress Event

Description: Board members ask corporate CEOs to wait tables at various restaurants in the community. Invitations to the dinner are sent to other business leaders in the community. Funds are raised through the waiters' tips.

Special features/attractions: The waiters and waitresses are well-known people in the community. By inviting other business and community leaders to the restaurant and event, dozens of capable donors are in one place at one time.

Revenue raised: $17,500 from tips that guests leave their waiters and waitresses (when held at a restaurant able to serve 500).

Estimated cost of hosting the event: $850 for postage, awards, and gag gifts.

Net funds from event: $16,650.

Expenses covered or underwritten by sponsors/companies: $550. This organization solicits a corporation to print the event's name and logo on aprons waiters and waitresses wear at the event. The corporate sponsor also pays for the printing of the invitations.

Time needed to coordinate the event: Five months.

Number of staff involved: Three to five, to develop a plan of action, assign tasks to volunteers, and make sure actions are being accomplished.

Number of volunteers involved: 30 to 40. Volunteers do everything from serving as waiters and waitresses to asking friends who are corporate or community leaders to attend or be involved.

Size of constituency needed to make the event successful: 2,000.

Number of participants needed to make the event successful: 500 to 600.

Tips to maximize event effectiveness: Ask two to three high-profile, well-connected people in the community to be servers. The balance of the waiters and waitresses can be corporate CEOs or mid-level managers. Train all servers prior to the event to avoid embarrassment.

Pitfalls to avoid: Don't limit the number of invited guests; send as many invitations as possible.

Additional information . . .

Many organizations hold celebrity waiter events, where people like the local TV meteorologist and mayor serve dinner to participants, usually at an upscale restaurant. The money raised from these events comes from tips the waiters and waitresses receive.

But board members at this organization increased profits from their celebrity waiter event when they recruited a new group of "waiters"—corporate CEOs! The most recent event netted $16,650!

The high-profile CEOs generate bigger tips than media personalities or other managers or community volunteers, largely due to the people they invite—other leaders in the business community, says St. Louis Crisis Nursery's administrator.

"Besides the increase in tips, our organization gets an additional bonus: These 'big spenders' are put on our mailing list for other fund raisers, like our annual campaign—and many of them make additional contributions."

Plus, board members set the stage for future corporate contributions when they recruit the CEOs as waiters and and waitresses. "They tell these CEOs about our programs and services," explains the administrator.

"Once they understand everything we do for the community—and get them involved in this special event—they come to like us. That puts us in a position to solicit their companies for grants."

Contact: St. Louis Crisis Nursery

continues

Exhibit 17–2 continued

Planning List

Five months prior:

- ❏ Meet with board to discuss special event and develop a plan of action
- ❏ Set event date, time, and location
- ❏ Develop a list of potential participants (honorary chair and celebrity waiters)
- ❏ Contact a restaurant that can serve a large number of people to host the event
- ❏ Meet with board members to determine potential corporate sponsors
- ❏ Write and send proposal letter to corporations to support event

Four months prior:

- ❏ Send letter to corporate CEOs asking them for their participation
- ❏ Complete final potential celebrity waiter list
- ❏ Recruit celebrity waiters (have board ask potential celebrity waiters to participate)
- ❏ Send follow-up letter to those interested, explain event and their duties
- ❏ Have honorary chair sign letters
- ❏ Send letter to celebrity waiters with specific response date
- ❏ Ask corporations to consider corporate matching funds for tips earned by the CEOs
- ❏ Make follow-up phone calls to celebrity waiters, PR contacts, etc.

Three months prior:

- ❏ Mail "thank-yous" to celebrity waiters for agreeing to participate
- ❏ Mail follow-up letter to those who can't participate or who declined
- ❏ With celebrity waiters' help, develop a list of potential people to invite to dine at the restaurant
- ❏ Ask board to review invitation list
- ❏ Write and get printer bids for invitation, response card, receipt cards, and thank-you cards (solicit a printer to donate printing services)

Two months prior:

- ❏ Assign celebrity waiters to shifts and seating sections
- ❏ Deliver invitations to board members to prepare
- ❏ Design aprons for celebrity waiters to wear at event
- ❏ Get bid to produce aprons (ask company to underwrite this cost)

One month prior:

- ❏ Mail packet of information to celebrity waiters with their shift time and invitations
- ❏ Do phone follow-up with celebrity waiters to confirm schedules
- ❏ Determine and buy awards and gifts:
    - ✓ Celebrity Waiter of the Year award
    - ✓ Gift to honorary chair
    - ✓ Gift to restaurant (plaque)
- ❏ Send out news release announcing date, time, location of event, and celebrity waiter list

continues

Exhibit 17–2 continued

Three weeks prior:

- ❏ Mail or hand-deliver invitations to guest list
- ❏ Pick up aprons

Two weeks prior:

- ❏ Mail reminder letters to celebrity waiters noting shift times and providing names of those who have made reservations in their sections

One week prior:

- ❏ Phone celebrity waiters as needed to inform them of reservations made
- ❏ Discuss who will collect tips
- ❏ Assign staff member to handle media (take photos, work with reports, etc.)

One day prior:

- ❏ Fax/call media reminding assignment editors about the event

Day of:

- ❏ Set up a location for hors d'oeuvres and beverages for celebrity waiters
- ❏ Greet celebrities as they arrive, hand out aprons, review shift times and other instructions

Follow-up:

- ❏ Prepare cost analysis
- ❏ Report results of the event to board members
- ❏ Send "thank yous" to celebrity waiters, board members, guests who made contributions, sponsors, and restaurant

Source: Reprinted from C. Elliot, *Aspen's Guide to 60 Successful Special Events: How to Plan, Organize & Conduct Outstanding Fund Raisers*, pp. 64–69, © 1996, Aspen Publishers, Inc.

Chapter 18

How Can You Enjoy a Worry-Free Event? A Word to the Wise

Today is unique. Don't let its wonderful moments go by unnoticed and unused.

Pat Boone

You've been in high gear for the last several weeks. How can you enjoy this event so that others will enjoy being with you? This chapter is just for you. What you really need the day of your event is a relaxing day off. However, the likelihood of this occurring is, at best, minimal, so it helps to think ahead about YOU. If you've planned well, there won't be a great deal to do. So, step outside yourself, relax, and watch it all happen around you. All of the work you have done in preparation for this event will now pay off as *you* become a guest at *your own* event!

Dressing for the Event

You've no doubt predetermined your attire for the evening of your event. But the key to dressing at home (or away from home) is to make time the night before to plan your routine for dressing. That means go through the steps required to dress, from studs and bow ties to stockings, jewelry, and purses. Review everything you'll need and lay them out together on an extra bed or chair. If, however, you do not live close to your destination, it could take too long to go home to dress and return in reasonable time. If necessary, by all means find a substitute place! It may be a friend's house, a locker room, or a dressing room. The closer you are to your event, the less pressure you'll put on yourself to hurry. This routine will guarantee that ultimately you'll be calm, cool, and collected.

Arriving Early

Plan to be on site at least twenty to thirty minutes before the first volunteers are due to arrive. They will appreciate the fact that you are there early to greet them, and will probably have numerous questions to ask you. This is important time with your volunteers. If you absolutely cannot be there due to last-minute preparations, be certain that a staff member in whom you have utmost confidence will handle the volunteers and early arrivals.

Reviewing Lists

Become familiar with and keep reviewing your volunteer and guest lists. The more people you can address by name, the more confident and competent you'll feel, and the more welcome the guests will feel. A list with names and affiliations will help you recognize people. It even helps with those people you've never met. When you introduce yourself, they will, in turn, introduce themselves. Upon hearing the name of the guests, you may even remember the name of the host and hostess who invited them and possibly bring them together, or at least comment on whether or not the hosts have arrived.

Greeting Volunteers and Guests

Greet your volunteers and participants. Even the people you don't know will appreciate a friendly, smiling face. It's not unusual for some of your volunteers to feel they might rather be a guest at this point. This is when making them feel comfortable about their participation is most important. After all, these people are now the power and energy behind this event. When they work like a team, everything runs smoothly. Unfortunately, if they are not working well together, or if someone would rather be talking with the guests, you have a potential cog in the wheel. Such a situation is simple to prevent by reinforcing your participants and volunteers. You'll then be providing an especially meaningful appreciation of their roles in making this a most successful event.

Greet your guests. It sounds so obvious, but the more you can do for your guests, the more comfortable they become and the better time is had by all. This applies even when you don't know all the guests. When people are greeted by a smile and a welcoming person, they feel pleased to have made the effort to come. On the contrary, when someone walks into an event, doesn't know many people there, and finds everyone occupied and involved, the first feeling that person will have is one of discomfort. This is unfortunate when a simple warm greeting will do so much to put each arrival at ease.

Be warned. You absolutely *must* be ready for those early arrivals. You can be certain that there *will be* early arrivals! They will come as early as thirty to forty-five minutes before you are ready for them. In fact, the older the audience, the earlier they will arrive! This is not so surprising since most are concerned about how long it will take them to reach

their destination. Although they typically move slowly, when they have an exciting destination, their motivation serves to accelerate their pace. When this happens, you'll be fine as long as you've taken this warning seriously and are there to greet them. Welcome these early birds and encourage them to be a part of the scene. This is also your opportunity to thank people for coming, and to let them know what a difference they are making. Not only will they be pleased, but they'll begin their experience feeling happy and comfortable about their decision to attend.

Be aware and be cautious. Of prime importance is being attentive to the amount of time you devote to your guests. Although it is important to greet your own friends, it is also important to spend time with as many other guests as possible. You represent your organization as a host or hostess at these events and guests will expect acknowledgment from you. They want to be certain that you are aware that they have supported your event.

Encouraging Exploration

Encourage guests to explore. Once greeted, it's helpful and prudent if you can direct your guests to another area so that your entryway doesn't become too crowded. You might choose to send them to a specific place to meet friends or order a drink. Whatever the case, get your guests involved promptly by encouraging participation.

Taking Notes

This may sound like a strange thing to do, but taking notes bears fruit. Certainly, you won't want to walk around with a pad and pencil, but having them available and accessible nearby can help you. In spite of all of your careful planning, there will be glitches that you can and should change. Perhaps a specific plan might not have worked exactly as you had determined it would; it's then helpful to be able to annotate it. This is especially true if your event is one that may be repeated in the future. Jotting a note down at the time will jog your memory later when you need to remember that terrific idea you once had.

Have Fun!

You have placed your plans in motion. You now have the opportunity to see them unfold and enjoy them just as you have arranged for others to appreciate and enjoy them. With a deep breath, with the confidence you have in your volunteers and yourself, you now have the keys to a perfect event. Further, a splendid, satisfying, heartwarming experience is yours to savor.

Points to Ponder

A frequently heard comment from fund-raising professionals goes something like, "I don't do special events." This is most likely due to the stress of event management and demands of time and energy, all with no ensured positive outcome. All the proverbial eggs are in one basket, a basket that can be dropped at the last moment. The golf tournament can be canceled because of rain or lightning. The Black and White Ball can be upstaged by an earthquake. The award dinner can lose its honoree to a last-minute illness or a business emergency. The gala can lose its celebrity host to delayed air travel. Dessert can be a soupy mess because the refrigerator came unplugged. Any disaster one can imagine has probably happened to some event at some time.

The best advice is check, double check, and triple check everything. Have a written contingency plan with names, phone numbers, and deadlines for implementation. Prepare yourself mentally to meet emergencies on your feet, to do whatever becomes necessary from pitch-hitting for a speaker to sending staff for last-minute purchase of dessert substitutes. Resolve to keep your sense of humor, and to appear calm and in control at all times. Panic, fear, and anger are both contagious and ruinous at an event.

Summary

The best advice for enjoying a worry-free event is to have a plan, implement the plan, cover all the details, and then sit back and enjoy the unfolding. There is wisdom in the philosophy of doing your best and then letting go.

The day of the event should include a little personal pampering so you can appear as the calm, cool professional in charge. Structure your time to allow deliberate but unhurried dressing, travel, and arrival well before the first volunteers and guests. Greet the first arrivals as if this production was done with ease and grace. Become a guest and enjoy what you have created. Enjoy from the perspective of an honored guest and you will be a gracious host and a more effective representative of the organization.

Chapter 19

Where to End?

There is a wild, splendid, intoxicating joy that follows work well done.

Elbert Hubbard

Chapter Outline

- Expressing Appreciation

- Event Evaluation

- The Final Report

- The Future of Your Event

- Does It Ever End?

- Converting Attendees to Donors

- Points to Ponder

Surprise! Your event isn't over yet! Your plans have been executed, you've had a terrific success, and it's now time to congratulate all involved, say thank you again, and evaluate what you have accomplished. This chapter will cover concepts for expressing your appreciation to all concerned; it will discuss the next step, that of evaluation; and lastly, it will cover the final report plus recommendations. In this chapter, you'll also find a discussion regarding the longevity of events.

Expressing Appreciation

Are thank you notes all the same? Not really. There will be times when it's appropriate to send the same letter to everyone. But, there will be certain volunteers who have given service far above

and beyond the call of duty. These are the heroes and heroines of your event, and you'll want to be sure that they are appropriately recognized. It's been said that a donor should be thanked at least seven times. Well, volunteers certainly fall in the donor category. They have donated time, effort, support, and encouragement. It is incumbent upon staff to find as many ways as possible to thank these invaluable people. For example, a phone call the next day (while the glow of success is still bright), might come from someone who is not writing a note. Certainly, hand-written notes are imperative. However, if you have so many volunteers that you can't possibly thank them all by hand-written notes, consider a special way to have the notes signed. For *Fantasy Flight 1029*, every thank you note was signed by each member of the steering committee. That involved considerable coordination and included driving batches of notes around town, then collecting them to take to the next signer. The result was a brightly colored note, signed personally in different colors by many people who added original thoughts. The signatures ran all around the edges of the paper and when each note was finally finished, it was folded with colored sparkles added and enclosed in the hand-addressed envelope.

Formal notes are appreciated when signed by the CEO or other dignitary. However, hand-written notes are still the most personal expression of appreciation. For the key volunteers, a relaxing, informal lunch is welcome and appreciated. And once again, you'll want your paper and pencil nearby during the lunch. These are the times when ideas come pouring forth about how to improve a good thing.

A dinner is a special way to express particular appreciation. Such a dinner may have nothing to do with the theme or evaluation or anything else. It's simply a gracious opportunity to get important people together and say thank you.

Thank you plaques or other gifts can provide a permanent reminder of your appreciation of someone's work and involvement.

Such thank yous and recognition may extend far beyond the week after the event depending upon the organization and the materials printed for the constituency. Any newsletter or other publication informing a constituency about happenings and activities at your organization provides an excellent opportunity for recognition. In the publication, you might list the volunteers and their contributions. You might also include a photograph or story, certainly the financial results, and/or the programs and services made possible by the funds raised.

Even if you have a regularly published newsletter, you may want to consider a special edition. This decision must be made well in advance. Check the cost, plan the layout, determine what photographs you'll need, and determine what purpose you'll want this special edition to serve. If you've done your homework and have planned what you want the guests of this special event to do in the future, a special-edition newsletter might be the vehicle for informing them, keeping them involved, plus beginning a real relationship with them.

After *Fantasy Flight 1029*, a special insert was included in the university's faculty and staff paper. This insert had pictures and stories about the dedication and the event and an explanation of the use of the dollars raised. Extra inserts were printed and every volunteer received one with a follow-up note. Every guest received one with a letter and a calendar of events for the schedule of the fine arts department. This encouraged people to go back and see more of what they enjoyed the night of the event.

The College of Fine Arts has become the envy of the campus because they have managed to keep the community involved with them. Members of the administration have noted that every Fine Arts

> If you've done your homework and planned what you want the guests of this special event to do in the future, a special-edition newsletter might be the vehicle for informing them and keeping them involved.

event is well attended by members of the community, many of whom were first introduced to the College and its activities at *Fantasy Flight 1029*. The plan worked then and continues to work now.

Event Evaluation

Evaluation sounds like a technical exercise and usually implies work. Consider the possibility that you just might want to produce your event again. For events, it's not uncommon to begin to plan for the next event as soon as the first is completed. You'll find that many areas will need to be evaluated, which means contact is imperative with those people who were deeply involved. No doubt they have already been thinking about how things could be better accomplished the next time around. Consider giving them the opportunity to share their ideas and suggestions with you. You'll find it most helpful to develop a form to record the volunteers' evaluations. The form then can be mailed to all volunteers with a postage-paid return envelope. Exhibit 19–1 presents an event evaluation form.

The Final Report

This is the document that will ultimately determine the strategy for the next event. It will document the following ingredients:

- the goals for the event

- the planning process—its adequacy plus recommendations for change

- recommendations for staff to fulfill the required roles

- the numbers of the following and a recommendation regarding the adequacy of each:

  –volunteers required to produce the event

Exhibit 19–1 Event Evaluation Form

Event Name:_____ Date: _____

Location: _____

   Rate each question on a scale of 1 to 5. Circle the number, with 5 being the best response, and scale your answers down to 1 according to your experience. Some questions will require a written response as well as a numerical rating.

Invitations and Guest Lists

Were the lists gathered and used effectively?   1   2   3   4   5

Should the same lists be used again?   1   2   3   4   5

Would it be more effective to add names?   1   2   3   4   5

      Or should a whole new list be developed?   1   2   3   4   5

Were the invitations received in a timely manner?   1   2   3   4   5

      Or should they be mailed earlier?   1   2   3   4   5

Guest Check-In

Did the process go smoothly?   1   2   3   4   5

Are there opportunities for improvement? _____   If so, please state them.

_____

_____

Were guests with special needs accommodated well?   1   2   3   4   5

If not, what improvements could be made? _____

_____

Entertainment

Were participants in place and on time?   1   2   3   4   5

Do you have any suggestions for making it easier for guests to participate?

_____

Did the entertainment concepts work?   1   2   3   4   5

Do you have any suggestions for additional events in the future?

_____

continues

Exhibit 19–1 continued

Technical and Planning

Were electrical and other technical needs handled well?   1   2   3   4   5

Do you have suggestions for changes in this area?

_____

Was the schedule of meetings adequate?   1   2   3   4   5

       Were there too many meetings?   1   2   3   4   5

       Too few?   1   2   3   4   5

Did you receive information in a timely fashion?   1   2   3   4   5

Do you have suggestions to improve communications?

_____

_____

_____

Did you think that there was a good process for problem solving?   1   2   3   4   5

How would you change the process for the next project?

_____

_____

Do you have any suggestions for facilitating your personal participation? For making it simpler to manage?

_____

_____

Was the food service managed well?   1   2   3   4   5

If not, can you make suggestions for future events? _____

_____

Did the planning for this event adequately address all of the issues and concerns you may have had?

_____

_____

Were you provided adequate information to help you be prepared for your work?

Name (optional) _____

_____

What suggestions would you make for planning a repeat of this event? _____

_____

–guests accommodated

–dollars expended and raised

- a recommended timeline

- the recommendations for future events (from the evaluation forms)

The Future of Your Event

You've had a success. The guests enjoyed it, and the volunteers are willing to do it again. How many times can you repeat an event before it becomes so commonplace that it is no longer attracting an audience? The proliferation of repeated sports events is an apparent byproduct of the baby boomers who have supported much of the increased focus on exercise. But one would be wise to question the longevity of such events as walks, runs, bikathons, and triathlons. Although there will always be an audience for each of these events, a question remains about the size of that audience and, therefore, a question concerning the potential profit from producing such an event.

"Tastings" have been popular over the past ten years or so. However, they are now on a decline because the restaurants that have been asked to participate are finding the event to be more work than benefit. And the number of ticket buyers, who once thought these events were fun is also decreasing. Suddenly, the experience, from some points of view, has become more of a feeding frenzy than a manageable and pleasant tasting that brings recognition to the vendors providing the tastes.

You'll be wise to evaluate the longevity of your event. When will it become too predictable for most guests? Will it sustain the interest and involvement of the community? A well-produced event can sustain interest for a long time, but do consider other events in your community. Are they changing? Do they mimic your event? Keep an open mind to the potential for change. Decide whether you're filling a place in the market, or whether you'd be better off making changes that will continue to draw an audience.

Does It Ever End?

Yes, your event will finally come to an end, and if it was rewarding and successful, there will always be a group supporting a repeat performance. If you have achieved your goals, you will have done the following:

- brought a new external market into contact with your organization (cultivation)

- raised the dollars and the awareness that you were seeking (income)

- created significant visibility for your organization (visibility)

You'll also have developed a plan for the follow-up to this event. How will you engage your guests with your organization in the future? What communication plan do you need to ensure that your guests will remember your organization and possibly consider future involvement? It is legitimate to simply plan to ask your guests to attend the event the following year. There may be people who have no desire to be further connected in any way. But that decision should be a conscious one.

Converting Attendees to Donors

One of the first opportunities to begin this conversion is when the ticket order is placed. For *Fantasy Flight 1029*, a special letter was sent to those ordering business and first class tickets. These prospects were especially important because they clearly had the capability to make significant gifts. The letter presented in Exhibit 19–2 offered these patrons preferential treatment for future performances in fine arts.

The letter in Exhibit 19–2 accompanied the boarding passes that were sent to those who purchased tickets. For patrons who bought tickets at the coach class rate, the letter ended after the first two paragraphs. The example is included to demonstrate the cultivation opportunity extended at the time the ticket was purchased.

Exhibit 19–2 Thank-you Letter

THANK YOU!

The Faculty of Fine Arts gratefully acknowledges your recent ticket order for

Fantasy Flight 1029

The journey that you are about to take will be an adventure in the Fine Arts. You will begin your adventure when you step out of your car in the parking garage (at Speedway and Park). It will continue on the patio in the Fine Arts Complex and will end there as well. We thought you might want to know that your dinner will be served in two seatings, at two different sites, each offering its own unique ambiance, cuisine, and performances.

Each guest will experience at least twelve different performances during the evening. If it is especially important for you to sit with your friends, please plan to arrive with them so that you will be assigned the same itinerary. If you don't happen to sit in the same rooms, you will enjoy comparing notes at the finale.

As a special patron of this event, it is our pleasure to offer you assistance with your future ticket orders for performances in the Theatre, Music, and Dance Departments. For your future reference, when you wish to attend a scheduled event, you may call the following people:

For Theatre Arts and/or School of Music Performances

Paulette Cauthorn 555-1162

Hours 9:00 a.m. to noon

For performances of the Committee on Dance

Michaline Cardella 555-4698

Hours 9:00 a.m. to 5:00 p.m.

Please identify yourself as a Gala Patron. Both Paulette and Michaline will have your name on a special list. They will assist you with the best available seating for your chosen performance. Please be aware that performances often sell out, so try to call as far in advance as possible.

No matter which of the three goals of visibility, cultivation, or income was primary in the decision to launch a special event, the opportunity to convert attendees to donors is present. Considerable planning and effort have gone into the outreach function. New faces have been sought and identified. New points of contact have been created. New spheres of influence have been established. All present new opportunities for increased giving by existing donors and for first-time gifts from new supporters. The true responsibility of the development department is to raise money in support of the cause. Seeking financial support for the mission and program undertaken by the organization is the ever-present burden.

Generally speaking, the attendees at any event fall into two groups—those who are already supporters and who asked others to join them at the event, and those who have not contributed in the past and were persuaded to attend the event out of a desire to be with the other attendees (friends, associates, or celebrities).

Those who are already supporters should be thanked graciously for their loyalty and participation. Their presence was noted and appreciated as one more indication of their continued interest and investment. Special recognition should be given to the supporters who sold tickets and tables or who otherwise were active in making the event a success. These supporters should receive a report on the success of the event, perhaps with a vignette, an endorsement, or even a copy of a news clipping.

Those who have not previously given a philanthropic gift should be identified and segmented for appropriate cultivation. Although some will never become donors because their interest was to see and be seen, others have taken the first step up the pyramid to becoming first-time donors, repeat donors, and perhaps major donors. Indeed, some events target only individuals who have the capacity to be major donors. As with other prospects under cultivation, each attendee should be evaluated and assigned to a specific plan for cultivation and solicitation. Some will be assigned to the process used for those new contributors obtained through donor acquisition. Others will be assigned to the process used to cultivate high-end prospects. Whatever the segmentation, all should receive a

graceful acknowledgment of their attendance, an official receipt for their ticket purchase, and an invitation to make suggestions about future improvements. Consider asking selected individuals if they would consider an invitation to join the committee for the next event. They should be added to the newsletter recipient list, the holiday greeting card list and, most importantly, to the invitation list for the next event.

All the post-event activity intended to cultivate, interest, and attract those who have the capacity to give a philanthropic contribution will be for naught if the attendees have missed the connection between the event and the organization. Although events are enjoyable and entertaining by design and emphasis on the cause and its programs are kept light, the organization and its cause must be identified and identifiable. Each activity must add to the visibility of the organization. One of the largest and most successful events in California, The Black and White Ball, is held every second year in San Francisco. The streets surrounding City Hall are blocked off, scores of tents are set up, and dinner is served to guests who come in formal dress, always black and white. After dinner, the music from four to six bands and orchestras entice the diners into the streets to dance the hours away under the stars and soft air, the scene gently illuminated by street lamps. The Black and White Ball is anticipated for months and discussed weeks afterward. Tickets are in great demand and sold through newspapers and ticket agencies. Singles and youngsters are encouraged to attend through reduced prices. The caution? Experts believe that fewer than 50 percent of the attendees know the event is produced by and benefits a local performing arts company!

Points to Ponder

No matter what the primary goal of the event (cultivation, visibility, or income) the real oppor-

> As with other prospects under cultivation, each attendee should be evaluated and assigned to a specific plan for cultivation and solicitation.

tunity lies in building long-term relationships with the attendees—as repeat attendees, as supporters, as volunteers, as advocates, and as major donors. Everything should be done to strengthen the tie, especially because the original connection was tenuous. Most people attend events because of who else will be there. They attend for the event, not for the organization. Although information about the organization is contained in the program, many people fail to make a strong connection, even if they remember the event fondly.

The connection now needs to be focused on the organization and its mission. Start with a "thank you for joining us" statement. Include information on how the money raised was used to make a difference. Mention the van that was purchased to transport clients, the number of books purchased for the library, the number of meals provided for the homeless, etc. Consider including a low-level request for an outright gift as part of the thank you, which can include a report and an update.

Consider mailing a post-event evaluation questionnaire. Ask questions such as the following: What was the thing you liked best? The thing you liked least? How can the event be improved? What other charity events have you attended this year? Will you consider attending the next event? Would you consider serving on a host committee in the future?

Add the new names to the organization's mailing list. Send newsletters, bits of information, annual reports that show the result of the event, etc.

Mail early notices of the next event, informing them of the plans, asking them to save the date, and offering early bird opportunities to purchase tickets at the same price as the event they previously attended.

Summary

Just as any social event, the cycle of a special event begins with the concept and ends with the thank you. The difference is the number and vari-

ety of thank yous. Volunteers, honorees, sponsors, attendees, and donors of gifts-in-kind all receive acknowledgments for their special contributions. The form of appreciation is determined by their role in the event.

Key leadership may have a celebratory luncheon; publicity may be arranged for sponsors; volunteers may get a special token that commemorates the event. Just as the thank you is the first step in getting the next gift, it is the first step in recruiting for the next event or in attracting a guest to attend again.

Evaluation is a planning tool that comes at the end of the process. It guides the determination of success and the decision about the event's worthiness. Evaluation is the first step toward the next event. During the evaluation, consider asking the following questions:

- Were goals met?

- Were guests pleased?

- Were volunteers satisfied?

- Was administration gratified?

- Was the mission furthered?

- Should we, or can we, do it again?

Conclusion

Your adventure into the world of special events has been filled with detail and drama, highs and lows, and has likely generated more stories and experiences than you might ever have imagined. Hopefully, you have discovered the value of events, and, more important, the value of planning.

When your events successfully fulfill your goals, you will be providing critically important help to your organization. Happy dreaming, happy planning, and may all your special events bring you and your organization satisfaction and success.

Bibliography

Arledge, R., and D. Friedman. *Dynamic Fund Raising Projects*. Chicago, IL: Precept Press, Inc., 1992.

Aspen's Guide to 60 Successful Special Events: How to Plan, Organize and Conduct Outstanding Fund Raisers. Gaithersburg, MD: Aspen Publishers, Inc., 1996.

Axiom Information Resources. *1997–98 Star Guide*. Ann Arbor, MI, 1997.

Brentlinger, M., and J. Weiss. *The Ultimate Benefit Book*. Cleveland, OH: Octavia Press, 1987.

Cicora, K. *Marketing and Managing Special Events/ Research Report No. 125*. Melbourne, FL: Krieger Publishing, 1990.

Cloud, D., ed. *Lets Celebrate: A Public Relations and Special Events Guide for Non Profit Homes and Services for the Aging*. American Association of Homes & Services for the Aging, 1988.

Connelly, A., and M. Winter. *Going...Going...Gone: Successful Auctions for Nonprofit Institutions*. Greenwich, CT: Target Funding Group, 1993.

DeSoto, C. *For Fun & Funds: Creative Fund-Raising Ideas*. New York: Parker Publishing Co., 1984.

Devney, D. *Organizing Special Events and Conferences: A Practical Guide for Busy Volunteers and Staff*. Sarasota, FL: Pineapple Press, 1990.

Dexter, K. *Bazaars, Fairs & Festivals*. Wilton, CT: Morehouse, 1978.

Ernst & Young. *The Complete Guide to Special Event Management: Business Insights, Financial Advice and Strategies*. New York: John Wiley & Sons, 1992.

Everett, D., ed. *Broadcaster's Guide to Special Events and Sponsorship Risk Management*. Washington, DC: National Association of Broadcasters, 1991.

Farb, C. *How to Raise Millions Helping Others Have a Ball*. Austin, TX: Eakin Press, 1993.

Farmington Public Library. *Fundraising 101*. Farmington, NM, 1993.

Franks, A. and N. Franks. *Cash Now! A Manual of 29 Successful Fundraising Events*. Vancouver, British Columbia: Creative Fundraising, 19xx.

Freedman, H., and K. Feldman Smith. *Black Tie Optional: The Ultimate Guide to Planning and Producing Special Events*. Rockville, MD: The Taft Group, 1991.

Geier, T. *Make Your Events Special: How to Produce Successful Events for Nonprofit Organizations*. New York: Folkworks, The Public Interest Production Co., 1986.

Goldblatt, J. *Special Events: Best Practices in Modern Event Management*. New York: Van Nostrand Reinhold, 1996.

Greenfield, J. *Fund-Raising: Evaluating and Managing the Fund Development Process*. New York: John Wiley & Sons, 1991.

Harris, A. *Raising Money and Cultivating Donors Through Special Events*. Washington, DC: Council for Advancement and Support of Education, 1991.

Hopkins, B. *The Law of Fund-Raising*. New York: John Wiley & Sons, 1991.

Kraatz, K., and J. Haynes. *The Fundraising Formula: 50 Creative Events Proven Successful Nationwide*. Anaheim, CA: KNX, Inc., 1987.

Kaitcer, C. *Raising Big Bucks Through Pledge-Based Special Events: How to Plan Successful Walks and Bike Tours*. Chicago, IL: Bonus Books, 1996.

Leibert, E., et. al. *Handbook of Special Events for Non-profit Organizations.* New York: Association Press, 1972.

Liebold, L. *Fireworks, Brass Bands, and Elephants: Promotional Events with Flair for Libraries and Other Nonprofit Organizations.* Phoenix, AZ: Oryx Press, 1986.

Mixer, J. *Principles of Professional Fundraising.* San Francisco, CA: Jossey-Bass, Inc., 1993.

National Hole in One Association. *Million Dollar Shootouts: A Proven Fund Raiser for Charities.* Dallas, TX, 1993.

Nelson, D. *Getting the Payoff from Special Events.* Presented at seminar. San Francisco, CA: May 1996.

Paton, R., and S. Kumar. *Mobilizing People and Organizing Events: Winning Resources and Support.* Dorchester, England: Henry King Ltd., 1993.

Plessner, G. *The Encyclopedia of Fund Raising: Charity Auction Management Manual.* Arcadia, CA: Fund Raisers, Inc., 1986.

Plessner, G. *The Encyclopedia of Fund Raising: Golf Tournament Management Manual.* Vol. 1. Arcadia, CA: Fund Raisers, Inc., 1980.

Plessner, G. *The Encyclopedia of Fund Raising: Golf Tournament Management Manual.* Vol. 2 Arcadia, CA: Fund Raisers, Inc., 1986.

Plessner, G. *The Encyclopedia of Fund Raising: Testimonial Dinner and Luncheon Manage-ment Manual.* Arcadia, CA: Fund Raisers, Inc., 1980.

Prior, O. *Planning the Big Bash, a Systems Approach to Special Events.* New York: Caxton of New York, 1983.

Rice, W., and M. Yaconelli. *Creative Socials and Special Events.* Grand Rapids, MI: Zondervan Publication House, 1986.

Seltzer, M. *Securing Your Organization's Future: A Complete Guide to Fundraising Strategies.* New York: The Foundation Center, 1987.

Sheerin, M. *How to Raise Top Dollars from Special Events.* Hartsdale, NY: Public Service Materials Center, 1984.

Shotwell, M. *Creative Programs for the Church Year: Help With Planning Holidays, Special Emphases, and Seasonal Events.* Valley Forge, PA: Judson Press, 1986.

Strangland, R. *The World's Funniest Roast Jokes.* New York: Meadowbrook Press, 1992.

Weinberger, J. *Please Buy My Violets: How to Raise Money for Your Cause.* Mt. Desert, ME: Windswept House, 1986.

Weiner, S. *Bring an Author to Your Library.* Fort Atkinson, WI: Alleyside Press, 1993.

Williams, W. *User Friendly Fund$Raising: A Step-By-Step Guide to Profitable Special Events.* Alexander, NC: Worldcomm Press, 1994.

Index

About the Authors

BARBARA R. LEVY is the Executive Director of the Arizona Children's Foundation. Her 25-year career in development has included service with The University of Arizona, The Arizona Theatre Company and Arizona Opera. She is one of thirty individuals in the nation to qualify for and earn the credential of Advanced Certified Fund-Raising Executive.

Ms. Levy is a frequent national speaker on board and fund-raising issues. She has been active on the National Society of Fund Raising Executives Society and Foundation boards, currently sits on the Foundation Board and chairs the Advanced Certification Board.

Ms. Levy is the editor of the *NSFRE Fund-Raising Dictionary,* published by John Wiley & Sons in 1996.

Ms. Levy is listed as a biographee in several publications including *Who's Who in Emerging Leaders in America, 2000 Notable American Women,* and the *International Who's Who of Professional and Business Women.*

BARBARA H. MARION entered the fund raising field in 1963, was President of FRA, Inc. for eighteen years, and is now Principal of Marion Fundraising Counsel, a San Francisco based consulting firm which specializes in feasibility and planning studies, capital campaigns, board and staff training, and fund development plans.

Ms. Marion is also adjunct faculty at the University of San Francisco's Institute for Nonprofit Organization Management, where she teaches the theory, philosophy, and history of philanthropy and fund raising.

As guest editor, she wrote the chapter on decision-making for *Ethics in Fundraising: Putting Values into Practice,* New Directions for Philanthropic Fundraising Series, a quarterly publication sponsored by The Indiana University Center on Philanthropy, Jossey-Bass Publishers, Winter 1994. She also served as guest editor of *The NSFRE Fundraising Dictionary,* published by John Wiley & Sons, 1996. A nationally known professional, her activities include numerous speaking engagements at fund-raising conferences and seminars.

A member of the National Society of Fund Raising Executives since 1972, Ms. Marion has held various national and chapter offices, including Chair of the National Board of Directors, Chair of the NSFRE Foundation, and President of the Golden Gate Chapter. As a long-term member of the Ethics Committee of NSFRE's national organization, she was active in the development of NSFRE's current Code of Ethics and its enforcement procedure.

In 1994 Ms. Marion received the Henry A. Rosso Award for Lifetime Achievement in Ethical Fundraising presented by the Center on Philanthropy at Indiana University; the NSFRE National Outstanding Fund-Raising Executive of the year in 1995; and NSFRE's award for Leadership in the Society and Distinguished Service to the Minority Outreach Committee in 1992. Ms. Marion also received the Fund Raising Executive of the Year Award from the Golden Gate Chapter of the National Society of Fund Raising Executives in 1989 and its Distinguished Service Awards in 1985 and 1988.